F. R. LEAVIS

F. R. LEAVIS

WILLIAM WALSH

INDIANA UNIVERSITY PRESS

BLOOMINGTON & LONDON

Library of Congress Cataloging in Publication Data
Walsh, William,
    F. R. Leavis

    Includes bibliographical references and index.
    1. Leavis, Frank Raymond, 1895–
    2. Criticism – Great Britain.   3. English
    literature – History and criticism.
    PR29.L4W34   1980   801'.95'0924   80–7971
    ISBN 0–253–19426–1
    1 2 3 4 5 84 83 82 81 80

Contents

Foreword

The purpose of this book is not to hark back over old controversies
or to engage in new ones, but to define and substantiate the positive
achievement of F. R. Leavis, whom I see as the fourth critic in the line
of English critics inaugurated by Johnson and continued by Coleridge
and Arnold. I should make clear that the study has no official or
authorised status and is based solely on Leavis's published work and
the publicly known facts of his professional career. I am grateful to
Mrs Q. D. Leavis and the literary executors of F. R. Leavis for
permission to quote from materials protected by copyright. I am
indebted to Chatto & Windus for permission to make use of my
essay 'A Sharp Unaccommodating Voice' from *A Human Idiom;*
to George Core, editor, and the *Sewanee Review* for permission to
use my essay 'On the Personal Side' which appeared there; to Ian
Robinson, editor, *The Human World,* and the Brynmill Press for
permission to quote from Leavis's contributions to that journal; to
A. D. Peters & Co. Ltd for the extracts from *Cambridge Between Two
Wars* by T. E. B. Howarth; to the *New Statesman* for permission to
include extracts from contributions by D. J. Enright and John Bayley;
to Boris Ford, editor, the *New Universities Quarterly,* and Blackwells
for permission to quote extracts from the Winter 1975 commemorative
number on F. R. Leavis; to the *Listener* to quote from the number of
24 July 1975; and to New York University Press for permission to
quote from *The Importance of Scrutiny* by Eric Bentley, 1948. I am
grateful to the University of Leeds which enabled me to undertake
this work, and to the Rockefeller Foundation which enabled me to
complete it at the Research Center at the Villa Serbelloni. I thank
Professor T. A. Birrell, Director of the Instituut Engels-Amerikaans
in the University of Nijmegen, for advice on the typescript, and Mrs
Winifred Leonard for secretarial and research assistance stretching
over many years.

I

On the Personal Side

Frank Raymond Leavis was born on 14 July 1895, of French Huguenot descent, the scion of a line of Little Englanders, and among his earliest memories was the Boer War. When Leavis died in Cambridge on 14 April 1978, he had spent, apart from service in the First World War, fleeting visits and holidays abroad, and part-time work at York, Wales and Bristol Universities after his retirement, the whole of his life in the one town. He was brought up there – his father was a Cambridge townsman – he went to school there, attended the University there, he married there, his family was raised there, his academic career was almost wholly passed there. There is on the positive side an affinity between the character of the place and the temperament of Leavis, each manifesting concentration, austerity, subtleties of flatness and complexities within a restricted range, and a clean sense of a precise and distinctive English tradition. (No doubt there are less impressive qualities in each, too.) There is another respect in which the two are alike. Leavis was a Cambridge townsman, and anyone who has lived and worked in the University of Cambridge (certainly this was true twenty or thirty years ago and I believe not by any means untrue now) will be aware of the way in which townspeople are regarded as not belonging; the town being parochial and semi-rural, the University sophisticated and cosmopolitan. I do not claim that there is any cause or effect here, but Leavis, in spite of his eminence, his world-wide fame, and his extraordinary influence on the literary and educational scene, carried for most of his life within the University the mark of the unestablished and disconnected, and, it must be said, the feelings to be expected from one in such a position.

It is not surprising, then, that in later life one contention more than most caused Leavis to feel a scalding indignation. This was the charge that somehow his criticism represented a menacing and dominant orthodoxy in Cambridge, which more independent spirits had later to loosen and displace. As he wrote in the *Spectator* in 1961, '. . . it is not noble, when you are bent on perpetuating an orthodoxy that has long been in possession, to point to the heretic who has survived, somehow, as the Establishment you are bravely displacing.'[1]

Leavis's father Harry, a man of principle and cultivation to whom Leavis was deeply attached, owned a family musical-instrument business in Cambridge, and it was natural that the son should attend the excellent local grammar school, the Perse School, thereby binding himself still more firmly into the provincial nexus. The school, which had a strong academic leaning, was in a particularly lively phase during Leavis's time. The headmaster, Dr W. H. D. Rouse, was a classicist who believed in teaching the dead languages as though they were living ones – the direct method so-called – which is a splendid way of teaching, given the personality of a Dr Rouse. Leavis remembered writing excuses for lateness and pieces on the repair of bicycles in the ancient tongues:

> ... I had what Mr. Hutchins[2] (to judge by his account of the conditions he is familiar with) would judge a comparatively good education. I left school with a very good start in French and German. I spent a great deal of time as a schoolboy writing Latin proses, some of which were commended by my headmaster, Mr. Ezra Pound's correspondent, Dr. Rouse. I could in those days (so soon left behind!) explain in Greek, observing quantity, stress, and tonic accent (the precise value of which Dr. Rouse knew), that I was late for school because I had a puncture in my back tire. With my Form I read through semi-dramatically the plays of Shakespeare. I worked enough at history (I remember reading, among other things, Trevelyan's *History of the American Revolution*) to win a university scholarship in that subject. At the university I took the Historical Tripos Part I and the English Tripos, both successfully. Then I was able to spend three years in post-graduate research.[3]

Any prejudice he might have shown in later life towards the classics as the centre of a humane education was not therefore to be based on ignorance. English at the school was taught by H. Caldwell Cook, in his time a well-known reformer of methods of English teaching, who firmly advocated creative and dramatic methods. Leavis himself took part in school productions of Shakespeare, with some degree of success – as indeed he did in games. He played rugger in school and became later at the university a fine cross-country runner.

A vivid glimpse of Leavis as a schoolboy is given by Eric Warmington, one-time Professor of Classics in the University of London, and a contemporary of Leavis, in a memoir published in 1975. After speaking of the school's achievements in classics and foreign languages – many boys left school able to speak French perfectly – and the influence of

H. Caldwell Cook, who implanted a love for Shakespeare and taught the boys how to act, he writes:

> One of these dramas was *Macbeth* of which Cook staged Act 2 in 1912. In contrast with the few words uttered by Fleance (me), the part of the villain-hero was taken by a quiet boy who later became renowned as a teacher of English and an unswerving critic of English literature and of other experts therein – F. R. Leavis.

According to a critique of the occasion in the school magazine, the *Pelican*, Leavis acted 'extremely well', but it seems that he did not quite manage his voice so as to produce the required 'air of mystery and of the supernatural'. Yet he was nimble in body; I see that, two years later, the *Pelican* had a report on school rugger which referred to Leavis as 'the player who has made much the greatest progress in a short time: a very hard-working forward, but light.' A cleancut jaw, firm mouth, and deep-set dark-seeming eyes, are features which are unchanged in him even today. When you stared at him, he gazed back silently as if he already had you in scrutiny. I have heard that he did not like having to compose Latin and even Greek verse under Rouse; and when he won a scholarship at Emmanuel College it was not in Classics. I wish I could remember more about Leavis, but in those days he was, of course, quite unknown, though we were all familiar with the name Leavis because of an advertisement prominent in those days – LEAVIS SPELLS PIANOS. His father was in the piano business. [4]

Leavis remained all his life very conscious of the care of the body, disdainful of flab, and fastidiously opposed to any kind of physical immoderation. In spite of disabilities inflicted during the war, he was for most of his life a man of remarkable muscular stamina and wiry strength. His school life was crowned by a history scholarship to Emmanuel, and Leavis's relationships with students, always close, patient, and friendly, were notable for a particular feeling for scholarship boys, who in those days had to show exceptional prowess and independence.

Leavis had a shattering war. It began soon after he left school, and he served throughout in the Friends Ambulance Unit as a stretcher-bearer, work in which scenes of slaughter and risk to life were almost a routine. The war left a permanent effect on his health – he was gassed – and it is hard to believe that it didn't do something similar to his psychology. At least one can see that his experiences justified the sense Leavis always possessed, of enjoying a profound unity with ordinary people. One of the great values he appealed to – centrality, profound commonsense – was derived from this source. There is little in the way

of memory or comment about the war in Leavis's writing. The one
reminiscence, given characteristically in the course of a much more
general argument, appeared in a public lecture given at the University
of York in 1971, and later published.[5] It concerns an exchange Leavis
had with a young man of research student status in an Oxford Common
Room:

> He was an American – inquiring and obviously nice; and, concluding
> that I was old enough to have been contemporary with the 1914 war,
> he asked some questions about the moral impact on the country, and
> referred in due course to the Somme. I replied that, yes, I supposed
> the country *had* been profoundly disturbed; speaking as one who had
> found himself trying to tot up from the casualty-lists in the papers,
> and odd reports, the sum of school-fellows dead in a morning, I
> didn't see how it could be otherwise. I added, still dwelling on a re-
> called particular sense of the general realization of disaster that shook
> the country, and not meaning in the least to imply irony – certainly
> not prepared for the response I drew – that those innumerable boy-
> subalterns who figured in the appalling Roll of Honour as 'Fallen
> Officers' had climbed out and gone forward, playing their part in the
> attacking wave, to be mown down with the swathes that fell to the
> uneliminated machine-guns. The comment, quietly sure of its
> matter-of-fact felicity, was: 'The death-wish!' My point is that I
> didn't know what to say. What actually came out was, 'They didn't
> *want* to die.' I felt I couldn't stop there, but how to go on? 'They
> were brave' – that came to me as a faint prompting, but no; it didn't
> begin to express my positive intention; it didn't even lead towards
> it. I gave up; there was nothing else to do.

Some may think it ironic that this great proponent of the necessity
for academic and intellectual élites should have felt, as he undoubtedly
did, part of the people. His experiences of the war, just as of life in
the family, with its stresses, hazards, and hardships, also made Leavis
feel that he belonged to one part of the community, even if he felt, as he
always did, an outsider in another part. After the war he went up to
Cambridge to read History in Part I of the Tripos and then the new
English Tripos in Part II. He did not, oddly enough, enjoy the overwhelming academic success one would naturally expect from someone
of his gifts, zest, and application – he took a Second in Part I and a
First in Part II – and his frequently repeated view that first class men
did not always get first class places in the Tripos examination, confirmed as it was by years of teaching, must have been at least faintly
affected by his own experience, an experience itself affected by the

horror and danger of war, by shellshock and by a family tragedy in which his father was killed at his side in a traffic accident on the very day that Leavis was to begin examinations in Part II of the Tripos.

English as a subject of study started in Cambridge when the Chair of English Literature was founded in 1911. The Tripos itself began in 1917.[6] Its purpose was to make the study of English Literature displace the classics as the centre of a humane education. To this end, under the influence of the vivacious and perceptive Mansfield Forbes, and with the support of the distinguished Anglo-Saxon scholar Hector Munro Chadwick, the study was to be exempt from compulsory Anglo-Saxon. The occupant of 'the lonely and despised' Chair of English Literature, Arthur Quiller-Couch, a conventional and gentle-manly product of late-Victorian Oxford, sympathised with this new freedom. Leavis paid a notable tribute to Mansfield Forbes, who was responsible along with so much else for contriving I. A. Richards's association with Cambridge English:

It was Mansfield Forbes who, from the very outset, ensured that the opportunity should be taken. Accident determined that, at the moment when his gifts of character and intelligence could tell decisively, he was at hand: the circumstances of war-time Cambridge give him an unforeseeable chance – thrust it upon him. Young, convinced, contagiously charged with energy and irrepressible, he performed during those opening years of Cambridge English – the dark years of the war – the service he was unmistakably and irrepressibly fitted for. There was the charter, there was an examination to be held under it in two years time, there was no Faculty – no plausible team even, and there was Forbes, with the conviction, the drive, and the intelligence. Nothing further is needed to explain how he came to play so decisive a part and was discovered, in those first-post-Armistice terms, when the demobilized rapidly refilled Cambridge and inquiries multiplied into what 'English' might mean, *being* it – being the new opportunity in person.

Of course, he incidentally reinforced some conceits and exposed his influence to the charge of inspiring and equipping ambitious stupidi-ties and stark insensibilities to posture as something else. But what 'teacher' can be ensured against that kind of hazard? Where does safety lie – unless in nullity? We didn't need Nietzsche to tell us to live dangerously; there is no other way of living. Forbes, himself a vital force of intelligence, had, in the strong disinterested way, the courage of life and, it follows, the impulse and the power to stir intelligence into active life in others.[7]

Living dangerously – at least in one sense of the phrase – is exactly what the young graduate student Leavis in the early twenties was forced into. He had to hang about, to pick up what work he could, and support himself as best he might, while all the time hoping to make his mark. For that he needed not only talent and persistence but also luck in attracting the favour of the influential, and the diplomacy to profit by it. Capacity and stamina Leavis was widely recognised to possess, even if in the common judgement he would not score highly on the other items. The subject of his doctoral thesis was 'The Relationship of Journalism to Literature: Studied in the Rise and Earlier Development of the Press in England', a theme hinting at the social element to develop in his thought and one he made use of in *Revaluation*. In 1927 he got his first official appointment, that of probationary faculty lecturer, a post he occupied for three years, during which he married in 1929 Queenie Dorothy Roth, a brilliant Girton scholar whose own graduate work was to come to fruit in the astonishingly original *Fiction and the Reading Public*. This marriage brought Leavis great happiness, three children, Ralph, Kate and Robin, as well as intellectual companionship of a rare and creative kind. (How different in this respect was Leavis's fate from Coleridge's.)

During this period Leavis, by a peculiar symmetry, had a crazy experience, oddly reminiscent of Coleridge's pass with the police spy Walsh. He was lecturing on English Prose and wanted a copy of *Ulysses* to use in his course. Here is the event as he describes it in a letter to the *Times Literary Supplement* of 3 May 1963:

One day a conversation with my bookseller about the censorship exercised by the American Customs led to my saying: 'Well, *we* can't talk: there are books you can't get me.' The upshot was that, at his suggestion, I dictated a letter to the Home Office requesting permission to import a copy of *Ulysses* by James Joyce, for use by me at Cambridge in a course of lectures on English prose – I was down on the lecture-list for such a course.

A week or two later I received an invitation to call on the Vice-Chancellor. When, at the appointed hour, I introduced myself to him in the Master's Lodge at Downing (a college with which I then had no connexion), he handed me a typescript several pages long from the Public Prosecutor. This contained an account of me and my lectures (number of undergraduates attending, proportion of women, &c.), the product of investigations carried out by the Cambridge police. It contained also an account of the book ('indescribably filthy', &c.: 'We do not suppose you have read it, and shall be pleased to send you a copy for examination'). It closed with the expression of an undoubting confidence that I should be suitably and firmly dealt with. In fact, I couldn't help believing that Sir William Joynson-Hicks himself had drafted this descriptive and hortatory part of the document, and sent it round for the Public Prosecutor's use.

I told the Vice-Chancellor (Professor Seward) the facts about my application; said I had never entertained the absurd idea attributed to me by the Public Prosecutor – that of prescribing *Ulysses* for study for the English Tripos; remarked that I didn't see why anyone who wanted to read the book, which everyone interested in contemporary literature was expected to be able to discuss intelligently, shouldn't be free to read it – or to try, and that it was in any case widely current among Cambridge undergraduates: 'I happen to know,' I said, 'that there are copies circulating at both Girton and Newnham.' What I should have liked to eliminate, I added, was the glamour of the clandestine attending the cult – for there *was* a cult. 'I could easily have got a copy,' I said, 'by letting myself be put in touch with one of the disreputable agents every bookseller knows of.' 'I'm glad you didn't do that,' the Vice-Chancellor replied: 'letters get intercepted.' And he touched with an admonitory finger one of the pigeon-holes of the desk at which he was sitting. He didn't seem at all disturbed, and I think he replied to the Public Prosecutor in the terms of my explanation.

I heard nothing of any further official action, and (though not granted a licence to import *Ulysses*) used, and went on using, a passage of Joyce's prose in my lecture-course.[8]

The anecdote illuminates not only extraordinary changes in both taste and manners – the blend of Mrs Grundy and the C.I.D. of then, compared with the permissiveness and shrunken authority of now – but also the young Leavis's gift for striding into discomfort and even disaster. This particular fuss drummed on for quite some time, occasioning, for example, comments about the Leavis prize for pornography. It was during these years that Leavis developed the other art of which he was to become a master, the art of teaching.

The external facts of the academic career – if that is the word for it – in the course of which his art was refined, can be given quite briefly. At the age of 40 he had been without a salaried post for some years; even in 1945 he was a part-time lecturer of very junior standing. In his sixtieth year he was admitted to the Faculty Board but never had any voice in Faculty appointments. As he puts it himself, with what a detached observer must admit is forgivable bitterness:

At my superannuation I was indeed a University Reader: I had been advanced to that status in my sixth-fifty year. As for my previous official standing, I was appointed as Assistant Lecturer in my early forties and a full University Lecturer in my fifties. The financial consequences for my retired years, as well as for my previous life, of such an academic career constitute, in the nature of things, a fact that I and my wife (who also – though with even less recognition – devoted a life's service to Cambridge English) can hardly regard as negligible.[9]

As a teacher Leavis had a distinctive presence and manner. His personality was powerful but reined-in and gave the impression of disciplined inner resource and contained strength. He was a lizard for warmth, hunting the sun in summer and teaching in front of a huge fire in the winter. He preferred to take a small group rather than the conventional single pupil, which had the advantage of letting him see more of the many pupils who wanted to come to him and made, as well, for a more relaxed and more open atmosphere. His voice was thin in volume, blending the qualities of Cambridge cultivation and the slightly shadowed vowels of Cambridge town; and it was the subject of endless mimicry. It was a voice capable of the most sensitive reproduction of rhythmical effect. His spoken idiom was lucid and urbane and a characteristic rhythm of deliberately defining hesitation checked and rechecked the flow until the final compelling close. Loyalty to something superior to the tribe allowed him, he clearly felt, freedom to make wittily satirical comments about University colleagues – but in a curiously impersonal way. The most personal comment was in the service of a larger cause. Leavis was one of the few teachers, perhaps the only one, who never on any occasion bored his students. No doubt this was to be attributed to a unique combination of articulate conviction, spiritual vitality and profound concern. Leavis's great gift as a teacher was, by exhibiting as he did, year in, year out, the actual operations of a marvellous taste and a powerful intellect, to stir in his students the subjective passion which Henry James said was the aim of education, and to enliven them with his conviction that in grappling with literature they were grappling with life itself in its most significant, valuable and intense phases.

Fine teaching, that unfixable, most transient art, has much more to do with character than method, with the person rather than the means. I want to quote here three personal comments about Leavis as a teacher; the first and second were broadcast on the occasion of Leavis's eightieth birthday, the third written when he died:

He was really superb. I remember the feelings with which this other man and I would come away. We would be partly exhilarated, and partly a bit subdued and rueful, perhaps. Exhilarated because of the new insights and the fine discriminations he had made, and sobered because he kept such extremely high standards in insight, and one just realised how unskilled one was as a reader. At the same time, there was no feeling that he belittled you in any way – if you had difficulties or raised objections, then he met you on those. He could scrap what he was going to say and just meet you on whatever you were interested in.[10]

He was an extraordinary teacher. D. J. Enright said that he was one of the few teachers he had met who treated one absolutely as an equal, and this indeed was the case. He had about him a kind of well-scrubbed and athletic elegance, and corresponding to this physical attractiveness there was an astonishing electric quality about his mind. One always had the feeling that one was not simply discussing what was there on the page. Of course, one was. But, this had all sorts of roots and connections with life, with what one really felt might be important in one's personal emotions and values.[11]

As a teacher he was strong medicine. A few of his pupils resented so vigorous a personality, whose every word, tone, silence and gesture added definition and edge to his views – and fled. Some, with better minds, were taken over as if by a more potent form of being: they gained much, but the sense of entering into an embattled élite could entail losses too. Others, perhaps less sophisticated, or just unwilling to yield themselves even to patent superiority, profited less ambiguously, and greatly. Possibly FRL's greatest and most enduring influence travelled by way of his pupils' pupils, backed up by his writings, and spreading to countries remote from Cambridge, where in different conditions the bitter local intensities faded from the teaching.[12]

These bitter local intensities began early and festered during the inter-war years. This was the Cambridge of Rutherford, Trevelyan, Keynes, Moore, Wittgenstein, Leavis. Very many people around the world, many in England outside Cambridge, would accept this description and recognise that the names given belong to the same sphere of discourse. Not many people would take such a view in Cambridge at any time, and hardly any people at that time. The then view realised itself in the extraordinary situation – at least it would have been thought so at any other university – in which Leavis would have to spend the years from the completion of his Ph.D. in 1924 (except, as I say, for 1927–30 when he was a probationary lecturer) till 1936 when he was appointed Fellow, Director of English Studies at Downing, and an assistant university lecturer, as a freelance teacher with all that implies in patchy employment, economic strain and general uncertainty. The facts are hardly in dispute, although legal and administrative explanations for his not receiving promotions have been advanced.[13] It will still seem to most observers an astounding state of affairs. No doubt theoretical disagreements among the members of the English Faculty must have played their part – differences about the character and functions of the English school, and the nature of its central discipline, and there was clearly distinct and growing hostility to Leavis. Colleagues who would, if one's experience of universities is of any validity, naturally expect Leavis to behave as though he were on the same level as themselves, could not be expected to see what in fact they had in Leavis. He was after all a prophet not only in his own country, but also in his own town. He had, too, profound certainties about his own rightness, an unclubbable nature, a fervent sense of mission, a sharp voice and an unaccommodating viewpoint: none of which was likely to recommend him to his more ordinary and more fallible colleagues. Leavis, and, it seems, his wife, were grit in the oiled machine. This is how Basil Willey, at one time by no means unfriendly to Leavis, remembered them. He uses the rather hazy description 'Scrutineers' for what must essentially mean Frank and Queenie Leavis:

> Never for a moment straying to right or to left, never seeking refuge in religious or political dogma or in psychological explanations, they kept to the straight and narrow path, scrutinising each literary work as such and not as a product of something else, and judging it by standards which, though doubtless derived in the last analysis from religion or ethics, could yet plausibly be applied as if they were autonomous. I was often, as all non-Leavisites were, irritated by their arrogance, self-righteousness, disdainfulness and rudeness. Yet I recognised their integrity and zeal, and above all, of course, the distinguished critical perceptiveness of Leavis himself, as repeatedly shown in his subtle analyses of particular writers and passages. In those days, the days when he was still outside the Faculty and accounting himself ostracised, I always defended him against his detractors, even though sharing their exasperation at his obsessions.[14]

In spite of propitious beginnings, the inauguration of the new
Tripos and the context it provided for a wholly new spirit and approach, the presence of friends and collaborators and the circle in
which it became possible to develop *Scrutiny*, Leavis's career at
Cambridge was conducted against a background of 'obloquy, slander
and worldly disadvantage' as he puts it himself.[15] Something we can
write down to personal enmity, something to a nature that combined a
fastidious and fierce resolution never to back down or compromise,
with an intensity of commitment which is rare enough anywhere and
particularly, it seems, in the academic world. Roy Fuller, when asked
about this matter, replied:

> My own feeling about the strongest part of his opposition-rousing
> character would be the intense seriousness with which he takes
> literature and creativity. I think many writers and many critics,
> however serious they may be, have a kind of cosy side to their
> nature – at certain points in their criticism and their creation, they are
> inclined to drop their arduous view of life and say, 'Well, after all,
> things aren't so bad,' and 'We don't mind old Buggins or old
> Juggins.' Leavis has never done this.[16]

If one wanted a list of the charges made against Leavis's temperament – often advanced as grounds for opposing his views – we cannot
do better than look at what he has quoted from public prints about
himself, in which he provides a catalogue of such counts.[17] He has been
diagnosed, he says, as suffering from persecution mania (p. 37), as
being a rugged moralist (p. 35), as having a notoriously Puritan habit
of approach (p. 67), as demonstratively lower-middle-class, pro-
claimed such in . . . solemn critical labours by an ungentlemanly lack of
reticence (p. 73), as being one given to fanatical insistence (p. 74), even
as being a comic character (p. 96), as anti-political, anti-industrial and
anti-scientific (p. 114), as charting a roseate prehistory (p. 100), and as
exercising over students through his career a deplorable influence
(p. 105).

To these precisely framed defects we can add more general characteristics, which again can be taken from references in Leavis's own
work. He is both bleak and touchy, '*puritano frenetico*',[18] as an Italian
journalist, reporting on the English literature scene, called him. He is
said to be so dogmatically set in his ways as to be incapable of changing
his views or of recognising or profiting from disinterested criticism. If
he does change his views he is thought by one party to be guilty of an

act of treachery to some generally held, platonic idea of Leavis; or by
another, when charged with change, to be apt disingenuously to disguise or deny the fact of development or mutation.[19] He is, it is claimed,
an angry polemicist who delights in inflicting wanton damage on
literary reputations like Lord Snow's or academic reputations like
Lord Annan's. 'It would be dishonest of me,' writes D. J. Enright, 'not
to confess my own feeling, that Leavis has at times engaged in breaking
butterflies on wheels – and then gone on to break the broken remains.'[20]
He has been accused of despising scholarship in its purest form and of
breeding generations of students with a similar attitude. Above all he is
possessed by a fanatical and absolutist sense of inerrancy, which makes
any disagreement an offence, any questioning an insult.

Perhaps all these charges could be subsumed under or contracted
into one, that of arrogance. In this context it is interesting to recall
Leavis's relationship at Cambridge with a contemporary, Wittgenstein,
who is in the minds of many the very distillation of arrogance. Leavis
and Wittgenstein met at one of those conversaziones, common then in
Cambridge, at which people were regularly at home to friends, to
visiting scholars, to the interested, and to students, particularly graduate
students. On this occasion it took place in 1929 at tea-time on Sunday
afternoon, in the home of W. E. Johnson, the famous logician and
'supervisor' of Cambridge philosophers, and his sister Miss Fanny,
at Ramsey House, Barton Road. The meeting was in the little drawing-
room which was a quarter filled with a Broadwood Grand, at which the
old logician used to take his exercise playing Bach. Leavis, who had
been at school with Johnson's son Stephen, was an established familiar
in the house. Wittgenstein was coldly, cuttingly cruel to a young man
who had been asked to sing. When Wittgenstein at the end of the
young man's now tremblingly inadequate performance got up to
leave ('triumphantly – so I thought,' says Leavis), Leavis followed him
with his hands on his lapels of his coat as though – it must have
seemed – he were about to take it off, rebuking him forcefully. When
Wittgenstein said, 'I thought he was a foolish young man,' Leavis
replied emphatically, containing himself, 'You may have done, you
may have done, but you had no right to treat him like that. You've no
right to treat anyone like that.' To which Wittgenstein disconcertingly
returned, 'We must know one another.' 'I don't see the necessity,'
Leavis replied. In the piece in which he tells this anecdote, Leavis asks
the question whether arrogance is the proper word to apply to Wittgenstein. He writes:

Arrogance? I don't think that anyone who knew him would have rested on that as a suitable word. For the trait was a manifestation of the essential quality that one couldn't be very long with him without becoming aware of – the quality of genius: an intensity of a concentration that impressed itself on one as disinterestedness.

When one thought, as one often did, of 'single-mindedness' as a necessary descriptive word, there was apt to be some criticism in one's intention: 'He doesn't give one a chance.' From observation I conclude that that would have described my reaction if I had ever committed myself to a serious discussion with him. Argument once started, he exercised a completeness of command that left other voices little opportunity – unless (which was unlikely) they were prepared to be peremptory, insistent and forceful. In relation to philosophic discussion I heard it said: 'Wittgenstein can take all the sides himself; he answers before you've said it – you can't get in.'

I myself didn't offer to engage him in any serious argument of any kind, though I did on occasion take issue with him. And then I simply said, 'No, we mustn't do that,' and if he pressed for a reason, dismissed the matter with a factual representation as settled – as far as possible unanswerably. This might perhaps seem to indicate that any arrogance there might be was mine. Actually, I think it would be a misleading word to use of either of us, though it seems to me to apply, if at all, to Wittgenstein rather than to me: if you were not by nature 'recessive' you had, on occasion at any rate, to be firm and final with him.[21]

Recessive is certainly not what anyone has ever taken Leavis to be. Dominant – indeed excessively so – is the general, perhaps the universal description. And in this context Leavis's interpretation and refinement of the term arrogant seems both just and cogent, particularly as it applies to himself: an intensity of concentration that imposes itself upon one as disinterestedness and singlemindedness. That Wittgenstein and Leavis had in common this very rare quality helps to explain the continuance of an association begun so unpromisingly between markedly different personalities with totally disparate leading themes to their lives. (So different that at the end of one meeting Wittgenstein's advice to Leavis was, 'Give up literary criticism.') Perhaps the deepest part of the difference illuminated by this anecdote is that disinterestedness or singlemindedness in Leavis, of the kind he attributes to Wittgenstein, was qualified by human responsiveness, a more grounded moral sensitivity to others. Let me confirm this sense I have of Leavis's kind

of singlemindedness by recounting another memory recalled by him of
his relationship with Wittgenstein.

In spite of its acrid beginnings the relationship did develop and lasted
for a couple of years. Wittgenstein fell into the habit of dropping in to
the Leavises' home, sometimes at times highly inconvenient in a family
household. He would arrive unannounced, plunge into the record
cabinet, display a rather unflattering surprise at what it contained, and
fiddle with the settings of the gramophone till it suited his own require-
ments, a liberty one couldn't object to, Leavis thought, since Wittgenstein had perfect pitch. 'What was characteristic about the performance (Wittgenstein's) was not merely the aplomb with which he
ignored our – my wife's and my – apprehensive presence, but the
delicate precision with which he performed the manoeuvre. He was, in
fact, truly and finely cultivated, and, as part of his obvious cultivation,
very musical; and, having absolute pitch, had judged and acted instan-
taneously on hearing the opening bars.'[22] Here is the reminiscence:

I remember . . . one summer evening when he called on me and
suggested that we should go on the river. We walked the mile and a
half to the boathouse in the garden of what is now the Garden House
Hotel and took a canoe. We got in and Wittgenstein said: 'I'll do the
paddling: I need exercise.' I thought that there was no reason why
we shouldn't both take a paddle, and that I liked exercise too, but
forebore to say it. After paddling up the Granta for a quarter of an
hour he stopped the canoe under the bank opposite the University
bathing place, and said, 'Let's get out and walk.' 'There's no footpath
this side,' I replied, 'and, as a cross-country man, I can tell you that
you'll find the going rough and rather difficult.' Since he seemed to
regard the matter as decided in his sense, I got out with him, and
devoted myself to steering him towards gates and hedge-gaps and
helping him through barbed wire and across ditches.
We came finally to the plantation that bounds Trumpington Park
on that side. 'Let's go in there,' he said, turning towards the fence.
Night had come on by then, and I answered, 'No; it wouldn't be discreet.' 'Why not?' he asked challengingly. 'Because,' I said, 'the Hall
is just behind – it's there as a screen.' 'Oh' came unconcessively
from him, and we went along the cart-track that borders the wood,
and emerged, by the stone bridge, on the road that runs from
Grantchester to Trumpington. Leftwards a noise as of steam-organs
made itself heard in the middle distance, and there was a glow in the
sky. 'What's that?' asked Wittgenstein. 'It must be Trumpington
Feast,' I answered. 'Let's go,' he said. With a finality as unprovoca-

tive as I could make it I said, leaving the 'But Wittgenstein!' to be conveyed by the quiet firmness, 'It's by now about eleven.' 'I'm often out later than that,' he replied. 'Yes,' I said, 'but we've left a canoe by the river-bank a good way back, and then, considerably beyond that, there's a man waiting for us at the boathouse.' 'Oh!' he said in the same tone as before. But we turned and retraced our steps to where the springboard of the University Swimming Club pointed to our canoe. We got in; Wittgenstein took up his paddle, and we arrived at the Belle Vue boathouse towards midnight.

The man came forward and held our canoe as we got out. Wittgenstein, who insisted imperiously on paying, didn't, I deduced from the man's protest, give him any tip. I, in my effort to get in first with the payment, had my hand on some money in my trousers pocket, and, pulling it out, I slipped a couple of coins to the man. As we went away, Wittgenstein asked: 'How much did you give him?' I told him, and Wittgenstein said: 'I hope that is not going to be a precedent.' Not, this time, suppressing the impatience I felt, I returned: 'The man told you that he had been waiting for us a couple of hours – for us alone, and there is every reason for believing that he spoke the truth.' 'I,' said Wittgenstein, 'always associate the man with the boathouse.' 'You may,' I retorted, 'but you know that he is separable and has a life apart from it.' Wittgenstein said nothing.[23]

Between Wittgenstein, who was 'a troubled soul, a fact that he neither advertised nor concealed' and Leavis, whose 'trouble' was of an essentially different kind, there was, in spite of a vivid, mutual interest, a degree of intellectual and personal antipathy. Wittgenstein demonstrated that he admired Leavis's character rather than his intellect or his particular literary addiction, which he thought pseudo-intellectual, while Leavis, though he was clear that Wittgenstein *was* a genius, also believed that Wittgenstein's genius was no more relevant to his own intellectual problems than a passion for chess. And while Wittgenstein needed, as Leavis points out, what even a genius of his kind needs, namely some corroborative human presence, he was much more characteristically a solipsistic personality, agonisingly conducting his profound intellectual struggles in extreme isolation, and seemingly almost incapable of real human engagement. He was not, for example, a good teacher. His influence as a teacher, according to Leavis, was not the kind that fortified the intellectual powers of his listeners or resulted in improved understanding of Wittgenstein's theme: '. . . the wonder and the profit for the lecture-audience lay in the opportunity to witness the sustained spontaneous effort of intellectual genius wrestling with its self-proposed problems. I was never present at one of those occasions, and I know, of course, that if I *had* been, the profit could hardly have been mine: I wasn't qualified by training and experience – or by interest in the mode of thought.'[24]

Leavis himself, on the other hand, was a natural teacher for whom education was a constitutive part of his concept of criticism as teaching was a principal means of putting his critical intentions into practice. In Leavis's eye the critical function existed within an educational context. In the same way the values informing and determining each critical act derive from that same world of values which governs the general moral life of human beings. The foundation and development of *Scrutiny* undoubtedly support this contention. Those who founded *Scrutiny* were a set of research students and undergraduates who used to meet at Leavis's house in the early thirties. In one sense it was, as Leavis called it, 'an outlaw enterprise' founded on faith and conducted on a shoestring; in another it represented, as this group saw it, the essential significance of Cambridge. On the one hand it provoked suspicion and hostility in the official academic world; on the other, its ethos attracted all those for whom Cambridge English was one of the most original and living concerns in the literary world of the day. 'We were, and knew we were, Cambridge – the essential Cambridge in spite of Cambridge.'[25]

The *Scrutiny* group included, as well as F.R. and Q. D. Leavis, L. C. Knights, Donald Culver, D. W. Harding, J. L. Russell, Bruce Pattison, James Smith, Henri Fluchère, Denys Thompson, W. H. Mellers, Adrian Bell, W. A. Edwards, John Speirs. In the remoter background of the *Scrutiny* ethos were Matthew Arnold, Henry James, George Santayana, Eliot, and I. A. Richards's 'cleansing analysis of the received vocabulary of criticism.' In the immediate background there was as an influence Q. D. Leavis's highly original research thesis, *Fiction and the Reading Public*, written as a dissertation in the Cambridge School of English, and at first supervised by I. A. Richards, and a penetrating study of the historical sociology of literature.[26] In the background as a model was *The Calendar of Modern Letters* which offered strong and lively contemporary criticism. Even the name of *Scrutiny* was a gesture of respect towards the *Calendar*, recalling its various scrutinies of contemporary writers. Of the *Calendar* Leavis wrote: 'At the core of its contributing connexion was a group of half-a-dozen intelligent critics who really were, it was plain, a group. Discussion playing over a body of common interests could be felt behind their writing. And a quick perceptive responsiveness to the new creative life of the time had determined the interests, the idiom and the approach.'[27] It was clear to the group, the fate of the *Calendar* which lasted two and a half years (1925–27) confirmed it, that the collapse of an intelligent reading public and the development of mass circulations and all that is associated with Northcliffe made it impossible for any serious review to conduct itself on business lines. There could not be a critical review but there must be one. On this assumption it was clear that *Scrutiny* must be the product of a band of able, devoted, uncommercially motivated, totally disinterested writers. Its extraordinary characteristic was to be both anti-establishment and anti-Marxist. The root of the whole enterprise was a conviction that literature mattered crucially to civilisation, representing 'a human reality, an autonomy of the human spirit, for which economic determinism and reductive interpretation in terms of the Class War left no room.'[28] *Scrutiny* had no theoretical orthodoxy or philosophy, but what it offered was a conviction about the state of civilisation and the function of criticism. In fact early contributors were remarkably varied in creed and interest. But they were all simultaneously concerned for conservation and were radically anti-academic: 'We were concerned to promote that which the academic mind, in the "humanities", hates: the creative interplay of real judgements – genuine personal judgements, that is, of engaged minds fully alive in the present.'[29]

Leavis's presence as *Scrutiny's* impulse and directing force was signalled in a curiously inconspicuous way. He appears in the first number as a contributor and a reviewer, and only in Number 3 as a co-editor with L. C. Knights, Donald Culver and Denys Thompson. The name of Q. D. Leavis who was, between 1932 and 1947, a brilliantly original contributor *and* always the anonymous essential background worker, never appeared as a member of the editorial staff. The names of those writing in the first few numbers are surprising both in range and, indeed, in the fact that some of them should have appeared in *Scrutiny* at all, when one remembers the treatment they received once the journal got into its proper stride. (I am thinking of W. H. Auden and I. A. Richards in particular.) But names such as that of the radical conservative philosopher Michael Oakeshott, and Edmund Blunden, H. Butterfield, M. C. Bradbrook, Christopher Dawson, H. J. C. Grierson, Herbert Read, Adrian Bell, William Empson, Edmund Rubbra, G. Lowes Dickinson, and George Santayana, suggest that the excitement of a new venture will attract those whose sympathies express a general good will rather than firm, precise and sustained conviction. As the journal settled down, it was clear that apart from the Leavises the principal collaborators were W. H. Mellers, H. B. Parkes, H. A. Mason, D. A. Traversi, James Smith, Geoffrey Walton, Martin Turnell, Henri Fluchère, Denys Thompson, and perhaps most important of all, D. W. Harding. To this group were to be added later the names of R. G. Cox, Marius Bewley, R. G. Lienhardt and D. J. Enright. There were other, infrequent contributors, some it must be said distinctly lightweight, and no doubt this fact demonstrates the great difficulty *Scrutiny* had in the later post-war years in recruiting contributors of the appropriate quality.

If one wanted definitive evidence of the attitude towards *Scrutiny* and the Leavises prevalent among the Cambridge establishment in the thirties, it can be found very clearly, though not always by design, in T. E. B. Howarth's *Cambridge Between Two Wars*. It was a blend of distaste, uneasiness and amazed exasperation at their sheer awfulness. Leavis is taken to be one of many, among E. M. W. Tillyard, Basil Willey, George Rylands and F. L. Lucas, and one, to boot, who simply would not accept his proper place. Howarth writes:

> Tillyard, built up as an arch-intriguer by the hagiographers of Leavis, disliked sectarian controversy and anyway was busy producing in the thirties three books on Milton and one on Shakespeare; Willey gave courses on the English Moralists, which he worked up into two notable books; and Rylands, whose highly acclaimed lectures drew almost as many outsiders as members of the English Faculty, was still in his heyday as a theatrical producer.
>
> So it was that the spotlight centred increasingly on Leavis and the name of the play changed, as John Gross has epigrammatically put it, from the meaning of meaning to the value of values. Leavis was (and still is) a controversialist to the very core of his being. In that respect the only foeman worthy of his steel was Lucas – immensely well read in classical and modern European literature, a traditionalist in literary taste and a radical in politics, stylish and witty both verbally and on paper and afraid of no one, least of all Dr and Mrs Leavis.[30]

What F. L. Lucas – hardly a name to conjure with now – was not afraid to say about the Leavises was that they were

> 'latter-day Puritans, intent on imposing exclusive and salvationist beliefs and values on the impressionable young ... Tight-lipped Calvins of Art, teaching the young to love literature by first loathing

nine-tenths of it, and carrying their white and lofty foreheads with the self-important anguish of waiters staggering under towers of exquisitely brittle crockery.' Himself knowledgeable and at ease in Classical culture, Icelandic saga, French and German, Lucas found Leavis narrow, insular and the very reverse of life-enhancing.[31]

According to Howarth (who gives the impression that he thinks it distinctly unfair), Leavis, not Lucas, won the day because of 'the great hold he exercised on generations of undergraduates, who propagated his views in schools and universities throughout the country; and secondly because of 'the solid platform he provided for himself by the publication of *Scrutiny*, which first appeared in 1932, the year in which he became director of studies at Downing and four years before he at last became an assistant lecturer and published his immensely influential *Revaluation*.'[32]

This last observation seems to suggest that Leavis's teaching career and *Scrutiny* itself were elements in a campaign designed to defeat F. L. Lucas, which apart from elevating Lucas to a quite disproportionate significance absurdly underrates the positive purposes to which Leavis devoted his life. But there is, nevertheless, a grain of truth lodged in the corner of what Howarth says. In so far as Leavis's work had a negative aim, and wasn't, as it was, the realisation of a rare gift, it was intended to oppose, and if possible to defeat, what F. L. Lucas and those of his world stood for. What that was Leavis explained on many occasions in many different ways. Sometimes when explaining it, carried away by passion and anger, he gave the impression – particularly in the tone in which he wrote – that he felt himself to be the victim of some organised conspiracy. There is evidence to that effect in some of his letters to the public press,[33] in spite of explicit disclaimers. He wrote, for example, in December 1953 to the *Manchester Guardian*:

> I do not, then, in my valedictory article, or anywhere, speak of any 'conspiracy' against myself; and to speak of 'conspiracy' in any case, is to ignore (as Dr Daiches follows all the precedents in doing) the actual analysis that has been presented and documented again and again in *Scrutiny* – the analysis of the state of literary culture in this phase of our civilization. I have not accused the British Council of enmity towards *Scrutiny* or myself. What I have said is that, as things are, an organisation financed by the State for the promotion of British culture will inevitably work to impose the social-personal 'currency values of metropolitan literary society and the associated University milieux' as the distinctions and achievements

of contemporary England, and so to repress the stir of genuine life. Of this truth, I have pointed out, those British Council 'Surveys' present unanswerable and readily accessible evidence.

That the prevailing state of affairs has involved discrimination against *Scrutiny* no one who considers the plain facts can deny. Many people (to adduce a clear representative instance) have copies – I enclose one, sir, – of the correspondence I had with the Editor of the *Times Literary Supplement* in 1950, when a special 'Survey of Contemporary British Writing for Overseas Readers' included an otherwise very comprehensive account of 'Literary Periodicals' in which there was no mention of *Scrutiny*. My letter calling attention to the fact was not published. A short while before that a Third Programme talk on the literary reviews of our time by Mr Pryce-Jones had also, though it ranged from *New Verse* to *The Criterion*, left out *Scrutiny*. Mr John Raymond in a later talk on contemporary literary criticism achieved a similar discrimination: it has, in fact, been routine. And I am surprised that Dr Daiches, after his participation in a fairly recent series of talks on 'Literary Criticism in Our Time', feels himself able to report a general readiness in B.B.C. performers to recognise, on the due occasion, any such order of achievement as he has just attributed to *Scrutiny* and *Scrutiny* authors in your pages.[34]

Scrutiny, then, was unpopular and in a worldly sense unsuccessful. This was as much to be attributed to such influences as the inept amateurism of British artistic and literary life, to the British fear of the deeply engaged, to the British suspicion of the unengaging oddity, and of course to the fine threads which make the impalpable British Establishment into a potent unity, as to anything like a deliberately concerted hostility. The weight of a wasp-like Leavis settling on the gossamer structure was more than enough to alarm and agitate it. *Scrutiny* in another sense was extraordinarily successful,[35] running for twenty years on nothing but the intense devotion of its collaborators, selling out every copy, and becoming in the course of time one of the strongest and most productive literary intellectual centres of the day. Sometimes men of good will must wish that Leavis could have been more content with the second and less disturbed by the first. (It is, no doubt, easy for the uninvolved to take this lofty attitude.) One of *Scrutiny*'s most important functions, and surely one that accounted most for its success, was to act as the workshop and theatre for Leavis's own criticism. In the course of twenty years the substance of most of his books appeared first in *Scrutiny* and, indeed, their shape frequently betrays their periodical origin.

Leavis's literary career, stretching from 1929 to 1976, began rather later than one might have expected, but it went on much longer than usual and he was in fact producing significant work in his eighties. His first publication, a piece called 'T. S. Eliot: a Reply to the Condescending', appeared in the *Cambridge Review* in 1929, and was reprinted in 1970 in a collection called *The Cambridge Mind*. It shows a sensitive intimacy with everything Eliot had published to date and, very early, a firm sense of the critical function and material:

> The critic must cultivate this sense of fact in regions where there are no facts that can be handed round or brought into the laboratory. He must aim, in so far as he is a critic, to establish the work of art as a fact, an object existing outside of, and apart from himself. Actually, of course, this cannot be done, and there is no one demonstrably right judgement. But a critic is a critic only in so far as he is controlled by his ideals.[36]

In 1931 he published some reviews, a piece on Donne, and a general critical review for *The Bookman*. Other early essays, some of them of a more general and social kind, were published by The Minority Press, a company founded by Gordon Fraser while still an undergraduate in St John's. These and some related *Scrutiny* pieces were collected in a volume *For Continuity* which appeared under the Fraser imprint in 1933. Some of the titles of these pieces have a significance for the future. One of them, for example, is called 'Mass Civilization and Minority Culture', another, 'What's Wrong with Criticism', another, 'Restatement for Critics', and there are two essays already on Lawrence. Eliot, who had liked 'Mass Civilization and Minority Culture' when it came out as a pamphlet, asked Leavis to write a piece on contemporary criticism for his *Criterion Miscellanies* but in the event it was rejected and printed in *For Continuity*. The rejection must have been a deep disappointment to Leavis and may well have been the origin of that sense of personal inadequacy in Eliot which grew stronger in Leavis over the years. The comments about Leavis's incapacity to write, so unjust about the mature work, do get some warrant from these early performances, which show insufficient precision in the idiom and an uncharacteristic and premature generalising habit. The true stamp of the Leavis attitude, approach, and style, appears first in a small seminal book *New Bearings in English Poetry* in 1932. *New Bearings* was followed by the second original and authentic work *Revaluation* in 1936. During the next forty years these two books were to be succeeded by a series of volumes which were to establish Leavis as the most notable of English critics since Arnold, and as one of the most significant writers on the English literary scene. I am thinking of *The Great Tradition: George Eliot, Henry James, Joseph Conrad* (1948), *The Common Pursuit* (1952), *D. H. Lawrence: Novelist* (1955), *Anna Karenina and Other Essays* (1967), *Dickens the Novelist* (1970), *Nor Shall My Sword: Discourses on Pluralism, Compassion and Social Hope* (1972), *The Living Principle: 'English' as a Discipline of Thought* (1975), and *Thought, Words and Creativity* (1976). I shall turn in due course to the detailed consideration of these works, but I want to pause here to make a number of general preliminary comments on the body of the work.

The spirit that breathes in the best, and particularly in the latest, of these books is that of an austere Cambridge liberalism, one at once worried by the attrition of history and strengthened by an intense, protestant or rather protesting ethic. This was the spirit which had in it, as Richard Poirier puts it, 'the Arnoldian – later to be the Leavisian – sense of English letters: that it was a carrier of as well as a clue to the state of the culture as a whole, that cultural values depended upon an alert sense of the function of literature and of criticism.'[37] The English quality of this ethos was modified in Leavis, as in Arnold, by a fine sense of European civilisation. An illustration of this point occurs in a reminiscence given by Leavis in his essay on Montale's *Xenia*:

> I have found Montale's poetry peculiarly congenial. What makes it so congenial I can begin to suggest by recalling the occasion when, a couple of years ago, I had the honour, at Milan, to meet Montale. How it was that someone present came to quote from *Le Cimetière marin* I can't now remember, but Montale and I found ourselves reciting, in relays, Valéry's poem. How far we got I again can't remember, but it was plain that, between us, we could easily have reproduced the whole poem from memory.[38]

It is peculiar, then, that Leavis, whose criticism best articulated the mind of this liberal, English protestant sensibility, should have been accused both at the beginning of his career and at the end of suffering some Marxist infection. In 1933 in of all places the *New Statesman*, Calder Marshall represents him as advocating Marxism 'so that a Communist tyranny can impose the reading of *The Calendar* on an unwilling proletariat,'[39] an accusation which turns upside down the anti-Marxism, implicit and explicit, in what Leavis wrote. It is odder that at the end of his life the same extraordinary suggestion should have been made, and referred for justification to a rather youthful and euphoric remark made in *Scrutiny* in 1932. T. E. B. Howarth wrote:

> Dr Leavis in a long life has frequently boasted, and on the whole rightly, of his imperviousness to the infection of Marxism. Yet in *Scrutiny* (December 1932) he wrote: 'Let me say, then, that I agree with the Marxist to the extent of believing some form of economic communism to be inevitable and desirable in the sense that it is to this that a power-economy of its very nature points, and only by a deliberate and intelligent working towards it can civilization be saved from disaster.' Some of the Scrutineers' most cherished values have not particularly thrived under that form of economic organisation.[40]

In fact, Leavis and *Scrutiny* offered the only strongly articulated opposition to the developing strength of Marxist criticism in the English speaking world.[41]

In essence Leavis, for all his courtesy and charity to religion at large and his many Christian students in particular, was a protestant – or more accurately – a protesting humanist. He belonged by nature to the tradition of angry dissent. A secure sense of human value of a profoundly English kind was at the base of a sensibility which expressed itself, on the one hand, in discerning in literature what corresponded to its intuitive grasp of reality, and on the other, in rejecting whatever did not, rejecting whatever did not, that is, both in literature and life. Given his period, Leavis's life-long opposition was not primarily to the Marxism which, had he lived later, might have been his most obvious enemy, but to the British Establishment, to the many forms and institutions through which it influenced society, and to the ethos it spun and the assumptions it supported. Leavis had to have an opposing force before he could gather his own strength. So much of his best and most positive work takes off from a position of disagreement with some inert conventional view or some unwarranted and arbitrary estimation.

But Leavis, true to his conviction of the necessary intermingling of life and literature, by no means confined himself to literary questions. He was a vigorous and pertinacious polemicist who used *Scrutiny* itself for many years as a platform from which to criticise society, education and the press, as well as the peculiarly bland hypocrisy of English life, and after the demise of *Scrutiny* he made the press itself serve a similar purpose. His polemical letters to the papers were collected in a volume *Letters in Criticism* published in 1974. It encompasses a great variety of subject and tone.

Topics treated in these letters are literary, educational, sociological, and personal. They stretch from the filming of *Women in Love* to the debate about joining Europe and from the meaning and existence of an organic community to the deficiencies of classical education, from the nature of parody to the trial of *Lady Chatterley's Lover*. Writers written about include Lawrence, Mark Twain, Conrad, Orwell, Eliot, Auden, Dickens, Shelley, Henry James, Ezra Pound, Milton, George Eliot, Chaucer, and Shakespeare. Many of them have to do with correcting misapprehension or misreading of Leavis's own treatment of these writers. Some are painfully personal self-defences, particularly of Leavis's own questioned consistency, e.g. on James and Dickens. Others, perhaps some of the most valuable, are on educational themes, on the function of the university at the present time, on university student unrest, on the qualities likely to be well regarded and rewarded in contemporary Schools of English 'journalistic brightness, glibness and unselfcritical confidence,'[42] on the critical function in the modern world, on the particular deficiencies of the University of Cambridge and its English School. He gives on one occasion strenuous support to Hugh Trevor Roper's plea for more intelligent methods of examination and 'better ways of determining a student's worth than the end-of-course race against the clock.'[43] A leading theme, letters on which frequently ring with a Lutheran scorn and anger, is the concerted reaction of hostile solidarity towards *Scrutiny* and Leavis himself among the powers of the metropolitan world, the academic milieux, and its associated cultural organs. It was the flourishing state of this metropolitan literary world that Leavis was most conscious of and appalled by. Its success was possible because there no longer existed a coherent, educated and influential reading public to judge and diminish it. Its power lay in its capacity to impose social-personal values in place of serious criticism:

> For if it is a small world, it is, as a system of personal and institutional connections, comprehensive: it virtually controls the currency of accepted valuations and the climate of taste. Since its *raison d'être* is to ensure the kudos (not to speak of the profits) of literary distinction against exposure to standards, it is inevitably disastrous for English literature, in the present and the future. Standards having been once banished, such a system will resist with all its resources the reinstatement of the offensive presence.[44]

In these letters Leavis could be caustic, mocking and witty, answering V. S. Pritchett's witticism, 'It is not enough to be pained by Dr. Leavis's telling Thackeray to leave the room because he is only a greater Trollope – quite a good throwaway line for the classroom,' Leavis remarked, 'this assured and vivacious pronouncement . . . may not be addressed to the classroom but it has the air of relying confidently on the right response from the "boys".'[45] Of Graham Hough's use and misreading of a passage in *The Great Tradition* he asks: 'Or is it just possible that, in the course of his unimpressed perusal, the gist of what I say lodged in Mr. Hough's mind, and was disguised from his recognition when he came to write it down by the difference between his idiom and mine?'[46]

But if the fact of literary sociology I have referred to above was what most disturbed Leavis, the two classes of person connected with it who most provoked his ire are the academic politician and the literary journalist, whom Leavis clearly considered to be either friends, or at least close acquaintances of, the mammon of iniquity – although most people will recognise that they have their decent, modest, middle-man's part to play. But as Leavis saw it they combined a deadly lack of seriousness about standards and an appalling air of being in the know with a habit of deriving considerable kudos from their avocation. Leavis's most ferocious irony was applied to the academic administrator like Lord Annan or the literary journalist like Philip Toynbee.

Leavis's remarks on Lord Annan have a peculiarly personal antipathy and a strong Cambridge bite. Perhaps I may quote a substantial piece from a letter written in 1961 in *The Observer*, in which Philip Toynbee, dealing with the question of literature and morality, had rebuked Leavis and his school for its grimly moralising bias. The passage shows the nimbleness of Leavis's ironic play, the characteristically weighty and mobile style, the teacher's capacity for lucid expository skill, and, as well, the passionate seriousness which was the ground of each, and which in Leavis's eyes wholly justified the strongly personal concern:

Mr. Philip Toynbee believes that the 'superiority of modern American poetry to our own' is due to America's happy immunity from my influence, which (we all know) does incalculable harm in this country. So much, at any rate, readers of his article in *The Observer* for January 8 will have been able to comprehend and carry away. . . . Yet may not some readers have asked, and have not I a right to ask, what ground he can point for offering to justify a disapproval of me with this?:

My own inclination is to use a much-travelled quotation against –
why not mention them? – Dr. Leavis and his proliferating
disciples, *Nihil humanum mihi alienum puto.*
This formulation gets no added virtue from its context in what,
being as polite as possible, one might call the succession of formula-
tions, there being nothing in the article that can be called a sequence
of thought. Mr. Toynbee was too preoccupied with establishing his
own enlightenment and eliminating the possibility of reply to have
any thinking left for logic or paraphrasable argument. He carefully
demonstrates his mature adequacy to the difficult theme of Art and
Morality. No one today, he tells us, can be an aesthete; no one can
take the Tolstoyan moralistic line; and every one can see that there
must be some relation between the artist as man and the quality of
his art. Mr. Toynbee himself sees it: his, we are to understand, is the
central, the truly enlightened, position. What is there left for the
sinister influence (with his proliferating disciples) whom Mr.
Toynbee, from his poised centrality, is placing? The Latin tag. The
Latin gives a wise and judicial air to the insinuation.

The insinuation – for Mr. Toynbee himself has had to rely on
insinuation, the stated charge would look too silly – could, if given
an explicit meaning, only be that my criticism favours the kind of
'moral' attitude that figured classically in the prosecution of *Madame
Bovary.* I notoriously, he implies, have shown that I need confront-
ing with the truth he has made it his life's mission to vindicate and
enforce: the principle that 'everything which has been thought, felt,
done or experienced by man should be accessible material for the
poet or the novelist.' This is his gloss on the Latin tag. He adds,
however, italicising the phrase: '*without condemnation or praise.*'
Hamlet, he tells us, 'is the greatest work ever written in the English
language. The judgement is a more arresting one than (to all appear-
ances) he suspects, for he offers it in his modesty as an accepted
commonplace. But more surprising still are the triumphant question
and reply that follow. 'And who is condemned or praised in that
great work? Not even Claudius, surely?'

And that settles it: Shakespeare, like all great artists, is morally
neutral; he merely *represents*, and there are no questions to be asked
about implicit evaluative attitudes. Mr. Toynbee (though he takes
the category 'great' seriously, and seems to think he means something by calling *Hamlet* great) clearly thinks that he has said all that
need be said about the relevance of moral sensibility to the appreciation of Shakespearean tragedy. It is almost incredible; there is a kind
of sublimity about Mr. Toynbee's journalist-insouciance.

For he means his whole article to lead up, or to have the air of leading irresistibly up, to this conclusion, the formulation of the moral he himself draws from his reflections (it is to dispose of me and the proliferating disciples): 'if we underestimate the extreme complexity and indirection of the relations between morality and literature we encourage a backhanded flippancy of judgment. . . . We over-estimate the literary merits of Lawrence.'

This completes the placing of myself. I, the reader is to understand, have, with my well-known timidity or conventionality of moral, or moralistic, *parti-pris*, my crude externality of approach, and my inability to appreciate the extreme complexity of the relations between morality and literature, committed myself to proclaiming Lawrence a great writer – an overvaluation the absurdity of which Mr. Toynbee could expose if he had time.[47]

Most of Leavis's letters to the press were written between 1953 and 1973, that is, after the demise of *Scrutiny* and the incessant, exhausting labour of running the journal without money or support other than his wife's. Although other names appeared, for example that of L. C. Knights, among the editors throughout the journal's existence, this seems to have been no more than a formal gesture or a polite recognition of past services. Leavis wrote for example to *The Times Literary Supplement* in 1972: '. . . after the early days his [L. C. Knights's] connexion with *Scrutiny* was not merely negligible but deprecatory and the effective editing and the major contributions like the actual work, were carried out by my wife and myself.'[48] As an editor Leavis, in his relations with contributors, was, according to D. J. Enright who began to write for *Scrutiny* as an undergraduate, 'exceptionally courteous and unintrusive . . . his intervention was limited to a comma less a comma more; he never argued about length, and he would insist on paying for a book one had bought to review.'[49] As a professional writer he kept the admiration and loyalty of his publishers, Chatto & Windus. Ian Parsons, who dealt with Leavis's work from 1932 until his retirement from Chatto's, reported that he had had very few disputes and these had been conducted with 'complete frankness on both sides, and resolved without rancour. . . . Much too busy doing his own work, teaching and writing, he has been content to leave us to do ours, and has never badgered us about sales or breathed down our necks about publicity, as so many others do.'[50] Ian Parsons's work was taken on by D. J. Enright who discovered Leavis as a writer to be 'prompt and patient, scrupulous in thanking me for catching minor slips' and willing even to rephrase some passages. 'Concerning the Leavisian style which has caused so much pain in some quarters,' Enright goes on, 'he could take a firm line: "I'm afraid I'm obdurate." When I suggested a way of rewriting a particularly involved sentence, he replied, ". . . nobody would believe it was *me*!" True, I had brought out "the meaning", but lost the tone of voice, the cast of mind, and hence part of what he meant.'[51]

One of the events – I think it can be called an event – which gives one the opportunity to observe the Leavis style in a Johnsonian context, was the famous – or as Snow supporters would say, the iniquitous – Richmond Lecture given in private in Downing College in 1962 and provoked by a rather flimsy meditation by Lord Snow on 'The Two Cultures and the Scientific Revolution', which was itself a Cambridge lecture, the Rede Lecture given in 1959. Snow's own lecture offered no more than some superficial observations about the mutual incomprehension of scientists and non-scientists, cast in a characteristically unrigorous way and expressed with insensitive vulgarity. Leavis's retort, news of it having leaked out to the press, was published in the *Spectator*, furbished with cartoons which Leavis had not been warned of and about which he protested indignantly. There are those, and not by any means only friends and supporters of Snow's rather bumbling complacencies, who thought there was a disproportion between the force applied and the object attacked. Lionel Trilling, for example, deplored the tone in which Leavis wrote and the manner calculated to cause unnecessary pain and offence. Leavis insisted that his treatment of Snow was not generated by personal animosity. It was strictly impersonal:

My lecture has no personal animus in it: the kind of drastic finality I aimed at in my dismissal of the Intellect and Sage was incompatible with that. But, of course, if by a sharpness, clarity and cogency of challenge that make it hardly possible not to see the 'cruel' truth you undo the publicity-work that has made a great public figure out of a person of undistinguished capacities, that person must inevitably feel that he has suffered an odious experience – one that he will identify with an unfeeling and destructive 'attack.'[52]

Snow was a portent of a frivolous and superficial age, in which there had been the supersession of serious intellectual criteria by media-created publicity-values. That someone as undistinguished as a writer and thinker as Snow could be elevated into the position of sage and intellectual authority was what passionately concerned Leavis. The blend of personal anger, intellectual disdain, moral scorn, and suppleness and individuality of expression, remind one of Johnson on Chesterfield:

> ... anyone who offers to speak with inwardness and authority on both science and literature will be conscious of more than ordinary powers, but one can imagine such consciousness going with a certain modesty – with a strong sense, indeed, of a limited range and a limited warrant. The peculiar quality of Snow's assurance expresses itself in a pervasive tone; a tone of which one can say that, while only genius could justify it, one cannot readily think of genius adopting it.[53]

There is, then, a trinity of critics collected in the Leavis we know. The first is the Johnsonian deliverer of certainties,[54] moral, literary and commonsensical. Next there is the Arnoldian writer who was at once the subtle analyst of literature and the missionary to society. And then there is the Coleridgean theoretician of language, cultural continuity and decline. These critics did not follow one another in neat succession – there are elements of each in every phase of Leavis's career – but it would not be wholly inaccurate to say that the earliest work, as well as the educational writings, belongs to the Johnsonian *persona*, the longer middle to the Arnoldian, and the final period to the Coleridgean. Perhaps we could say that Leavis was Johnsonian in temperament, Arnoldian in the practice of criticism, and Coleridgean in his conclusions.

He had, an amazing thing when one thinks of our age of uncertainty, anxiety, and doubt, a swift and untroubled, a positively Augustan, self-confidence about his deepest judgements of value and an unworried certainty in their application in the exercise of his craft. As a critic his manner, in which positives are unmistakably implied by every point in the exposition, is in keeping with Arnold's dictum: 'Here the great safeguard is never to let oneself become abstract, always to retain an intimate and lively consciousness of the truth of what one is saying, and the moment this fails us, to be sure that something is wrong.'[55] In the great critical work of Leavis's middle period, there is an uninterrupted, supple flow of movement between principle and fact. And finally he came, in the books of his latest years, to a Coleridgean position about the vital significance of language in human life and culture. *Nor Shall My Sword* (1972), *The Living Principle* (1975), and *Thought, Words and Creativity* (1976) are directly related to the philosophy implicit in Coleridge's dictum: 'For if words are not things, they are living powers, by which things of most importance to mankind are activated, combined and humanised.'[56] And since 'the best part of human language properly so called is derived from reflection on the acts of the mind itself,' attention to the combinations, relations and the mutual accommodations of words gives us direct access to the intimate operations of the mind. When these are the words of a great writer, we have the liberalising experience of being made free, luminously free, of a mind infinitely more subtle, complex and powerful than our own. And by mind, of course, is meant not just intellect but the whole concourse of cooperative mental powers, of thought, feeling, purpose and imagination. One says made free of. But this is not to imply that it is easy. It is something Leavis showed that we have to struggle towards with discipline and abnegation.

The great critics – and it is a measure of Leavis's stature that it is impossible not to think of him in this context – had their personal and professional deficiencies. Johnson's truculently narrow dogmatism went with an Augustan incapacity to appreciate the nature of the poetic drama and the Shakespearian use of words. Coleridge's undisciplined self-pity and indulgence allowed the philosopher constantly to emerge to throttle the critic. And a certain blanched gentility in Matthew Arnold accompanied a romantic blindness to the power of Dryden and Pope. Leavis is said by many to have suffered from a species of paranoia or persecution mania and a sensibility lacking in generosity to anything but the very best, and that of a certain kind. But as D. J. Enright pointed out, paranoia is precisely a delusion and it is very hard for the impartial observer to conclude that the hostility shown to Leavis throughout his career, and particularly at Cambridge, was something he simply imagined. Moreover, as D. J. Enright writes again, 'When men have been treated as outcasts, they can hardly be expected to show the dispassionate sobriety of the law-abiding citizen.'[57]

What is clear is that Leavis, while on the one hand he received a strong devotion and lasting affection from his own pupils and sympathisers, provoked dislike and even hatred in as many others. To his own pupils his attitude combined cordiality, abstinence about interfering in their own careers – he never saw himself as a kingmaker – but also unstinted generosity if called on for help. His creation of the Downing School which gained him a world-wide reputation took place at the same time as an increasing alienation from members of the English Faculty at Cambridge, and indeed from many of those who were his early friends. He received very little in the way of public recognition or honours. He was once a defeated candidate for the Chair of Poetry at Oxford, an election he entered for because he thought of it as Matthew Arnold's Chair. When he retired in 1962 a fund collected to endow a lectureship in his honour had a disastrous conclusion when the appointed person, H. A. Mason, turned out in Leavis's eye to be wholly at odds with his views, while the journal associated with his group aimed, as Leavis declared, 'not the less so for deferential shows, at the undoing of all one has worked for.'[58] The fund was finally transferred to the University of York to help in academic publication. He received an honorary degree from the University of Leeds, and one from the University of York where after his retirement he became a Visiting Professor. He performed the same function at the University College of North Wales. In 1967 he was invited to give the Clark Lectures at Cambridge which were later published as *English Literature in our Time and the University*, and in the year of his death he was made a Companion of Honour. Even the honorary Fellowship to which he was elected on his retirement from Downing he felt it necessary to resign from when he saw what the College intended to happen to English Studies there. This was a pretty modest handful of distinctions for a man of his genius and influence.

It was not neglect, Leavis once drily remarked, that he had to complain about in the press over many years, and his death again illustrated the truth of his observation. He was as much a draw in death as in life. The press reaction exhibited the same great range to him dead as living. To one he was a teacher of genius, 'a critic of the first rank' who 'gave new aspects to the map of feeling and recognitions' (George Steiner), to another whom his writings affected 'like cold lino worn thin in a January bathroom' he was deficient in 'discernment, vigorous enjoyment and love, and lucidity' (Geoffrey Grigson). To another he represented and presented 'a critical and personal position perpetually on a war footing' (Kingsley Amis), to another his pre-eminence among modern English critics was a cultural phenomenon, 'in Arnoldian terms, a convergence of the Man and the Moment' (David Lodge). Another pointed out the irony 'in the fact that his lasting achievement as critic and teacher was not to have made disciples and converts but to have persuaded not very clever or subtle pupils to read and really respond to extremely clever and subtle authors – authors like George Eliot, Henry James, Conrad and D. H. Lawrence' (John Bayley). To another, while his own criticism, 'his engagement with specific texts as opposed to his overall view of the literary tradition – could be marvellously flexible and subtle, . . . it was regularly depressing to see just how much mediocrity his polemical fervour permitted him to sanction' (Ian Hamilton). For another, 'F. R. Leavis is one of that very, very tiny handful of critics in our time who will take an essential and significant place in the great tradition of literary criticism which he did so much to make explicit and then urgently and actively to extend' (Malcolm Bradbury). The most balanced and vividly intimate epitaph appeared in *The Times*, and I will quote some illuminating lines from it:

> When all bitterness is forgotten, Leavis will be remembered for his devotion to the cause of education and literature. He regarded the second in the light of the first, and therefore bred teachers and critics rather than artists. Outside his professional and family circle he developed few interests and no relaxations; in his youth he had shewn prowess at cross country racing and the loneliness of the long-distance runner adhered. A certain spartan frugality and fine intensity of living marked him with a mixture of vitality and asceticism; something at once very fragile and very wiry in his slight figure, but above all the flame-like nimbleness of his speech and glance, compelled attention. While to some he seemed a rare talent grown painfully awry, to others he assumed almost Socratic powers. His influence extended far beyond the boundaries of the subjects to which he confined himself.[59]

2

Educational Purposes

Leavis's first pieces were collected in a volume, *For Continuity*, which was published by his friend Gordon Fraser's Minority Press at Cambridge in 1933. A still earlier pamphlet, also published by Fraser, *How to Teach Reading*, was a lively riposte to Ezra Pound's *How to Read*. It was reproduced some years later in 1943 in *Education and the University*. Leavis referred self-mockingly to his reply to Pound as a descent into pedagogy, and it is a phrase which makes a cogent comment on the early volume, *For Continuity*. It has markedly corrective and educational aims. Leavis contends – persuasively, I think – that the pieces in it for all the occasional circumstances of their production compose more than a collection. They illustrate and develop the preoccupations and arguments of the early pamphlet, *Mass Civilization and Minority Culture*. They are also unified by the distinctive personality of the writer, a drier, lighter and more courteous Leavis than that which developed later. The contents of the book include Leavis's earliest sketch of an analysis of social and cultural decline, and his response to the Marxism of the thirties which – hard as that is to believe now – seemed to offer to many at the time so promising an alternative. He makes a first 'serious attempt at stabilising and defining a reaction' to the Lawrence who became very much a source of his positive values. He puts forward his first proposals on the nature of criticism. His registration of the symptoms of cultural decline are given point by short and perceptive analyses of a number of writers, Arnold Bennett, John dos Passos, James Joyce, and such current poets as Auden, Spender, C. Day Lewis and Roy Campbell.

It is curious that Leavis who in his middle, and greatest, period was more than once taken to task for his untheoretical and densely particularised kind of literary criticism, began his career in a mood of near-Johnsonian generality. The earliest pieces were much concerned with the nature of criticism and with the social and historical conditions in which it has to be practised. He deals more frequently than not with large, philosophical issues. The central theme is the nature of criticism:

What is the function of literary culture – its *raison d'être*? Why do we read, and why should we? By what standards, what criteria, what principles can we bring order into our reading (in so far as it doesn't belong with smoking) and establish it safely as something other than elegantly virtuous dissipation or (what is much the same thing) accumulation?[1]

This key question brings in contemporary conditions and deficiencies. No doubt that is why in more than one of these early essays Leavis is concerned with Marxism. It was extremely difficult, Leavis acknowledged, to determine what precisely the orthodox Marxist doctrine of culture was, and he himself pleaded guilty to the familiar charge that he had not minutely studied the Bible. He is, however, clear that for most of the time one of the great attractions of Marxism was its simplicity: '. . . it absolves from the duty of wrestling with complexities; above all, the complexities introduced if one agrees that the cultural values – human ends – need more attention than they get in the doctrine, strategy and tactics of the Class War.'[2] Moreover, he noted the paradox that what one commonly found in Marxist writing was oblivion of or indifference to the finest values of bourgeois or capitalist culture, and, as for example in the case of Theodore Dreiser, a contemporary hero, complete acceptance of the crude, completely unleavened bourgeois world that it was attacking. If the Marxist, quoting the example of Russia, retorted that economic maladjustments had to have priority and once dealt with they would produce cultural regeneration, Leavis replied that 'In such a country, illiterate, inert and economically primitive, a drive for literacy, economic efficiency and social righteousness together might well be expected to bring, along with mechanisation, a cultural awakening.'[3] The different conditions of America and Britain did not cry out for literacy and mechanisation. Literary talent and literature in these countries suffered from other kinds of thwarting and starvation than the economic. Leavis announced with that absolute certainty which is the other Johnsonian attribute of the early work, 'There *is*, then, a point of view above classes; there *can* be intellectual, aesthetic and moral activity that is not merely an expression of class origin and economic circumstances; there *is* a "human culture" to be aimed at that must be achieved by cultivating a certain autonomy of the human spirit.'[4] The Marxist, in fact, in matters of literary value turns out to be a very good 'bourgeois'. The Marxist loves machinery and capitalism – State capitalism in his case – as much as any Ford, whereas Leavis insisted that, in a civilisation of which the machinery becomes more and more overwhelming, the life and authority of this extra-individual mind – consciousness, sense of value and memory – must be worked for consciously.

The Marxist view, incomplete in its analysis and as crassly Philistine in its solution as what it opposed, nevertheless connected literature and society, experience and culture. In our own world there was only a vast inattention to this relationship. We live with hardly a nucleus of an educated public in the midst of a process of cultural dissolution and of machine-induced change so catastrophic that the generations themselves find it impossible to adjust themselves to each other: 'The standards that, maintained in a living tradition, constituted a surer taste than any individual as such can pretend to, have gone with the tradition.'[5] There were those aware of the results of disintegration and decay who still showed nothing like an adequate awareness of what has been lost. This was not merely bourgeois or capitalist culture, but the organic community. We have neither a rural community nor a town community but almost universally suburbanism. 'The organic community has virtually disappeared, and with it the basis for a genuine national culture; so nearly disappeared that when one speaks of the old popular culture that existed in innumerable local variations people cannot grasp what one means.'[6] This is not merely a matter of literary taste, since.

> The culture in question, which is not, indeed, identical with literary tradition but which will hardly survive it, is a sense of relative value and a memory – such wisdom as constitutes the residuum of the general experience. It lives only in individuals, but individuals can live without it; and where they are without it they do not know what they miss. And the world, troubled as it is, is unaware of what is gone.[7]

We have no centre, no authority, no discerning minority to keep alive the subtlest and most perishable parts of the tradition. Those to whom Johnson appealed when he spoke of rejoicing to concur with the common reader no longer exist. Taste in Johnson's time was in the keeping of the educated, who shared a homogeneous culture. An essential task of the literary critic is to maintain or revive, however tenuously, a connection with this almost vanished reality. This function is not, Leavis admits, the whole duty of man, or the whole duty of the educated man. But, the more seriously one is concerned with literary criticism, the less possible is it to be concerned with that alone. This predicament concerns us all but particularly the critic:

For it is true that culture in the past has borne a close relation to the 'methods of production.' A culture expressing itself in a tradition of literature and art – such a tradition as represents the finer conscious-ness of the race and provides the currency of finer living – can be in a healthy state only if this tradition is in living relation with a real culture, shared by the people at large. The point might be enforced by saying (there is no need to elaborate) that Shakespeare did not invent the language he used. And when England had a popular culture, the structure, the framework, of it was a stylisation, so to speak of economic necessities; based, it might fairly be said, on the 'methods of production' was an art of living, involving codes, developed in ages of continuous experience, of relations between man and man, and man and the environment in its seasonal rhythm. This culture the progress of the nineteenth century destroyed, in country and in town; it destroyed (to repeat a phrase now familiar) the organic community. And what survives of cultural tradition in any important sense survives in spite of the rapidly changing 'means of production.'[8]

In conditions of loss and decay, of a culture declining as the tradition which informed and sustained it declines, Leavis argues strenuously for the value and cogency of the critical function, particularly of the literary critical function, and above all of that properly understood. The inert practice which passes in academic circles, Leavis notes, was dismissed with scornful unceremoniousness by Ezra Pound in his *How to Read*, though not, says Leavis, too scornfully.[9] As one devoted to the study and teaching of literature, as he describes himself, he asks 'why do I think this devotion, in an age of "crises," a worthy one?'[10] In the first place it is upon a very small minority that the discerning appreciation of art and literature depends. There is also a larger min-ority capable of endorsing by genuine personal response the discern-ment of the critic: 'The accepted valuations are a kind of paper currency based upon a very small proportion of gold. To the state of such a currency the possibilities of fine living at any time bear a close rela-tion.'[11] Culture depends upon an unimpeded flow of communication and understanding between this few and the general public through the medium of an educated class. The culture which the literary mind – the intelligence trained in the study of literature – must be in touch with and make available is 'the culture that transcends the individual as the language he inherits transcends him.'[12] Implicit in that culture are standards surer and sounder than any an individual can pretend to. His possession of it gives the critic's personal choices a more than personal validity. Moreover, Leavis believes that if the critical function, now so inoperative, is not revived and refined, the interest in literature itself as an influence upon feeling, art and standard will die and where that happens, creation itself will not long persist. The existing state of affairs can be described, according to Leavis, like this: 'no one interested in poetry can suppose that if all the serious poets now writing died within the year the newspapers would register any noticeable shock. The world is not interested; and this lack of interest must seem to those concerned about culture more frightening than hostility.'[13]

Already, then, in the early thirties at the beginning of his career, Leavis was reflecting on the nature and purpose of the critical act. He was clear that it had both to be controlled by a strict conception of its nature and method and also that it had to have more than merely literary purposes. Not much help was available, Leavis considered, as he looked around at the current scene, to help to train one in strictness of literary conception and practice. There are many names in the history of criticism but there are few that helped to improve one's equipment and one's efficiency as a reader.

At least two of them are of our time: Mr. Eliot and Mr. Richards; it is a very large proportion indeed of the total. Mr. Richards has improved the instruments of analysis, and has consolidated and made generally accessible the contribution of Coleridge. Mr. Eliot has not only refined the conception and the methods of criticism; he has put into currency decisive reorganising and re-orientating ideas and valuations.[14]

The critic is given his essential data by his capacity to discern and fix differences of quality and degree. It is an art which has to be developed by immediate and particular acts of choice following upon a real and appropriate responsiveness to the thing offered.

Without a free and delicate receptivity to fresh experience, whatever the criterion alleged, there is no judging, but merely negation. And this kind of negation, persisted in, with no matter what righteous design, produces in the end nullity: the 'criterion,' however once validated by experience, fades into impotent abstraction, the 'values' it represents become empty husks. The safety sought in this way proves to be the safety of death.[15]

The critic has to note and register with conscious attention what was implicit in his response. This is particularly important for the critic who is apt to be tempted simply to extract and categorise abstract ideas.

Leavis gives two examples, Wordsworth and Lawrence, whose work is peculiarly susceptible to this mishandling. Certainly Wordsworth had ideas, but his philosophy, as Arnold said, was certainly an illusion. 'But the only way to fix anything for discussion in the shifting verbosities of his abstract "thinking" is to start from the concrete and never lose touch with it. What is successful as poetry is obviously "there"; its abstractable implications, or those encouraged by a general knowledge of Wordsworth, may be coaxed out as far as seems discreet into the Wordsworthian philosophic fog and the poetry made the solid nucleus for such organisation in terms of "thought" as seems worth attempting. But we ought never to forget that Wordsworth matters as a "thinker" only (if at all) because he is a poet.'[16]

The second example, that of Lawrence, is peculiarly interesting in face of his later views. Lawrence's thought, or prophecy, Leavis declares, matters because he was an artist of genius:

> His gift lay, not in thinking, but in experiencing, and in fixing and evoking in words the feelings and perceptions that seemed to him most significant. Lawrence's commentary on experience, his doctrine, must be approached by way of the concrete, the successful art; criticism of the doctrine cannot be separated from judgements concerning literary success or failure; discussion, to be intelligent, must be controlled by the critical sensibility.'[17]

It is clear that anyone holding such views of the purpose of criticism, anyone with this attitude to Marxism, anyone with a strong leaning towards the particularised response and the concrete judgement, anyone with a powerful moral impulse in his nature, would find it natural to think that literary criticism should issue into educational activity. 'We assume an "inner human nature", and our recognition that it may be profoundly affected by the "economic process" persuades us that it must rally, gather its resources and start training itself for its ultimate responsibility at once. A cogent way in which the human spirit can refute the Marxian theory and the bourgeois negative lies open in education.'[18]

It was, then, very much in keeping with Leavis's controlling assumptions and with the bent of his talent for him to have made expressly educational applications of his critical practice. The first was in *Culture and Environment*,[19] a small, unpretentious volume for schools, written in collaboration with a schoolmaster friend, Denys Thompson; the second, in *Education and the University*, which I shall take up shortly, which was directed to the problems of Higher Education.

Leavis addressed *Culture and Environment* to a sensitive place in the unfolding national consciousness, to the eighteen-year-olds of the Sixth Forms, the future university students and especially the future teachers. It is they who will in the long run intimately affect the assumptions and the practice of the nation. Part of Leavis's long-term influence is attributable to an unremarked but important characteristic of our educational system, that the current of ideas between school and university is open and direct, much more, for example, than in the United States where the connection is slack and meagre. The degree of intelligence in Sixth forms, the kind of study undertaken, the lively interest in ideas, dispose them to welcome strong and relevant conceptions originating in the University. And one has to add that there is something in Leavis's work peculiarly attractive to the intelligent young, something to which the 'unestablished' intelligence is genuinely responsive. It lies, I think, in the combination of reference to a more organic, a more 'human' society with a severe critique of empty, fashionable forms, an equilibrium of positive and negative, answering both to the desire for reform and the impulse towards belief.

If the intelligent sixth former and undergraduate take to Leavis, if his work calls up so full a response, that is because the young, with their unfatigued sense for what is living, recognise vitality. Vitality is the consequence or concomitant of the natural movement of Leavis's thought. His profoundest concern is with life, with quality in living – with what he calls in *Culture and Environment* 'an art of life, a way of living, ordered and patterned, involving social arts, codes of intercourse and a responsive adjustment . . .' This is at the base of his preoccupation with language, since it is through language, which is never merely individual, that individual action is transformed into human experience. And both concerns inform his attitude to literature, which is at once the most powerful and inclusive use of language, words with their roots in life, *and* always more than simply an aggregate of individual words. The criticism of literature for Leavis is an activity which begins deep down among our ultimate convictions and carries along with it our habitual modes of thought and feeling and all our constant operative relations with words. Implicit in our response to literature is our attitude to life. To educate through literature, therefore, is to cultivate, through that sensitive application to words which is together an extension of consciousness and a refinement of feeling, a growth of human life. This requires singleness of purpose and the discipline of relevance, since 'literature is literature and not another thing.' But it also means that the aptitudes encouraged, the intentions promoted, the values endorsed can never be only literary ones: 'a real literary interest is an interest in man, society and civilisation, and its boundaries cannot be drawn . . .'

Culture and Environment was designed principally for school use, as a text book for Sixth Forms, and it consists of a series of exercises and examples organised under such heads as Mass Production, Advertising, Levelling-Down, The Supply of Reading Matter, Fiction and the National Life, Progress and the Standard of Living, The Use of Leisure, The Organic Community, Tradition, Substitute Living, the Business Ethos, Education. It doesn't perhaps sound very exciting, but the plain fact is that this modest little book has become an educational classic. It is a modern *Culture and Anarchy*, spare and trim, smaller in scale, more intimate in tone: a textbook instead of a discourse. There is no touch of Arnold's grand manner in it, but it has a similar sense for contemporary fact and a comparable sureness of grasp of standards. Like *Culture and Anarchy* it gets its strength from turning on current conditions a mind trained in literary analysis, which means a mind with a fine touch for what is actually there before one *and* a thorough understanding of relevant criteria: and it gets its influence from the clarity with which it shows how to use a supple and productive method of social analysis.

Criticism, as Leavis conducts it, is the relevant, delicately attentive analysis of a complete response to literature; it is a commentary upon the act by which one enters into as full as possible a possession of the experience given in the words. When sensibility is made articulate there will be found in it elements of judgement and discrimination. But they are explicit in the account only because they are implicit in the response. They are distilled by the experience itself, not items carted in from outside. The method of *Culture and Environment* is the prolongation of this activity into the business of daily life. *Culture and Environment* shows a mind skilled and scrupulous in the critic's art interrogating its experience in the face of contemporary conditions, and finding there grounds for particular judgements and for a consistent general attitude. Without this poised attention to the texture of our experience – Leavis insists – the unavoidable accommodation to the environment becomes, in the context in which adjustment has to be made today, a helpless and total assimilation.

To help the young student to discover what resources are available to him for constructing his own critical attitude is an important part of

Leavis's intention. His suggestions are made with an economy and definition very grateful to a beginner. And they are miles away from anything that might be suggested by taking literary studies as a noviciate preparing select spirits for the aesthetic life. The student is to discover the necessary resources in the language and especially in those places where the language used is the function of a living community, a fine corporate consciousness. He is sent to key passages in *Pilgrim's Progress*, George Sturt's *Change in the Village* and *The Wheelwright's Shop*, and D. H. Lawrence. The thing all three have in common is that they offer incontestable evidence – its presence in the words – for the existence of an organic community: a habit of life, sanctioned by tradition, exquisitely adapted to local circumstances but expressive too of a central humanity – the whole constituting a set of conditions, relations and influences capable of transforming an environment into a culture and a biological organism into a human person. And the second thing they share is their demonstrating that this was a culture of the people, the common possession of the common folk, racy, robust, but making too for a highly developed form of civility. To grasp what this meant, as well as to recognise what has been lost in its disappearance, is a primary aim of education, if education is to give, as Leavis holds it should, 'command of the art of living.' It is also a possible and reasonable aim. For while the physical existence of the organic community has been shattered beyond recall, its meaning, its ideal significance continues diffusely throughout the whole language and with concentrated intensity in certain works of literature. What was once given simply by the rhythm of life has now to be come by, can only be come by, through the systematic exercise of trained intelligence. Such a training supplies the essential axis of reference to which the conditions of contemporary life can be referred, and in relation to which they can be placed in an order of decency and humanity.

It is against 'a norm of humanity' brought from such resources that Leavis tests the effect of a modern environment. Of the myriad influences, physical and intellectual, which have combined to produce it, two have been especially weighty in fixing its tone and manner, namely machinery, the use of applied power, and universal literacy. And the topics which the student is invited to reflect on are those which markedly exhibit this double influence. There is a minimum of exposition and a plenitude of examples, and the generalisations and conclusions are made much less by abstract statement and much more by the eloquence of instances. The effect is first to bring home to the learner, insistently, strikingly, and from many points of the compass, the fact that while 'culture' and 'environment' were once identified they are now divided; and second, to make distinct an active idea of culture which will qualify him to discriminate among the elements of his environment. Since language is at the centre of our culture, 'and language is not merely a matter of words – or words are more than they seem to be,' this entails constantly turning the students' attention to the way words are used, and especially to representative and decisive uses. It means eliciting the assumptions lurking in these, detecting the impulses they appeal to and exposing the real purposes they serve. The result is to heighten awareness of language as the essential agency of civilisation, and of the degeneration of language as a distraction of human capacity and a contraction of human possibility.

Leavis's effort, then, was to open a connection between sensibility and practical judgement, and to deploy the resources of literary taste in the interests of general civility; and to do this by bringing into conscious relation and articulate contrast the structure of our finest responses with the assumptions of our daily action. His purpose, in accord with his empirical, very English habit of mind, was not to recommend a system of general ideas but to cultivate skill in grasping an essential continuity. It was an undertaking, he hoped, in which 'the many intelligent men and women who every year go into schools might find assurance of vocation . . . The instinct towards health – the instinct of self-preservation – that we must believe to be in the human spirit will take effect through them or not at all.' I think it will be recognised that this hope has been remarkably justified during the more than forty years of the book's existence. It has produced its immediate effects in the grammar schools and in the universities by communicating to students a much clearer and juster conception of the critic's office in a modern society. It has also helped to prepare an audience able and ready to follow the extra-curricular activities of literary criticism, especially in social analysis and the theory of education. But its influence has also worked more profoundly at the place where presupposition is affected and the premises of action are established. *Culture and Environment* has sharpened the convictions of several generations of the intelligent young, including a whole cluster of young writers. It has offered them an intellectual stance, a radically critical attitude, and a vocabulary of value capable of being dissolved into their own idiom. In doing so, this small book has helped to keep alive, in a world of the irresistibly encroaching context, 'a truth of resistance'.

How much, one is bound to wonder at this point of time, how much of Leavis's conception is still valid? Won't forty-odd years of active work have put it inevitably into the class of the superannuated? Isn't it now interesting, not for its intrinsic vitality but because it represents the mind of a major critic at a formative phase in his career? On this there are two comments to be made. In the first place the social process which now controls us – the saturation of every fragment of life by the spirit of a commercial civilisation, and within that main drive, most emphatically by the influence of the entertainment industry – this was well in train in the thirties. Our environment is different from that of the thirties only in being more thoroughly, completely and successfully materialistic. What we have now is what we aspired to then. So that the passage of time has made Leavis's essential intention the more necessary and the more relevant. But one has also to note this: that intention, to be realised, required not only an ideal of society but a vivid sense of current actuality, a real closeness of contact with the subject. *Culture and Environment* very strongly gives the impression of being an accurate representation of the contemporary scene. One is sure that here the exact tone of the thirties is being listened to by a just ear and being made audible through a true voice. But the tact necessary to ensure this success may also be sufficient to guarantee a failure of understanding in the future. The names and details, the scheme of reference distributed throughout the body of the book, which convincingly evoke the thirties for someone coming into adulthood then, can hardly have the same suggestive force for a generation brought up wholly since that decade. To the contemporary student the names of periodicals like *The Saturday Review, The Weekend Review, The New Leader, The Strand, Windsor, Royal Magazine*, the names of writers like Marie Corelli, Hugh Walpole, Warwick Deeping, Robert Lynd, the names of prominent figures like Thomas Bata or Horatio Bottomley, lie in the obscurity of a locked code. He will make as little of them as he does from his well-sprung comfort of the economic theme running through the book, which links business with poverty, boom with slump, materialistic ostentation with actual want. To suggest a revision here is easy enough; to think that if it were done there would still be left that rare combination of positive, personal flavour and general application is quite another matter. It may even be that the names and terms in *Culture and Environment* may last simply because they are there, coming to have the mythical significance of Colonel Dickson and Mr. Beales, The Licensed Victuallers and The Commercial Travellers in *Culture and Anarchy*, and being preserved in a similar amber.

No such air of nostalgia enfolds Leavis's writing on the University, which is edged, tense, packed and rappingly present. We live in a world which suffers from a rupture with its own past; it is 'as if society, in so complicating and extending the machinery of organization, had incurred a progressive debility of consciousness and of the powers of co-ordination and control – had lost intelligence, memory and moral purpose.'[20] On the other hand, it is still true that we can call on the remnant of a cultural tradition. 'I assume,' Leavis maintains, 'that the attempt to establish a real liberal education in this country – to restore in relation to the modern world the idea of liberal education – is worth making because, in spite of all our talk about disintegration and decay, and in spite of what we feel with so much excuse in our many despondent moments, we still have a positive cultural tradition.'[21] This cultural tradition exists – or is potentially present for the disciplined, attentive and trained mind – dispersed in its elements in our language and organised and coherent in our literature. The conscious effort to recover it means first, resisting the bent of current civilisation, and second, using the one institution capable in our world of working for a 'cultural tradition still conceived as a directing force, representing a wisdom older than modern civilization and having an authority that should check and control the blind drive onward of material and mechanical development, with its human consequences.'[22] The idea of the university as Leavis saw it combined the condition of being a historical institution, which Coleridge insisted on, with that of possessing 'a conscience in intellectual matters', 'a deference to a standard higher than one's own habitual standard' which Arnold praised in the European institution of the Academy. If we associate, that is, Coleridge's requirement of an historical institution with Arnold's conception of the educational possibilities of the Academy, we have the grounds for Leavis's choice of the university as the one established institution now capable of re-attaching society to its past. It is still one of the few, and among the few the strongest and most esteemed, of the traditional organs of consciousness remaining in the current world.

And this institution, Leavis insists, working very much against the grain of contemporary educational assumption, is meant for a minority: 'it is disastrous to let a country's educational arrangements be determined, or even affected, by the assumption that a high intellectual

standard can be attained by more than a small minority.'[23] Leavis
believed that the supply of good university students was limited and
that it is only by actual concentration that the standards could be maintained. He argued, of course, that they should be maintained above all
at Oxford and Cambridge, and he sometimes wrote as though these
were the only universities, an attitude he relaxed when he had more
experience of other places. But his essential contention both in general
and particular cannot be gainsaid. If Oxford and Cambridge creamed
the country that was good not only for them but for other university
institutions which had in them a model and standard. Unless the
democratic axiom that everyone is capable of the highest in education
is dropped, then it is, in Leavis's view, 'a poor look-out for liberal
education.' Leavis had no time for the democratic axiom that it is an
offence against democracy to advocate for anybody anything that
everybody cannot have. He speaks of the 'extravagance of this unreal-
ity of democratic faith' and believes this to be a central cause of the
collapse of educational standards in America and in Britain. The special
education of an intellectual *élite* can only be 'undemocratic' if it is
assumed that democracy entails the lowering of standards. 'And if
democratic equality of opportunity,' writes Leavis, 'requires that
standards should be lowered, then I am against democracy.'[24]

The *raison d'être* of the university is to be, says Leavis, 'amid the
material pressures and dehumanizing complications of the modern
world, a focus of humane consciousness, a centre where, faced with the
specializations and distractions in which human ends lose themselves,
intelligence, bringing to bear a mature sense of values, should apply
itself to the problems of civilization.'[25] The mind required is to be
formed, he goes on, essentially by a literary training:

> ... a training of intelligence that is at the same time a training of
> sensibility; a discipline of thought that is at the same time a discipline
> in scrupulous sensitiveness of response to delicate organizations of
> feeling, sensation and imagery. Without that appreciative habituation
> to the subtleties of language in its most charged and complex uses
> which the literary-critical discipline is, thinking – thinking to the
> ends with which humane education should be most concerned – is
> disabled. And the process of evaluative judgement, implicit or ex-
> plicit, that is inseparable from the use of intelligence in that dis-
> cipline is no mere matter of a 'taste' that can be set over against
> intelligence.[26]

There are other studies, linguistic, semantic, philological, historical, of strictly subordinate and instrumental importance, which claim, or have even attained, the key position in the study of English.

All these candidates, both the more and the less respectable, are, in relation to an English School, *Ersatz*, [Leavis insists], and are to be resisted as inimical to the recognition and practice of the essential discipline. The essential discipline of an English School is the literary-critical; it is a true discipline, only in an English School if anywhere will it be fostered, and it is irreplaceable. It trains, in a way no other discipline can, intelligence and sensibility together, cultivating a sensitiveness and precision of response and a delicate integrity of intelligence – intelligence that integrates as well as analyses and must have pertinacity and staying power as well as delicacy.[27]

In an age of illiberal technicians and technical humanists we have to develop a central intelligence, to train the accomplished non-specialist mind. For two reasons literary criticism is eminently qualified to be the discipline by which this mind is perfected. It is of course an integral study, informed by its own ends, possessed of its own methods, expressed in its own idiom. But the complexity of its undertaking is such that it is bound to take a ranging view of its function and to reject any rigid limitation of its sphere of interest. It is impelled at all times to go beyond its own frontiers into the provinces of other disciplines. 'One of the virtues of literary studies,' writes Leavis, 'is that they lead constantly outside themselves, and . . . while it is necessary that they should be controlled by a concern for the essential discipline, such a concern, if it is adequate, counts on associated work in other fields.'[28] 'The scrupulous and enterprising use of intelligence' which literary criticism excites and enhances is not to be confined to the literary mode. The criticism, the intelligent reading, of a single poem can set up an enquiry into the whole world which speaks in the poem and this enquiry, while still answering to the control of every canon of critical relevance (if it doesn't, it isn't literary criticism or anything else worthwhile), is bound to be concerned with much that formally belongs to different studies. Some may offer as an objection, what others would regard as a tribute, that this is to favour the merely amateur mind. 'Call him what you like,' Leavis replies, 'we want to produce a mind that knows what precision and specialist knowledge are, is aware of the kinds not in its own possession that are necessary, has a maturity of outlook such as the study of history ought to produce but even the general historian by profession doesn't always exhibit, and has been trained in a kind of thinking, a scrupulously sensitive yet enterprising use of intelligence, that is of its nature not specialized but cannot be expected without special training.'[29]

The other characteristic of literary criticism which fits it so admirably to be the appropriate discipline for educating the free intelligence, is that the powers it appeals to, the capacities it exercises, are those deeply involved in the serious conduct of life. Penetration of mind, tact of address, subtlety of response, concern to refer to a mature standard, deliberation in judgement and responsibility in decision – these are the qualities essential in literary criticism as they are those most required in the important commitments and refusals, elections and acceptances of humane living. 'The more advanced the work,' writes Leavis with relation to the literary critical student, 'the more unmistakably is the judgement that is concerned inseparable from that profoundest sense of relative value which determines, or should determine, the important choices of actual life.'[30] And bringing the whole argument to its climax he concludes: 'It is an intelligence so trained that is best fitted to develop into the central kind of mind, the co-ordinating consciousness, capable of performing the function assigned to the class of the educated.'[31]

In the impressionistic sketch of the English School which was to perform the function of intellectual centre, Leavis proceeds in his characteristic way; not, that is, by a carefully plotted argument advancing step by logical step, but rather by communicating his urgent and linked convictions. There is a passage in which D. H. Lawrence, analysing the thought of Giovanni Verga, makes an observation which seems to me to apply very much to the character of Leavis's own thought and the manner in which he expressed it:

Now the emotional mind, if we may be allowed to say so, is not logical. It is a psychological fact, that when we are thinking emotionally or passionately, thinking and feeling at the same time, we do not think rationally: and therefore, and therefore, and therefore. Instead the mind makes curious swoops and circles. It touches the point of pain or interest, then sweeps away again in a cycle, coils round and approaches again the point of pain or interest. There is a curious spiral rhythm, and the mind approaches again and again the point of concern, repeats itself, goes back, destroys the time-sequence entirely, so that time ceases to exist, as the mind stoops to the quarry, then leaves it without striking, soars, hovers, turns, swoops, stoops again, still does not strike, yet is nearer, nearer, reels away again, wheels off into the air, even forgets, quite forgets, yet again turns,

bends, circles slowly, swoops and stoops again, until at last there is
the closing-in, and the clutch of a decision or a resolve.[32]

'The emotional mind,' Lawrence adds, 'however apparently muddled,
has its own rhythm, its own commas and colons and full-stops. They
are not always as we should expect them, but they are there, indicating
that other rhythm.'[33] That other rhythm is very evident in these pages
on the English School and English studies. Leavis exposes his profoundest beliefs, invites us to share them, and indeed assumes that we
do, that we must. What Lawrence called the clutch of decision and
resolve has in it always a sense of invitation, of implicit participation by
an audience. In this case Leavis, having declared that the special but not
specialist discipline of the new centre is to be literary-critical, argues
that its aim is to be real education, which he defines as 'that inwardness
with a developed discipline which can only come by working and
living into it';[34] it is meant 'to produce a mind that will approach the
problems of modern civilization with an understanding of their
origins, a maturity of outlook, and, not a nostalgic addiction to the
past, but a sense of human possibilities.'[35] These studies, leading constantly outside themselves, will include a particular scrutiny and
analysis of the seventeenth century, a period which at one end is in
touch with the world of Dante and which at the other shows us a
world irretrievably broken off from the medieval order.

> In the course of it capitalism 'arrives,' finally overcoming the
> traditional resistances, so that its ethos becomes accepted as law,
> morality and controlling spirit in the economic realm; the age of
> parliamentary rule begins, as does that of economic nationalism;
> crucial issues in the relations between Church and State, the spiritual
> and the secular, religion and the individual, are decided in a spirit
> going against the tradition of centuries – the principle of toleration
> is established along with that of 'business is business'; the notion of
> society as a joint-stock company; science launches decisively on its
> triumphant accelerating advance.[36]

Among the pieces of work the student will be expected to complete is
one on the process of change by which the England of the seventeenth
century turned into the England of today.

> In such a piece of work, clearly, it would be pre-eminently the
> unacademic virtues that would be demanded and tested: a pioneering
> spirit; the courage of enormous incompletenesses; the determination
> to complete the best possible chart with the inevitable patchy and

sketchy knowledge that is all one's opportunities permit one to acquire; the judgement and intuition to select drastically yet delicately, and make a little go a long way; the ability to skip and to scamp with wisdom and conscience.[37]

The student would be expected to see any literary history which was not a matter of sensibility, which simply consisted of 'facts about', as a worthless acquisition. He would study the history of literature more through the scrutiny of key passages, assigning them on analytic grounds to period and author. There would be other exercises testing perception, judgement and powers of critical analysis. The student would see that analysis has nothing in it of the nature of scientific laboratory method. Analysis has the poem to deal with only so far as the reader is responding delicately and appropriately to it. In pointing to the words in analysis,

> what we are doing is to bring into sharp focus, in turn, this, that and the other detail, juncture or relation in our total response; or (since 'sharp focus' may be a misleading account of the kind of attention sometimes required), what we are doing is to dwell with a deliberate, considering responsiveness on this, that or the other node or focal point in the complete organization that the poem is, in so far as we have it. Analysis is not a dissection of something that is already and passively there. What we call analysis is, of course, a constructive or creative process. It is a more deliberate following-through of that process of creation in response to the poet's words which reading is. It is a re-creation in which, by a considering attentiveness, we ensure more than ordinary faithfulness and completeness.[38]

Analysis is controlled by a sense of relevance and it is an exercise of the sense of value. If it engages with the metaphorical life of the work it will do so with a very clear understanding of the organic nature of metaphors and images.

> It will not do to treat metaphors, images and other local effects as if their relation to the poem were at all like that of plums to cake, or stones attesting that the jam is genuine. They are worth examining – they are there to examine – because they are foci of a complex life, and sometimes the context from which they cannot be even provisionally separated, if the examination is to be worth anything, is a wide one.[39]

The student must have a clear sense of that common misconception of technique as something distinct from sensibility. Technique is an expression of a given particular sensibility or it is nothing. 'Criticism involves analysis and abstraction, but the critic must see that his analysis is subtle enough, that his abstractions are the right ones, and that he does not, forgetting what they are, give them a status to which they have no right.'[40] Again, the student – the person training to be the reader – must see the importance of imagery, understanding it as being not limited to the visual, and comprehending that metaphorical realisation itself shows the poet's mastery not in the completeness of the realisation but in the precision of its appropriateness of realisation. In realisation we have to consider always the whole of some complexity, 'what we have to look for are the signs of something grasped and held, something presented in an ordering of words, and not merely thought of or gestured towards.'[41] A student trained in this way will be given the essential structure of literary experience. Such a training is not concerned merely with the 'culture' of individuals, or with 'adding to "the few who can talk intelligently about Stendhal, Proust and Henry James" (though the more of them there are the better).'[42] And a student so trained will understand that literature is not a matter of odd individual works or the illustration of processes and modes but it is above all an order, a tradition, a living consciousness. How much more vivifying would such an education be than the 'laborious and stupefying dissipation that usually passes for study.'[43] It starts with the training of sensibility, it engages with that constantly, its whole purpose is to that end:

> Armed in the ways suggested with a technique of reading, a trained sense for the significant, and types and analogues for dealing with further experience, the student may be left to educate himself (otherwise he is ineducable).[44]

3

Critical Directions

I want to open this section by referring to two of the leading ideas, which are both initiating conceptions and powerful intuitions, sustaining, expressly or by implication, much of Leavis's early writing. These were the two principal influences directing his criticism the way it went. The first has to do with the overwhelming importance of the English language itself. Literature is the most powerful, human, subtle and inclusive use of the language. A passionate conviction about this animates Leavis's work from the start, quickening his criticism of Shakespeare, providing the base from which to define the limitations of Milton's influence and Johnson's misapprehensions of Shakespearean drama, and supporting his analysis of Eliot's redirection and renewal of twentieth-century poetry. It was the growth of the English language in resource and range which made first Chaucer and then Shakespeare possible, and it was its increase in sophistication and suppleness and in its capacity to manipulate ideas which, together with a developing social interest in new forms of communication, encouraged in the seventeenth century the appearance of English prose, at a time, in fact, later than the beginnings of French prose. Compare, for example, as L. C. Knights suggested in *Scrutiny*,[1] the prose of Florio's translation, still thick and sense-ridden, with the lightness and the intellectual grace of Montaigne's French.

English literature can be read as the self-illumining chronicle of the state of the language. The life of language is recurrently refreshed by the people and by the poets who turn from its literary and mandarin forms to its use as a living tongue. New movements in literature are new uses of language, and this is as true of Chaucer, of Shakespeare, of Donne who brought into non-dramatic poetry the Shakespearean use of language, and of Pope in the eighteenth century, as it is of Wordsworth in the nineteenth and Eliot in the twentieth. The new mind requires the new voice, and the new voice is discovered by the poet's genius for intimately registering the idiom of his own time.

Language is the substance and material of literature, a poem being made of words and nothing else. Changes in language shape the development of literature, and the reader's attitude to language modifies his response to literature. To understand this is to understand in the most intimate way the relationship between literature and society, and a conception of society together with an ideal of civilisation is the other generating influence in Leavis's criticism. Dryden is the figure, in Leavis's view, who has a peculiarly representative and significant quality in relation to his age, standing as 'the Chinese wall between Shakespeare and the first age of bardolatry.' What Dryden did with *Antony and Cleopatra* demonstrated how the eighteenth century, aspiring to produce poetic tragedy, showed itself incapable of the tragic. And it was in Dryden's heyday that modern English prose was established. He represents a whole movement of civilisation just as the prose of his period is the product of a whole new world. In fact, 'All the forces of change that had been at work through the century had come together to inaugurate the triumphant advance towards the civilization, technological and Benthamite, that we live in.'[2]

The effect of Leavis's criticism of Milton, by tradition the second genius of English literature, is not, as seen from a later perspective, so very revolutionary after all since what it does is to enforce the immeasurable superiority of Shakespeare. The strength of Leavis's judgement, deriving as much from Keats as from Eliot, depends on his sense of the true and characteristic use of English. Its weight is conveyed succinctly in his account of the different ways with words of Milton and Donne, the latter judged to be endowed with the Shakespearean habit with words: 'one might say that it is the English use – the use, in the essential spirit of the language, of its characteristic resources.'[3] If in Donne the words seem to do what they say, in Milton they are doing so much less while they seem to be valuing themselves more highly. Milton's art is incantatory, his use of language remote from speech. 'Certain feelings are expressed, but there is no pressure behind the words; what predominates in the handling of them is not the tension of something precise to be defined and fixed, but a concern for mellifluousness – for liquid sequences and a pleasing opening and closing of the vowels.'[4] Compare this with what is said of Shakespeare's control over words in *Macbeth*. This is 'a complex dramatic theme vividly and profoundly realised – not thought of, but possessed imaginatively in its concreteness, so that, as it grows in specificity, it in turn possesses the poet's mind and commands expression.' It is Milton's deficiency in this respect not an incapacity to be interested in myth which makes us find him, as Leavis puts it, 'unexhilarating'.

Milton's poetry shows us what can happen to an overwhelming personality operating in isolation in a medium out of touch with the true run of the language and therefore, in a profound way, at odds with his society. Pope, on the other hand, exhibits the rare instance in which an exquisite symmetry of assumption, tone and manner exists between the artist and his time. Pope's vision of civilisation had a – just – sufficient ground in the reality of the Augustan period to orchestrate its ideal aspiration with solid good sense. 'When Pope contemplates the bases and essential conditions of Augustan culture his imagination fires to a creative glow that produces what is poetry even by Romantic standards.'[5]

Let me take a second example given by Leavis of the relationship of society and literature, that between literature and the ruling intellectual assumptions of the period, and use as an instance Johnson's response to Shakespeare. Johnson, that great writer, was at once the servant and the superior of Augustan conceptions. His criticism, and particularly his ambivalent reaction to Shakespeare, exhibited his own personal strength and freshness and also the loss suffered by the English tradition and the English language in the triumph of Descartes, of Locke and Newton, at the end of the seventeenth century. 'Born into Dryden's age,' writes Leavis, 'when "logic" and "clarity" had triumphed, Shakespeare couldn't have been Shakespeare and the modern world would have been without the proof that thought of his kind was possible.'[6] The strength in Shakespeare that Johnson praised, almost in spite of himself, was in essence opposed to the Augustan conception of thought and reality, which 'insisted that nothing mattered, or could be brought into intelligent discourse, that couldn't be rendered as explicit, clear, logical and grammatical statement.'[7] This was a matter of expressing passively received impressions according to authoritative rules in the clearest and best ordered terms. Decorous expression was the servant of morality and according to the Johnsonian morality Shakespeare appeared to have no moral purpose. That is, the Augustan ethos excluded from literature, and from thought itself, 'a range of subtleties and profundities central to human experience'; it was also incapable of realising that 'language is essentially heuristic; that in major creative writers it does unprecedented things, advances the frontiers of the known, and discovers the new.'[8] Such a concept of the relationship of thought to language makes it impossible even for so great a mind as Johnson's to grasp the poetic, creative use of language in drama – 'the use by which the stuff of experience is presented to speak and act for itself,'[9] and only too easy to fall into that moralising confusion which imagines that there is no moral stance in a play or poem unless it is explicitly and lucidly stated.

Wordsworth, in whom there was still a considerable weight of eighteenth-century good sense had, Leavis tells us, if not a philosophy – he agrees with Arnold about its being no more than an illusion – a wisdom to communicate. 'What he had for presentment was a type and a standard of human normality, a way of life; his preoccupation with sanity and spontaneity working at a level and in a spirit that it seems appropriate to call religious.'[10] How to distinguish the essentially Wordsworthian poetic experience was a critical problem which engaged Leavis's attention more than once, as early as *Revaluation* and as late as the Bicentenary Lecture at the University of Bristol in 1970. I use the latter source because it enables me both to give Leavis's most succinct version of his view of the matter and because it provides example of the tart wit I haven't sufficiently illustrated. Here, for instance, is how he writes when setting out to give an account of Wordsworth's greatness as a poet:

> Where there is so much claiming permanent value, inert concurrence in conventional valuations and reputations is to be challenged: they get in the way of life.
>
> There is too much of the merely conventional; perhaps it will be said there is too much literature. Most certainly it can be said with indisputable justice that there is too much Wordsworth. You can't tell a student to look through his copy of the Wordsworth in the Oxford Standard Authors and mark the poems that in his opinion are worth going back to. There are nine hundred small-print double-column pages. Wordsworth had a long life, and, though he didn't finish his great philosophic poem, he went on indefatigably practising his art. There are those acres of sonnets, and a great deal else. That formidable mass of printed paper contains things we wouldn't be without, as well, no doubt, as things we should have called memorable if we had ever found them.[11]

Both on the earlier and the later occasion Leavis makes use of the critical insight of Shelley in *Peter Bell the Third*, in which the commentary on Wordsworth is equal in its way to Eliot's on Donne. Shelley there registers exactly and decisively the difference between himself and Wordsworth. This is how Leavis puts it: 'Wordsworth seems static; poised above his own centre, contemplating; Shelley always moving headlong – eagerly, breathlessly, committed to pur-

suing his centre of gravity lest he should fall on his face.'[12] Shelley
finds Wordsworth unimaginative, cold and frigid, wholly deficient in
the Shelleyan quality of caressing and erotic warmth, whereas 'Shelley
always seems to *have* a temperature.'[13] On the other hand, Shelley also
noted with comparable acumen what made Wordsworth the great
generating presence for the Romantic poets. Leavis quotes these lines
from *Peter Bell*:

> He had as much imagination
> As a pint-pot; – he never could
> Fancy another situation,
> From which to dart his contemplation,
> Than that wherein he stood.
>
> Yet his was individual mind . . .

And Leavis concludes:

> There you have it; there you have what made Wordsworth
> decisive for the later poets of the Romantic period. They were very
> different from one another, and from Wordsworth; what they had in
> common was the need to escape – positively – from the habits and
> conventions of expression handed down to them by the eighteenth
> century. These made the expression of 'individual mind' impossible;
> they laid all the emphasis on 'social.'[14]

Wordsworth's career often seems to be a long decline from its
splendid beginnings, at least from its first ten years. That of Keats, on
the other hand, the other great poetic genius of the nineteenth century,
and according to Leavis the one with a peculiarly English sensibility, is
the example of a very different sort of poetic development. In spite of
his belief 'that if Poetry comes not as naturally as the Leaves to a tree it
had better not come at all,'[15] the truth was that Keats's best poetry did
not come 'naturally' at all. It came only as the result of a sustained and
deliberate effort of self-education. Indeed, an essential clue to the
understanding of Keats's poetic life, that astonishing passage from
cockney to classic, is an educational one, since Keats's career is the most
brilliant example in literature of the education of a sensibility.

In his account of Keats's transformation from cockney to classic,
Leavis remarks that the current evaluation, stemming from Matthew
Arnold, seems right in essentials and that what is required is a sharper
explication, a more purely literary critical explanation which will find in
the poetry rather than in the life or the letters the grounds for a higher

estimation of Keats's potential. With Arthur Symons, 'a representative of the Victorian tradition that has its main source in Keats,' who tells us that Keats was an artist 'to whom art was more than life,' Leavis is surprisingly in agreement, at least in respect of the poems up to the revised *Hyperion*. But then Leavis insists that the *Eve of St. Agnes* and the Odes 'transcend the appreciation of the "aesthetic" taste that, with justice, finds them congenial.'[16] That transcendence, Leavis reports in writing of the *Ode to a Nightingale*, is in part the result of an extremely subtle and varied interplay of motions directed 'now positively, now negatively.'[17] Indulgent relapse towards Lethe is balanced by a clear and open vitality, art as a drug by the breath of life. Leavis's analysis of Keats's Ode shows a characteristic percipience and the capacity to define, to achieve the desired greater sharpness, by qualification, pointing, and concrete illustration. It enables Leavis to give a much tougher meaning to the connotation of the term Art as applied to Keats. He brings out the qualities in it which show a critical intelligence, a sense of touch and grasp, and a strength manifested in the rapidity of the development between *Endymion* and the Odes. If Leavis calls the ode *To Autumn* Shakespearean, that is not to join in the extravagance of Middleton Murry but to stress the un-Tennysonian character of the poem, sustained as it is by a peculiarly English strength and a characteristic 'vigour such as is alien to the Tennysonian habit, and such as a Tennysonian handling of the medium cannot breed.'[18]

Let me at this point interpolate a summarising comment from the *Times Literary Supplement* in 1936, very early on in Leavis's career, which indicates in a partial but positive way some of the tendencies of the position I have been describing.

Roughly it appears that for him the norm of poetry ... proceeds from a certain harmonious combination of elements distinguished as intelligence and sensitivity. This is realised for him in the art of the early seventeenth century, when the line of the norm would pass somewhere between Jonson and Donne. This development comes to an end in Pope. It emerges often in Wordsworth whose connection with the Augustian tradition of the eighteenth century, Dr Leavis rightly insists, is more intimate than is generally allowed. A little later it emerges again in Keats whose derivation from Wordsworth ... is closer than is generally admitted. In this perspective Coleridge and Shelley are both aberrations: there is a divorce between their intelligence and their sensibility so that the former element finds inadequate expression in their poetry.[19]

The book which Leavis in his Preface to *Education and the University* had undertaken to write (some of its intended contents were published in *Scrutiny*), to demonstrate systematically in an ordered sequence the elements of criticism and analysis, and by implication the creative nature of language and his own concept of civilisation, he never in the event wrote in the form envisaged. And when, more than a quarter of a century later he published *The Living Principle*, in which he dealt with related topics though in a more philosophical way, he made clear this was not intended to fill that gap. He put aside for good the pedagogic and explicit treatment in order to engage directly with these problems in the texture and structure of English literature itself. He gave, that is, the most living kind of demonstration of the use of the instruments he had at one time intended to describe and of the beliefs and assumptions on which his practice depended. The three works in which he did this were: *New Bearings in English Poetry* (1932), *Revaluation* (1936), and *The Great Tradition* (1948).

Each of these exhibits that delicate but drastic discrimination characteristic of the critic which is, of course, the product of a profound knowledge not only of what is but of what is not recommended. Sometimes followers are apt to take up the one without having gone through the other, just as enemies assumed a wholly unwarranted ignorance in Leavis about what he excluded from favour. In each book we see two of the primary qualities of the critic, a sensitive feeling for what is there before him and a developed sense of the proper structure to which each thing he considers belongs.

A lively sense of the immediate, a feeling for the varied textures of literature, is the first qualification of the critic. And the second which should – and in Leavis's case does – grow from the first – is the capacity to discern amid the chaos of literature the true, substantial structure. This was the power to which Matthew Arnold gave the odd name 'justness of spirit,' and of which he said, 'To ascertain the master-current in the literature of an epoch, and to distinguish this from all minor currents, is the critic's highest function. . . .'[20] The sense of structure strengthens itself through innumerable particular engagements. When he realises as sensitively and completely as he can the work before him, the critic (says Leavis, enquiring into his own habit) asks explicitly and implicitly: 'Where does this come? How does it stand in relation to . . . ? How relatively important does it seem'?[21] And the structure which begins to define itself as a product of the concrete is itself a concrete 'thing', not a theoretical system or a system determined by abstract considerations. It is an order inwardly achieved. Its character, weight and form are the deposits of personal experience:

> What on testing and retesting and wider experience, turn out to be my more constant preferences, what the relative permanencies in my response and what structure begins to assert itself in the field of poetry with which I am familiar? What map or chart of English poetry as a whole represents my utmost consistency and most inclusive coherence of response?[22]

There are three works in which Leavis has committed himself to record his 'utmost consistency and most inclusive coherence of response.' Each of these attempts 'to ascertain the master-current and to distinguish it from all minor currents': for example, *New Bearings in English Poetry* for poetry after the first war, *Revaluation* for post-Shakespearean poetry, *The Great Tradition* for the English novel. The structures defined in these works – gradually and in the end powerfully defined – are unambiguous, coherent and finely organised. Whether they will prove to be acceptable to the future no one can say. Certainly some of them have become constituents in the mind of anyone who thinks seriously about literature today, and each of us will have his own view of them. But I am also sure they will stand as decisive and representative statements of the judgement of this period, on a level with, and as influential as, Arnold's view of the Romantics.

In *New Bearings in English Poetry*, published in 1932, Leavis addressed himself to the current poetic situation, its background, preoccupations and habits, basing himself on criteria drawn, as he says, from the *Calendar*, that 'uniquely intelligent review which, from 1925 to 1927, was, it is hardly excessive to say, the critical conscience of the younger adult generations.' He conducted his discussion, as was to become habitual with him, through scrutiny of particular examples, although he does not in any way neglect to define larger and more abstract influences, as he has often been charged with doing. The authors he chooses are those which seem to him to have a peculiar symptomatic importance on the one hand, and on the other to be those who will positively shape the future. It seems to him unlikely that the number of poets born varies much from age to age, and that what counts is the use made of the talent. The prevailing conceptions in the poetry of the period were derived from the practice of the great Romantics. These were defined by Joseph Warton as long ago as 1756, when he distinguished the man of wit from the true poet. The true poet was concerned with the sublime and the prophetic, and the supreme examples were Spenser, Shakespeare and Milton. Warton's view was echoed by Matthew Arnold whose assumptions in this matter were for all his critical acumen not much different from those he had inherited. Poetry was a matter of the tender and the exalted and there was no place in it for wit and intellect. By the end of the nineteenth century this attitude was bleached of all its romantic force. In the lesser poems of Keats, in the poems of Morris, Rossetti, O'Shaughnessy, this becomes a languid retreat from the roughness of the iron age. Poetry was a form of daydream and even poets of the quality of Tennyson had neither the strength nor courage to be rid of them. 'His case is well put by *The Palace of Art*: the explicit moral of this poem is that withdrawal will not do; but when he comes to the moral Tennyson's art breaks down: the poetry belongs to the palace.'[23] Arnold may have been conscious of the ineffectiveness of the concept of the poetic which ruled the age, but in his poetry he was wholly incapable of writing uncoloured by its moonlit glamour. The one Victorian poet who had the necessary genius and disinterestedness was Gerard Manley Hopkins – with Eliot and Pound he is one of the three major poets dealt with at length by Leavis – and his relations with Bridges show both that he had come long before his time and that he was to have no effect at all on his contemporaries.

The significant poets of the period, Yeats, Hardy, de la Mare, Blunden, Edward Thomas, Wilfred Owen and Isaac Rosenberg, Leavis treats with brevity, with sympathy and a still arresting freshness. Yeats began as a man of the nineties with the same late-Victorian sense of poetry as withdrawal, but behind the mist and trance there was an Irish resonance and validity. Yeats's poetry of exaltation in dream and despair with reality was of a subtler and more delicate sort than the other poets of his kind, and rare qualities of character, intelligence and disinterestedness enabled him to move to a new sensibility, that of the actual world, and to a new idiom, that of modern speech, a sardonic expression of bitterness and disillusion: 'The verse, in its rhythm and diction, recognizes the actual world, but holds against it an ideal of aristocratic fineness. It is idiomatic, and has the run of free speech, being at the same time proud, bare and subtle. To pass from the earlier verse to this is something like passing from Campion to Donne.'[24] But no Englishman, Leavis insists, could have profited from the sources of strength open to Yeats, nor could any poet begin where Yeats began, as we can see from the case of Walter de la Mare, whose poems, written from a child's consciousness, are remarkably skilful and delicate and expressive of a world of dreams nourished upon his memories of childhood. The insidious spells of his best poetry charm not only his audience but himself. 'He is the belated last poet of the Romantic tradition, and is already as remote as Poe from the present of poetry.'[25]

Hardy, a true Victorian, a poet of simple attitudes, depends for his rank as a major poet upon hardly more than a dozen poems: 'Hardy's great poetry is a triumph of character.'[26] He could, with the aid of a strong personal impulse, transform an innocent awkwardness into a bare and astonishing fidelity. Edmund Blunden stood out from the generality of the Georgian poets in that behind his rich rusticity there was a frankly literary quality, a concern with poetry as art. The combination of the pastoral and the psychological, so apt and individual in his earliest verse, particularly in the eighteenth-century meditative mode, became uncertain and stumbling later, where 'characteristic packed effects are apt to degenerate into cluttered obscurity.'[27] 'He was able to be, to some purpose, conservative in technique, and to draw upon the eighteenth century, because the immemorial rural order that is doomed was real to him. It is not likely that a serious poet will be traditional in that way again.'[28]

Of Edward Thomas, Owen and Rosenberg, Leavis remarks that even if they had been recognised they could hardly have constituted a challenge to the ruling poetic fashions. Thomas's achievement was really extraordinary. Having nothing in common with the Georgians, he succeeded in expressing in poetry a representative modern sensibility, but it wasn't of that order of greatness which could disturb the pattern imposed by the past.

It was Eliot who was to be the truly significant figure, the one who was to produce the new voice for the altered sensibility: Eliot, and not Lawrence, who like Blake seemed to exist outside and beyond the ordinary pattern of literary development. Even Eliot's earliest poems represent a break with the nineteenth-century tradition, requiring us to modify our traditional idea of the distinction between seriousness and levity in poetry, and to revise our idea of the canons of the poetical. The first poems themselves express a modern sensibility, 'the ways of feeling, the modes of experience, of one fully alive in his own age.'[29] The influences on Eliot were totally unlike those which influenced the Victorian and Georgian poets. His form derived from the later Elizabethan drama and from his study of the French poetry of Tristan

Corbière and Jules Laforgue. That Eliot could profit from such sources is itself, according to Leavis, a strong sign of originality and genius. In *Gerontion*, which he chooses as one of the best of Eliot's earliest poems, free from the heaviness and caricature of *The Love Song*, and from the slightly mannered use of urban imagery in *Prelude* and *Rhapsody on a Windy Night*, Leavis recognises an astonishing power and quality which had been absent from English poetry for 150 years. Eliot derived from the Elizabethans without using the agency of Milton in a way which was impossible for nineteenth-century poets and their successors. As the Victorian poets used a limited range of the resources of the English language, so their techniques had been limited and foreshortened. Eliot abolished the necessity for narrative and logical continuity and for anything that could be rendered in a prose paraphrase. In *Gerontion*, 'All the persons, incidents and images are there to evoke the immediate consciousness of the old man as he broods over a life lived through and asks what is the outcome, what the meaning, what the residue. This seems simple enough, and the transitions and associations are not obscure.'[30]

It was a method developed still further in *The Waste Land*, which appeared two years after *Gerontion*, and rendered with extreme precision an individual sensibility; it also expressed in an utterly new way the consciousness of the age, and above all the poet's awareness of the discontinuity and the uprooting of modern life, 'in which April is the cruellest month,' and sex breeds not life but disgust. The poem succeeds in realising the disorganised consciousness and the absence of inherent and positive direction. The method of the poem is characterised by a concentration and depth of orchestration, by the movement of themes in and out of one another, and by the shift of emphasis from level to level, from the individual to Europe to humanity itself. The organisation of *The Waste Land* is neither dramatic nor narrative nor metaphysical:

> The unity the poem aims at is that of an inclusive consciousness: the organization it achieves as a work of art is of the kind that has been illustrated, an organization that may, by analogy, be called musical. It exhibits no progression.[31]

The poem has weaknesses of obscurity, though less than used to be thought, occasions when Eliot seems to think he has succeeded where he has not. It is not likely that what we know of the part that Ezra Pound played in the final version of the poem would have much changed Leavis's analysis which is as apposite, persuasive and helpful as when it was written.

He apologises on more than one occasion for the elementary nature of his treatment, and although this may be put down to good manners on his part (it is hardly as elementary as all that), it certainly provides an admirable introduction to Eliot's sensibility and method. But the welcoming, even enthusiastic tone, does not prevent Leavis from discerning the significant quality in Eliot's writing which he was to return to again and again in his later and more discerning responses. 'Certain qualities of genius he undoubtedly has,' says Leavis, and we are bound to notice that warning 'certain' amid the compliments. The great technical interest of this most subtle poetry, Leavis said, was the problem of sincerity – for this is what technique meant to the poet. 'He had to achieve a paradoxical precision-in-vagueness; to persuade the elusive intuition to define itself, without any forcing, among the equivocations of "the dream-crossed twilight".'³² The technique of sincerity was essential in a poetry which was to be a new response, and a new utterance; it was all the more so since the poet's concern was to be specifically religious in a world which had renounced such a solution. It was necessary too, if Eliot the frequenter of Dante was not to conclude in a mere pre-Raphaelite trance. Dante had visions but we have only dreams. But Eliot

... no more supposes that Dante's mode of vision can be recaptured than that Dante's belief can. But his frequentation of Dante has its place in that effort 'to construct something' and that 'training of the soul' which he speaks of. And his leopards and unicorns seem to insist on the peculiar kind of 'disciplined dreaming' that he strives to attain in 'the dreamcrossed twilight' of *Ash-Wednesday*. They go with the formal quality of the verse, in which we have already noted a suggestion of ritual, and with the liturgical element, to define the plane at which this poetry works. The spiritual discipline is one with the poetical.³³

Nowhere is this 'equivocation of experience that produces agonising doubt' more deftly and delicately touched on than in Leavis's discussion of the *Ash-Wednesday* poems of 1930:

... the modern poet can make no pretence to Dante's certitude – to his firm possession of his vision. The ambiguity that constructs a precarious base for rejoicing in the fourth poem brings doubt and fear of inner treachery in the fifth. The breathless circling, desperately pursuing movement of the opening, with its repetitions and its play upon 'word', 'Word,' 'world' and 'whirled', suggests both the agonized effort to seize the unseizable, and the elusive equivocations of the thing grasped. The doubts and self-questionings are developed and the poem ends with a despairing recognition of the equivocal . . .[34]

Leavis was to develop over the years much that was latent in his attribution of subtle ambiguity to Eliot. In his earliest criticism it is the positive part of ambiguity that he concentrates on. As to Eliot, the supreme poetic influence of the period, Leavis's view was quite unqualified; his doubts, where they existed, had to do with certain intrinsic qualities of the poetry, qualities which both in the poetry and in Eliot himself were to provoke in Leavis in later years more strongly negative feelings.

Leavis agrees with Eliot about the impact made by Ezra Pound and about the pre-eminence of *Hugh Selwyn Mauberley* in his work. For the *Cantos* in which we have poetry where the principle of organisation is not intensity but extension or dispersal, details accumulating patiently and endlessly and the coherence of junctures abolished, Leavis never developed any sympathy. They seemed always to him to reflect the dilettante and frantic quality of Pound's disorderly sensibility – Pound he saw as essentially an aesthete. In *Hugh Selwyn Mauberley* he felt 'a pressure of experience, an impulsion from within,' and a projection of 'the miscellaneousness of modern culture, the absence of direction, of an alphabet of forms or of any one predominant idiom; the uncongeniality of the modern world to the artist; and his dubious status there.'[35] In this autobiographical poem he found both the impersonality of great poetry and technical perfection.

For the rest, Leavis praises half a dozen poems by William Empson, attributing to them a Donne-like quality which on re-reading I find now hard to acknowledge, and overpraises, perhaps because of a kindly personal connection, Ronald Bottrall, whose work certainly does not warrant the enthusiasm with which Leavis treats it. But the decisive thing that Leavis does here is to signal the end of the Victorian age and to recognise, define, and welcome the new.

What Leavis undertook to do for contemporary poetry in *New Bearings*, he accomplished with keener, more characteristic strokes for English poetry from the seventeenth century onward in *Revaluation*, perhaps the single most influential of all his critical books. The work had an occasional stimulus, appearing after the publication of *The*

Oxford Book of Seventeenth Century Verse. Most of the material appeared first as separate essays in the early volumes of *Scrutiny.* Leavis is generous throughout in his attribution to Eliot of the critical insight from which the book proceeds. Leavis's intention was to establish the line of wit, which runs from Ben Jonson through Donne to Pope, as the central and essential tradition, and to displace from this position the conventional predominance of Milton. Leavis's account of his response to Milton's verse was regarded by academic critics then, and frequently it is now, as provocative and perverse. He reports that after responding to the magnificent invention of the poetry of the first two books he finds himself protesting:

> . . . protesting against the routine gesture, the heavy fall, of the verse, flinching from the foreseen thud that comes so inevitably, and, at last, irresistibly: for reading *Paradise Lost* is a matter of resisting, of standing up against, the verse-movement, of subduing it into something tolerably like sensitiveness, and in the end our resistance is worn down; we surrender at last to the inescapable monotony of the ritual.[36]

It was the meditative and the melancholic manner derived from Milton's minor poetry which enfeebled the non-Augustan poetry of the eighteenth century and prepared by way of Gray and Collins for the less energetic and more sequestered strains in Romantic poetry. But Leavis is clear that during the eighteenth century the sensibility had changed and 'senses and faculties have been lost, a perceptive and responsive organization has ceased to function, a capacity for fineness has disappeared (Pope, of course, constitutes an exception – he is a genius, both belonging to his time and transcending it).'[37] From the Restoration onward England developed a culture which existed increasingly at a damaging distance from the moral bases of society. With the exception of Pope, whose best poetry was a union of Augustan correctness and metaphysical complexity, and later of Johnson, the dominant modes of the eighteenth century moved towards a pallid gentility. Blake, like Lawrence a unique genius for whom conventional orders were irrelevant and bogus, was uncompromisingly individual and outside the general development. Burns, who counts for so much in the *Lyrical Ballads,* derived his strength from a different tradition. Crabbe's strength, Leavis maintains, was that of the novelist and it was in Jane Austen's novels that the Augustan tradition achieved one of its most complete and subtle expressions.

Wordsworth's greatness, which rested on much that was still strongly eighteenth-century, was neither in his philosophy nor in his philosophic verse but in the poetry. The genius of the poetry was to define 'the sense of "belonging" in the universe, of a kinship known inwardly through the rising springs of life and consciousness and outwardly in an interplay of recognition and response.'[38] Wordsworth had a wisdom if not a philosophy to communicate, as the lives of men like Mill and Leslie Stephen demonstrated. 'What he had for presentment was a type and a standard of human normality, a way of life; his preoccupation with sanity and spontaneity working at a level and in a spirit that it seems appropriate to call religious.'[39]

Wordsworth, Shelley and Keats are Leavis's three great individual poets of the Romantic period. Coleridge as a poet he does not put on the same level. Shelley represents all that is to Leavis's mind distasteful in romantic poetry. It is not Shelley's exultant revolutionary doctrine and idealistic ardours that Leavis objects to so much as the poetry itself, in which a sweeping movement, a vague and general tumult, cancels the necessary critical consciousness of the poet, and reveals as an essential trait a weak grasp of the actual and the concrete. The emotion in Shelley's poetry forces the critic to invoke the idea of absence, the absence, that is, of critical intelligence. Spontaneity, inspiration, the medium, the quivering intensities, derive from an understanding of poetry as something 'not subject to the control of the active force of the mind', as Shelley himself says, implying, Leavis points out, not just that active powers alone are insufficient for creation but that poetry should have 'no more dealings with intelligence than it can help.' If the the verse of Shelley, the quintessential romantic, represents that decay of an organic and united sensibility characteristic of the nineteenth century, that of Keats, by an extraordinary reversal, represents its recovery. It was poetry which, while it appealed to the aesthetic taste, had within it capacities to transcend such limitations. The poems are subtler, finer, with a stronger intellectual structure (the quality Arthur Symons attributes to Shelley), and above all a 'rich local concreteness [which] is the local manifestation of an inclusive sureness of grasp in the whole.'[40] Leavis's complex, sympathetic and illuminating account of Keats is best summed up in his famous phrase: 'It is as if Keats were making major poetry out of minor – as if, that is, the genius of a major poet were working in the material of minor poetry.'[41] In the ode *To Autumn* and the *Introduction to the Revised Hyperion*, Keats reconnects the English tradition to Shakespeare, and Keats's second

Hyperion – quite apart from his explicit comments in the Letters – provides an irresistible warrant for Leavis's deepest conviction (which was also Keats's): 'Miltonic verse cannot be written but is [as ?] the verse of art. I wish to devote myself to another verse alone.'[42]

By this point Leavis had established his own strongly individual and positive sensibility, and in the exercise of it pointed to the qualities he valued most in English poetry. He required in it the active presence of critical intelligence so that his approved poetry was at the furthest remove from that produced by the divorce of intelligence and sensibility in the nineteenth century. Next he looked for a close relation with the natural spoken language – 'a strong idiomatic naturalness' as he says when speaking of Ben Jonson – and the widest use of its manifold resources. One of the best examples of Leavis's sense of this quality appears in his comment in *Revaluation* which analyses the momentary predominance in Milton of Shakespeare – the instance he gives is from *Comus* – where

> . . . the texture of actual sounds, the run of vowels and consonants, with the variety of action and effort, rich in subtle analogical suggestion, demanded in pronouncing them, plays an essential part, though this is not to be analysed in abstraction from the meaning. The total effect is as if words as words withdrew themselves from the focus of our attention and we were directly aware of a tissue of feelings and perceptions.[43]

Next he required a fullness of realisation, or better, the highest appropriate degree of realisation, 'liveness of enactment and a fullness of presentation.' It was this quality in Keats's poetry, its sensuous vitality and palpable presence, which he connects with the development of Keats's wisdom: 'It is clearly the expression of a rare maturity; the attitude is the product of tragic experience, met by discipline, in a very uncommonly strong, sincere and sensitive spirit.'[44] Maturity, indeed, is a constant canon of judgement. His treatment of Wordsworth's poetry, and of the wisdom it embodied, stresses that what Wordsworth offered was

> . . . preoccupation . . . with a distinctively human naturalness, with sanity and spiritual health, and his interest in mountains was subsidiary. His mode of preoccupation, it is true, was that of a mind intent always upon the living connexions between man and the extra-human universe; it was, that is, in the same sense as Lawrence's was, religious.[45]

The declared connection with Lawrence and Lawrence's intuition of 'the deep levels, the springs of life, the illimitable mystery that wells up into consciousness,'[46] points the way to Leavis's next significant critical exploration, namely into the structure, or the major tradition, of English fiction.

Leavis had now shaped for himself, or if that is too calculating, had become the user of a powerful and idiosyncratic prose which in its run and idiom was very close to his own speaking and teaching voice. If it was occasionally contorted by the pressure of complex thought or the necessity for responsible statement, or even by a quick sense of merit thwarted or injustice suffered, or if it sometimes left ideas embedded in thickets and densities of qualification, ellipsis and suggestion, it was always the servant of a profound seriousness; and the criticism frequently levelled at Leavis that he could not write can only have substance if the ideal against which it is measured is that of the practitioner of the enamelled or the fluently accommodating. He was concerned to get at 'the real naked essence of our vision,' to use a phrase he quotes as an epigraph from Lawrence's letters. Leavis's writing at any rate had the merit of engaging the reader's interest, if not always his sympathies. In *The Great Tradition* he announces 'not dogmatically but deliberately,' in Johnson's words: 'The great English novelists are Jane Austen, George Eliot, Henry James and Joseph Conrad – to stop for the moment at that comparatively safe point in history.'[47] The first thing to be said about this arresting declaration is that Leavis was well aware that critics found him narrow and that this opening proposition, whatever its justification, would be adduced in support of that view. The narrowness derives from the purpose Leavis had set himself, which was to determine the really significant creative achievement and to distinguish 'the few really great – the major novelists who count in the same way as the major poets.'[48] It is, therefore, a positive not an exclusive statement. Dickens and Lawrence were in due course to be added to crown and complete it. But there are other novelists, if not of such major rank, alluded to and on occasion discussed with insight and sympathy, whether they belonged to the earliest phase like Fielding and Richardson, or later ones like Peacock, Emily and Charlotte Brontë, Disraeli, T. F. Powys and L. H. Myers.

The two leading notes in Leavis's specification of the really great, the major novelists, are first, that they 'change the possibilities of the art for practitioners and readers,'[49] and second, that 'they are significant in terms of the human awareness they promote':[50] awareness of the possibilities of life. Such an insistence on the pre-eminent few, Leavis argues, is not to be indifferent to tradition but a way of grasping its true structure. Jane Austen is indebted to Richardson and Fanny Burney only in the way in which a great writer can be indebted. She affects not only what goes after but our view of what went before: 'Her work, like the work of all great creative writers, gives a meaning to the past.'[51] And again, she shows how in a great writer the concern with the intricacies of composition are inseparable from her moral impulses and canons. 'The principle of organization, and the principle of development, in her work is an intense moral interest of her own in life that is in the first place a preoccupation with certain problems that life compels on her as personal ones.'[52] Her technical originality is at one with, and the instrument of, her vision of life. Exquisite technical capacity goes with a vital capacity for experience, 'a kind of reverent openness before life, and a marked moral intensity.'[53] It is this characteristic which joins George Eliot to Jane Austen. Certainly she learnt from Jane Austen but again only in the way in which a great writer learns, in which part of the lesson is the realisation of his unlikeness: 'there is, of course, no significant unlikeness without the common concern – and the common seriousness of concern – with essential human issue.'[54] The same is true of Henry James. James's 'curiously transposed and subtilized ethical sensibility'[55] made him a displaced person in his own country. And English life supplied him with the material upon which this exquisitely analytical and strenuously moral sensibility could operate. 'James's wit is real and always natural, his poetry intelligent as well as truly rich, and there is nothing bogus, cheap or vulgar about his idealizations: certain human potentialities are nobly celebrated.'[56] There is, of course, plenty of evidence, as Leavis puts it, that James did actually go to school to the George Eliot who combined delicate psychological insight with a powerful moral understanding, gifts which served to illuminate her reverent attitude to life. James, who was intensely dependent upon literature, gained correspondingly from his contact with George Eliot, and Leavis, who is much struck by what he calls in a felicitous phrase, 'the cobwebbiness that afflicted him in his late phase,'[57] is convinced that his commerce with George Eliot influenced the incomparably superior concreteness of *The Portrait of a Lady* and *The Bostonians*.

James's material was the substance and the forms of highly civilised, indeed of an ideal, society. His strength lay in serving this interest with a technique informed by a 'clairvoyant moral intelligence.'[58] His weakness was that he did not live enough. He was, says Leavis with characteristic wit, 'a recluse living socially in the midst of society.'[59] The society he found in England, like that of America or France, failed to offer him the fineness he looked for except in glimmers and fragments.

It is about James that Leavis has most doubt, or about James that he is clearest as to the limitations in the later development: 'His registration of sophisticated human consciousness is one of the classical creative achievements: it *added* something as only genius can.'[60] But James's personal life was lived on too thin a diet of experience and relationship. The result, according to Leavis, was that vital subtlety turned into hypertrophied detachment. The characteristics of Conrad's fiction, concreteness and dramatic energy, made English a beautifully apt instrument for him. Conrad's genius was shown not in the purveying of oriental glamour but, like Jane Austen, George Eliot and Henry James, in his extraordinary capacity to render the actuality and the anguish of moral life, whether in the form of conflict between idealism and material interest in *Nostromo* or as moral isolation in *Chance* or the subtle relations of contrasting moral perspective in *The Secret Agent*. His great novels are not an exhibition of illustrated psychology but the marvellously adequate and concrete presentation of the reality of things, motives, values, weaknesses, in a subtly organised whole. He, like the others, was also an innovator in form such that the technical inventiveness and mastery expressed a moral sensibility and were not something separate from it. And he was, of course, profoundly influenced by Dickens.

It is in *The Great Tradition*, in an essay which first appeared in *Scrutiny* in 1947, beginning the notable series called 'The Novel as Dramatic Poem', that Leavis first outlined and then enforced in a critique of *Hard Times* his early view of Dickens: 'That Dickens was a great genius and is permanently among the classics is certain. But the genius was that of a great entertainer, and he had for the most part no profounder responsibility as a creative artist than this description suggests.'[61] It is true that the essay on *Hard Times* in its analytical skill and enthusiastic response implies a more complex and appreciative attitude than these comments suggest. The work in which Dickens was to be dealt with at length, *Dickens the Novelist*, a collaboration between Leavis and his wife, subordinated this idea of the entertainer to the great, the very great writer, the Shakespeare of the novel. It is a transformation in Leavis which he does not seem publicly to have acknowledged, but it certainly testifies to growth and development in his views. It also witnesses, I believe, to the powerful and creative influence exercised on Leavis's criticism by his wife, a point I shall return to.

4

The *Scrutiny* Years

The *Scrutiny* years stretched from 1932 to 1953, a period during which F.R., having moved from Emmanuel to become Fellow and Director of Studies at Downing, founded and sustained a Centre of English Studies of immense influence and international reputation, while Q.D., while she managed and wrote for *Scrutiny*, though her health was far from perfect, looked after her husband, kept a house, brought up three children, and uncomplainingly used the kitchen table both for cooking and writing: 'I myself, however, have generally had to produce contributions for this review with one hand while actually stirring the pot, or something of that kind, with the other, and if I have not done my thinking while rocking the cradle it was only because the daughters even of uneducated men ceased to rock infants at least two generations ago.'[1] And Leavis himself reported, 'My wife and I bore the major burden of *Scrutiny*: for two decades (including half a dozen years of war) we did the donkey-work and had the responsibility. We wrote more than anyone else – more than we should willingly have undertaken: it was unavoidable if *Scrutiny* was to be kept going.'[2]

As I said before, the earliest contributors included names that one is now surprised to find there. The settled connection which took only a few years to establish, chiefly depended – apart from the Leavises – on young research students at the time like D. W. Harding, James Smith, L. C. Knights, J. L. Russell, W. H. Mellers, John Speirs, R. C. Churchill, H. B. Parkes, H. A. Mason; it was later strengthened by D. A. Traversi, Marius Bewley and D. J. Enright.

The average size of an issue in the first seven volumes, that is up to 1938–39, was some 120 pages, in volumes 8 and 9 some 100 pages, and thereafter the size was nearer 80 pages. Even a glance at the index to the whole run will confirm that *Scrutiny* was by no means as narrow, and certainly not as fanatical, particularly during the early years, as its fashionable reputation would have one believe. Subjects dealt with from many points of view, and quite frequently, included not only English literary criticism and scholarship, but American, French, German, Italian and Spanish literature, education in many of its aspects, economics and advertising, arts, music, architecture and ballet, literary sociology of a very original and independent kind, newspapers and journalism, Marxism which received very considerable attention in the early years, general politics and psychology, problems of the university, particularly as these were illustrated by Oxford and Cambridge, the concepts of tradition, tragedy, cultural continuity, propaganda, and many more. As the connection settled and the scope of interest defined itself, it became clear, as Leavis said in his valedictory *Retrospect*, that 'What governed our thinking and engaged our sense of urgency was the inclusive, the underlying and overriding, preoccupation: the preoccupation with the critical function as it was performed, or not performed, for our civilization, our time, and us.'[3] This critical function was practised in an empirical and opportunist manner suitable to a particular group at a given place. It was a group that was anti-Marxist but certainly not from the beginning particularly pro-Capitalist. Its supreme value was 'a human reality, an autonomy of the human spirit,'[4] in which class war and economic determinism had no room or time. It had no clear separable philosophy and what it showed was an attitude, severity of standards, and devotion to continuity and the critical function. A clear understanding of the critical function, of course, implied a strong interest in the state of contemporary civilisa-tion, and an urgent commitment to opposing what the sharp analysis revealed, a drift towards the collective, the materialist, and the in-human. It was never subsidised, and indeed it received, as the history makes plain, no support of any kind from public institutions, and yet it sold out each of its 750 copies in the 1930s, a printing which had to be continued during the war at this level because of the rationing of paper, but which in the 1950s had risen to 1500. It came to an end after twenty years because the war disrupted and finally dispersed the group of active contributors and because the burden on two hard-pressed people became insupportable.

As the journal assumed its own character, as the idiom and ethos defined themselves, a threefold purpose strengthened in clarity and firmness. First, the aim was to define the nature and importance of the literary critical function; secondly, there was the necessity to practise the function in order both to determine the relative importance of the established figures in English literature and to explain the relations in which they stood to one another; thirdly, both these other intentions required a close analysis of the present state of the critical function and the conditions in which it had to be exercised. At the back of this part of the undertaking, as mature models and influences, were the concept of a critical function furnished by the deceased *Calendar of Modern Letters* and the researches of Q. D. Leavis which led to *Fiction and the Reading Public*. The first two I have referred to in a general way already, and I shall be returning to them again. (The central and creatively decisive feature here was the series of brilliant revaluations of major figures undertaken by Leavis, but contributed to by others, which went on throughout the journal's life.) For the time being I will concentrate on the third.

There is a marked and painful contrast of tone between the buoyancy of the manifesto with which *Scrutiny* first came upon the world in May 1932, and the bruised grimness of the *Valedictory* which introduced the last number in October 1953. The manifesto did not disguise from itself or the reader the state of affairs in which it was appearing. Hardly an intellectual journal had survived. Intellectual and critical standards were dissolving. *Scrutiny* was to be devoted to criticising the movement of modern civilisation, and while its centre was to be in the literary life it was not meant to be a purely literary review, and it would not confine itself strictly to literary matters. Its first duty was to publish good criticism and to be constantly aware of the present state of culture. *Scrutiny*'s insistence on standards of criticism was not meant only for the sake of the reader. The founders of *Scrutiny* believed that in a society without the highest critical standards the work of the creator became increasingly difficult and would finally prove impossible. They saw, too, like Matthew Arnold before them, that there were in fact scattered among the general public concerned and interested individuals. *Scrutiny* was founded on the assumption that a magazine could provide a focus of intellectual interest and education for such. *Scrutiny* had a critical policy but no intellectual or political orthodoxy. In all its critical endeavour analysis and interpretation would be used with a view to judgement. The standpoint of that judgement, the manifesto declared, would be clear when one or two numbers had been published. This was a claim which the review increasingly justified.

In 1940 Leavis looked back over the first eight years. He emphasised in this half-way review how difficult it was in the thirties for an intellectual not to be a communist: 'The assumption that not to be a communist required courage was at that time a natural one. The pressure was certainly tremendous – to wear red, or some colour recognized as its opposite.'[5] *Scrutiny*'s anti-Marxism was unhesitating and explicit because its positive position was that, though without doubt the human spirit was not to be thought of as expressing itself in a void of 'freedom', unconditioned by economic and material circumstances, nevertheless there was a great need to insist on the element of autonomy and to work for the preservation of the humane tradition – a tradition representing the profit of a continuity of experience through centuries of economic and material change.[6]

The liberal tradition that *Scrutiny* stood on was not to be identified with any particular religious creed or indeed opposed to any. The second point in his reflections on the decade – apart from its Marxism – was that it had been from a literary point of view a barren one, at least in comparison with the 1920s: 'The prevalent Marxizing and the barrenness might well seem to be in obviously significant relation, Marxist doctrines about literature and art being what they are.'[7] But Leavis is far from unsubtly suggesting any simple cause and effect here. The period of the depression filled the prospect with politico-economic problems, and 'certainly, the kind of political distraction that characterized the decade was very bad for creative work.'[8] The third head Leavis touches on is the growing power of the cliques, coteries and mutual admiration societies which ran contemporary letters, a state of affairs documented in detail by *Scrutiny*. Of course, there had always been such groups but never before had they held so unquestioned a sway. Leavis's feeling on this head derived in part from temperament and a personal history of felt injustice, but it was certainly not a merely subjective quirk. He was convinced, however, that *Scrutiny*, in spite of obstruction and hostility, had justified the intentions with which it began, above all in its success in reconstituting the fragments of an intellectual community, or another and different kind of élite characterised by intelligence, vitality and agreement. And he promised that *Scrutiny* would carry on while it could.

As indeed it did for the best part of a dozen years, 'without secretary, without business manager, without publicity manager, and without publicity,'[9] with editors and contributors unpaid and any losses met out of 'private and ill-furnished pockets,' during which it probably achieved the height of its influence and reputation. This period saw the production of some of F. R. Leavis's most brilliant criticism, including the working out of the seminal theme of the novel as dramatic poem, in which he enforced the deep *Scrutiny* conviction that the main creative force of modern literature had gone into the novel. This work gave rise to studies of Dickens, George Eliot, James, Lawrence, Conrad, and Eliot's later poetry. It also saw the production of Q. D. Leavis's highly original 'Critical Theory of Jane Austen's Writings', as well as her studies of the social context of literary work. (I shall look at the substance of these writings elsewhere.) In his understandably bitter *Valedictory* statement to the last issue, Leavis spoke with anger of the treatment of *Scrutiny*, which survived without any position or financial backing and which had from the beginning trained its own writers, and did so in spite of the hostility of the University in the centre of which it was placed, and the enmity of official organs like the British Council and the BBC, and semi-official ones like the *Times Literary Supplement* and the quality Sunday newspapers. *Scrutiny*'s relations with the British Council have their comic side. Leavis recalled the piquant fact that 'first we were asked to supply "spare" copies free, and then, when we replied that there *were* no spare copies, we were offered half-price. The working of bureaucratic machinery? – no doubt. And when you have millions of the public money to dispense in the interests of British culture you must economize in the right places.'[10] When *Scrutiny* finally ended, the distinguished retired military figure at the head of the British Council sent to Leavis a courteous, uncomprehending letter in which he wished him well and hoped that he might soon start another magazine! No new magazine was ever to be founded by Leavis himself. Two journals, however, thought, at least by third parties, to be imbued with the *Scrutiny* spirit were *The Cambridge Quarterly*, begun by a group of university teachers at Cambridge associated with the former *Scrutiny* contributor H. A. Mason, and *The Human World* which was edited at the University of Swansea by Ian Robinson. Leavis formally dissociated himself from the position of being the progenitor of these dutiful heirs, as they were called, and in respect of *The Cambridge Quarterly* expressed himself as wholly out of sympathy with its ethos and policy ('I had nothing to do with the conception, encouragement or planning of *The Cambridge Quarterly*'[11]) while explaining that the contribution by him in the first number (Leavis yielding to an urgent request for permission to print a lecture) would be found to be the last. And when P. N. Furbank in *The Listener* suggested that *The Human World* existed to propagate Leavis's views, Leavis wrote denying any such thing, and in particular objecting to the supposed affinity between himself and Wittgenstein which *The Human World* had discovered. One of the charges in *The Cambridge Quarterly* which most wounded Leavis was the accusation of *Scrutiny*'s failure with Shakespeare.

What in any case could success mean in treating so oceanic a subject?

Scrutiny's work on Shakespeare in fact was as lively and more varied and of a consistently higher standard than that produced on some of its other themes, for example on education. Some dozen writers took part in its Shakespeare criticism, including Leavis himself, L. C. Knights, R. C. Churchill, John F. Danby, D. A. Traversi, J. C. Littlewood, H. A. Mason, George Santayana, James Smith, A. A. Stephenson, F. C. Tinkler, and L. A. Cormican. Among the plays discussed in detail were *Antony and Cleopatra, As You Like It, Coriolanus, Cymbeline, Hamlet, Henry IV, Parts 1 and 2, Henry V, Julius Caesar, King Lear, Measure for Measure* and *Othello*. There was a constant review and analysis of traditional and current Shakespearean criticism. A student, or indeed any intelligent reader, could derive a very large part of his education in Shakespeare from a collected volume of the plays and the appropriate commentaries in *Scrutiny*. Shakespeare criticism in *Scrutiny* stood on a double footing, the effect of which was to displace the authority and prestige of Bradley. First, the plays were no longer to be thought of as illustrated biography or psychological novels written in verse according to established Victorian conventions. *Scrutiny* effected, as Leavis puts it, the relegation of Bradley 'by bringing home to the academic world, in the course of exemplifying positively a number of more subtle and intelligent approaches to Shakespeare, how inadequate and wrong the Bradley approach was.'[12] Leavis himself often wanted to give the main credit for *Scrutiny*'s post-Bradleyan approach to D. A. Traversi, and certainly his work was lively, alert and appealing, although it hadn't the profundity and complexity of Leavis's own writings, for example on *Measure for Measure*[13] and *Othello*,[14] or the scholarship and delicacy of L. C. Knights's earliest *Scrutiny* contributions. The concern of Traversi's criticism, said Leavis, 'was to prevent the hardening into accepted "rightness" of any supposed new method or approach or set of critical conceptions.'[15]

The other main ground on which the Shakespeare criticism was founded was a conception of the Shakespearean medium. It is elucidated by Leavis in a piece called 'Tragedy and the Medium'[16] which was the product of a disagreement with George Santayana's earlier essay 'Tragic Philosophy'.[17] In that characteristically witty and perceptive essay Santayana had written:

> . . . in Shakespeare the medium is rich and thick and more important than the idea; whereas in Dante the medium is as unvarying and simple as possible, and meant to be transparent. . . . A clear and transparent medium is admirable, when we love what we have to say;

but when what we have to say is nothing previously definite, expressiveness depends on stirring the waters deeply, suggesting a thousand half-thoughts and letting the very unutterableness of our passion become manifest in our disjointed words. The medium then becomes dominant: but can this be called success in expression?[18]

Leavis strongly objects to this phrasing. It reveals, he maintains, an essential misunderstanding of the Shakespearean use. It is not a question of ideas which are capable of being studied and extracted from a medium. It is arbitrary and uncomprehending to require, as Samuel Johnson did in similar vein, that poetry should be a medium for previously definite ideas:

What Mr. Santayana calls 'Shakespeare's medium' creates what it conveys; 'previously definite' ideas put into a 'clear and transparent' medium wouldn't have been definite enough for Shakespeare's purpose. . . . The control over Shakespeare's words in *Macbeth* . . . is a complex dramatic theme vividly and profoundly realized – not thought of, but possessed imaginatively in its concreteness, so that, as it grows in specificity, it in turn possesses the poet's mind and commands expression.[19]

The Shakespeare criticism was set firmly in a historical context (see, for example, the perceptive pieces by L. A. Cormican on the medieval idiom in Shakespeare).[20] This work was in the hands of John Speirs who brought to medieval studies buoyant enthusiasm, a sensitive critical mind, and a set of contemporary standards of poetic life all too rare in the bleaker scholarship – in the more linguistic severities of which he was sometimes held to be deficient – of medieval scholars. Most of his work on the Scots literary tradition, on Chaucer and on the non-Chaucer tradition in medieval literature, appeared in *Scrutiny*, later republished and enlarged in three notable volumes. His work, while immensely appreciative and indeed enlightening on Chaucer, went to show that there are also other literary traditions both in Scotland and England of a non-Chaucer kind which played their part in preparing the way for the Elizabethans. At the same time, John Speirs's mythological and anthropological interests very much extended and complicated our conception of medieval art. Speirs is one of the best of *Scrutiny* writers who have had the least general recognition. Speirs's criticism earned a special commendation from Leavis when reflecting on the history of *Scrutiny*:

Where medieval literature is in question, what Speirs did was to perform the characteristic *Scrutiny* office of taking it out of the hands of the specialists and professionals and laying it open to the cultivated reader as living literature. This is the offence which the specialists and professionals call lack of scholarship.[21]

No such charge could be levelled against the percipient, immaculately scholarly and occasionally tart Shakespearean criticism of L. C. Knights which appeared in the earlier numbers of *Scrutiny*: or against the acute and highly original contribution of D. W. Harding, some of which achieved a classical status, for example, 'Aspects of the Poetry of Isaac Rosenberg',[22] 'Regulated Hatred: An Aspect of the Work of Jane Austen',[23] and 'The Theme of "The Ancient Mariner"',[24] or against any of the work of James Smith, an extraordinary writer who combined deep erudition with powerful intellectual gifts and a philosophical approach and understanding, which greatly enlarged the scope of *Scrutiny*'s work, giving it a new kind of stretch and orchestration. Some of his essays, too, like the famous one 'On Metaphysical Poetry',[25] or 'Wordsworth: a Preliminary Survey'[26] became permanent sources of enlightenment on their subjects.

Another writer who extended the range of *Scrutiny*'s interests was W. H. Mellers whose musical critiques and reviews – succeeding those of an earlier musical contributor, Bruce Pattison – became one of the most attractive, as well as independent, elements in the *Scrutiny* pattern. Over the years Mellers wrote major studies of Edmund Rubbra, Mahler, Bartok and Fauré, on Michael Tippett, on American music, and particularly on his great passion, polyphonic music. Mellers wrote in a more fluent and personal manner than many of the *Scrutiny* writers and his work showed always a lambent and educational enthusiasm of a very positive sort which was by no means so common among the lesser *Scrutiny* figures, whose great fault was to take on something of the idiom and the attitude of the Leavises and their most distinguished intimates, in a way which neither talent nor experience warranted. Mellers, for example, was criticised in the pages of *Scrutiny* itself by two such lesser Scrutineers[27] on the grounds of an unduly ecstatic tone, on the inadequacy of Mellers's historical perception to his musical scholarship, on his over-estimation of polyphonic music, and on the superficiality and generality of his critical idiom, and above all on the overcapacious handbag of his recommendations:

Sibelius and Elgar (each of these Mr. Mellers has described as the last great composer to be endorsed by his society), Fauré, Berlioz, Vaughan Williams ('definitely a great composer'), Couperin le Grand (whose church music is 'as profound as anything written in the eighteenth century, not excepting Bach'), Bartok, Dvorak (whose D minor Symphony is 'among the supreme achievements of the nineteenth century'), are all composers on whom Mr. Mellers had indulged his weakness for the superlative.[28]

He was also criticised for changing his mind about Stravinsky and van Dieren. Why not? the innocent reader would be inclined to reply both to the accusation and the quoted observation. Mellers in a modest and sensible reply refused to accept that verbal facility was to be identified with superficiality. He enquired why he shouldn't change his mind when his experience justified his doing so, and insisted that his aim was to evolve a conception of a European musical tradition:

... into which one will be able to fit one's attitude to Bach, Mozart and Beethoven; not to define an attitude to these great composers on to which one can often quite irrelevantly hang everything else. I am convinced that this notion of the *totality* of the European tradition is of the utmost importance if we are ever to have again a musically-educated public; and this is the first step towards a more healthy relation between the composer and his public than inevitably obtains at present.[29]

He made also the valid point that musical education suffered as much from the pervasiveness of the nineteenth-century tradition as literary tradition had at the beginning of *Scrutiny*'s time. Nor did he think it part of his purpose to continue the negative criticism which had been a significant part of *Scrutiny*'s function in its early days.

The *Scrutiny* undertaking, then, had at its heart a fresh concept of literary criticism, and it brought this to bear in the most practical way on a large range of English literature, classical and contemporary, major and minor. A lively and distinctly original interest in musical life enlarged the context in which it operated, as did its sustained concern with French literature, with American life and literature, and with German literature. More than half a dozen critics contributed to a wide-ranging examination of the French classics. They included Henri Fluchère, R. C. Knight, James Smith, G. D. Klingopulos, and H. A. Mason. The most substantial contribution was from Martin Turnell, who appeared on many occasions between 1936 and 1948 writing on the major French classics as well as on less weighty but more clinically significant writers. The reports on American affairs came from Henry Bamford Parkes who was English born and educated and a naturalised American citizen, and they were notable for their combination of intimacy and detachment. American literature itself was written on by both the Leavises, by D. W. Harding, R. G. Cox and H. A. Mason, but some of the most impressive work came from Marius Bewley, who was much admired by Leavis. A great deal of his notable book *The Complex Fate* first appeared as contributions to *Scrutiny*. D. J. Enright, who wrote most of the German criticism, began to contribute to *Scrutiny* as an undergraduate. Even in these youthful contributions, Enright's disconcerting ability to jolt us out of routine appears again and again. Wittily and sometimes even flippantly, he defended a kind of orthodoxy and centrality of taste and judgement. Few English critics have written with such justice and delicacy about German writers as Enright, and above all, of Goethe and Thomas Mann.

I mention this range of critical work in *Scrutiny* (and one could add, too, its alert and intelligent concern with science as an influential habit of thought) to show that the general labelling of *Scrutiny* as fanatical and perversely narrow needs much qualification. *Scrutiny*, of course, was not simply a general intellectual organ. It was enlivened by a strong idea of what the critical function should be, it was supported by something like an intellectual community, and it engaged in the practice of its work with what can only be called passion.

Donne – if not a *Scrutiny* figure, one feels, at least a *Scrutiny* presence – once divided a sermon into pretext or purpose, context or setting, text or substance. If we apply these categories to *Scrutiny* we see the pretext as the will to correct the function of criticism in the light of a new concept of it, the context as the study of the literary society past and present in which this purpose had to be worked out, and the text as twenty years of pioneering, independent, and immensely influential literary criticism. While most of the better *Scrutiny* writers made some contribution both to one and the other, the one who made the greatest contribution to the text was F. R. Leavis; the one who made the greatest contribution to the context was Q. D. Leavis.

I shall look at each of these in turn later in this book. Here I may simply remind the reader of that great series of studies deriving from the concept of the novel as dramatic poem, in the course of which Leavis developed some of his most effective and shaping criticism, including the work that appeared as *The Great Tradition* and that which was given a final form in *D. H. Lawrence: Novelist*. The *Scrutiny* criticism of the novel was contributed to very significantly by others, by Q. D. Leavis herself in her studies of Jane Austen's art and her analysis of James's 'The Lesson of the Master' and her essays on Edith Wharton, Dorothy Richardson, Gissing and E. M. Forster. There were significant studies by R. C. Churchill on Dickens[30] and G. D. Klingopulos on *Wuthering Heights*.[31] These were essays picked out by Leavis himself as having a peculiar significance in the critique of the novel. (When Mrs Leavis, however, turned her attention to *Wuthering Heights* in 'A Fresh Approach to *Wuthering Heights*'[32] she found that Klingopulos's essay, though honest and sensitive, ignored or slighted elements and themes which seemed to her as of fundamental importance.)

On the other side, that of context, *Scrutiny* devoted much space, some will feel too much space, to the diagnosis of current literary life, its values, powers and hostility to *Scrutiny* itself. It analysed the domination of Bloomsbury and the spreading effect over the generations of that group. It offered particular opposition to the genteel forms through which the Bloomsbury ethos worked, in such centres of power for example as the ancient universities, the British Council and the B.B.C. Particular occasions may not always have warranted the intensity of rebuttal they received in *Scrutiny*, but there can be little doubt that *Scrutiny*'s view of the establishment's determined, skilful strategy of hindering, ignoring, and blunting its effect, was amply demonstrated. If the *Scrutiny* attacks on the establishment represented the negative side of its analysis of the context, the studies of Mrs Leavis on Leslie Stephen, Haddon, Chadwick, and Sidgwick which appeared between 1939 and 1947 offer a totally different concept of the intellectual life and a much more positive idea of the achievement and distinction of an intellectual class.

The documents putting *Scrutiny*'s case against the literary world of the day are scattered throughout its nineteen volumes. The most significant have been conveniently assembled by Leavis himself in Volume 1 of his *A Selection from Scrutiny* (1968). They begin with a number of placing pieces – 'placing', a characteristic and revealing *Scrutiny* term – by T. R. Barnes, H. A. Mason and Q. D. Leavis. These by processes either of graduated dissent from or discriminating realignment of, or even total demolition of, the reputation of current literary figures carry, both expressly and by implication, a condemnation of the error, frivolity, and corrupted judgement which has made these seem acceptable and even noteworthy. They are also in their different ways

extremely entertaining, a point not often made in discussion of
Scrutiny contributions. T. R. Barnes, writing on Wyndham Lewis as a
symptom not a leader of the age, shows how like a successful ad-man
he had come to believe quite uncritically in what he sold:

> Lewis's satire seems largely self-indulgence. It reminds one of
> Halifax's dictum: 'Anger, like drink, giveth rise to a great deal of
> unmannerly wit.' I read recently of a German tailor, who, annoyed
> with his employer, had the latter's portrait tattooed on his behind.
> He exhibited it, to the delight of his friends, and the discomfiture of
> his enemy. Mr Lewis's activity, in the *Apes of God*, and many of his
> other works, seems to me to be exactly analogous to the tailor's and
> just as valuable; though he is scarcely the tailor's equal in precision
> and economy of technique.[33]

H. A. Mason's sober reassessment of the T. E. Hulme myth makes
both the necessary positive and negative points about Hulme, emphasising his natural bent for trenchant distinction and for welding together
distinctions from different categories into positions of startling clarity.
Hulme was not of any creative importance but he was a stimulating
influence, probably more effective as a speaker than a writer. The fact
that many of his dicta can be found in T. S. Eliot indicates that Hulme's
strength lay not in any philosophic or critical originality but in the
success of those who came under his influence. T. R. Barnes tackled a
favourite *Scrutiny* subject, the Bloomsbury ethos as distilled in Lytton
Strachey. Strachey was the saint of contemporary letters. He had an
'impeccable' style, the cadences of which are echoes of Browne,
Gibbon and Johnson. The success of the Strachey character-essay
was based on Strachey's competent, Freudian-dressed appeal 'to that
desire for fantasy satisfaction through "characters" or substitute lives,
which is the basis of commercial fiction.'[34] His literary criticism was a
string of epithets without particularity or argument. He was excited
by the patina and not the form. The longest and wittiest pieces here are
by Q. D. Leavis who writes about E. M. Forster in a way which is
lively, sympathetic and pointed, and about Dorothy Sayers (an
extraordinary subject it will now appear to us but quite comprehensible
in 1937 when she figured among the clinical examples in the *Scrutiny*
treatment of best-sellers). She also deals trenchantly with Charlotte
Yonge. And again if we wonder why this should be necessary, that was
because of the strange influence at the time of a special kind of Christian literary criticism or Christian discrimination as it was called. In
Mrs Leavis's view the claims of Charlotte Yonge made by these

Christian propagandists should be investigated 'before the canon of English Literature finds itself permanently burdened with one of the prolific fiction-writers whom time alone has already expelled.'[35] The Anglican discriminator needed the same warning as the Marxist critic, namely that 'before certifying a work on the grounds of content or apparent orthodoxy it is as well to be sure that its actual "message", what it inevitably and essentially communicates, is what you thought it was.'[36] Mrs Leavis had maintained in her earliest work that there was a place for the best-seller. What she is objecting to in respect of Charlotte Yonge in the Victorian period and Dorothy Sayers in the thirties was 'this odd conviction that she is in a different class from Edgar Wallace or Ethel M. Dell . . .'[37] She is particularly incensed by Dorothy Sayers's success among academics which she had presumably observed at first-hand in Cambridge:

> Run your eyes over enough academic bookshelves – not those hous-ing shop but those where they keep what they really choose to read-and you get accustomed to a certain association of authors represent-ing an average taste which is at best negative: Edward Lear and Ernest Bramah's *Kai Lung* (delicious humour), Charles Morgan and C. E. Montague (stylists), Rupert Brooke (or Humbert Wolfe or some equivalent) . . . Dorothy Sayers can take her place alongside without raising any blushes; these or their kind are the writers she admires herself. But doesn't it raise some awkward questions? What is the value of this scholarly life Miss Sayers hymns if it doesn't refine the perceptions of those leading it? If your work was of any value to you would you want, would you be able to relax on Edgar Wallace (much less on Dorothy Sayers)? Miss Sayers innocently presents her typical admirable scholar and 'English' don engaged on her life's work of what but a History of English Prosody (an all too plausible under-taking)! Apart from the fact that the lady was engaged in perpetrating a sort of public nuisance, think of the effect on the teaching of English in her college of that attitude to the study of poetry. No education could take place there . . .[38]

Dorothy Sayers was easy if necessary meat at the time. But *Scrutiny* and Mrs Leavis are seen at their best in her piece in this section on E. M. Forster. She is writing on *Abinger Harvest*, Forster's mixture of auto-biography and criticism. Mrs Leavis understands Forster very well indeed. She sees how 'compared with the other major novelists of this century Mr Forster exhibits a lack both of personal vigour and of that intellectual strength which impresses as the best source of vitality.'[39]

She is gentle towards his niceness and not over-severe about his blind-spots which have 'none of Lytton Strachey's hateful qualities – the cheap irony, the vulgar prose effects, the assumption of superiority to his historical puppets.'[40] She is as clear about his weakness, 'an uneasy wobble in some of the ironic effects' as about his personal brand of wisdom, 'a deprecating refusal to be easily wise ... Along with this goes ... Mr Forster's courage – and courage is readily felt to be an important part of this writer's make-up – [which] is not associated with his irony so much as with his delicate emotional machinery. Certainly it is something in the nature of courage which provides the mainspring: courage to assert the virtue of the finer feelings.'[41] One side of Forster leans towards Ronald Firbank, 'a tiresome fribble to some of us'; the other towards a reticent boldness and probity of feeling.

The second set of documents analysing the literary world, again included in Volume 1 of the *Selection from Scrutiny*, is mostly contributed to by Leavis himself, although there is, as well, an engagingly witty note by Q. D. Leavis on the background of twentieth-century letters. The pieces by Leavis in this section have an altogether more abrasive rasp in the voice. His epigraph is

things rank and gross in nature
Possess it merely. That it should come to this!

It has come to this, he believes, because of the three-fold effect on publishing of 'the value of advertising, the reach and thoroughness of the Literary Racket, and the power and vindictiveness of the gangs.'[42] The world of reviewers is notable for its solidarity. 'See them fall upon the rash outsider who undertakes to remind the world what serious standards are.'[43] The pressure of advertising, the pressure of comradely feeling, and publishing turned into a large-scale commodity industry in which the market is raked for potential profit makers and wares boosted by commercial methods, these have succeeded in displacing the critical function and turned it into the supply of 'oil for the cogs of the publishing machine.' This was the situation as Leavis saw it in 1932. In *Scrutiny*'s specification of the causes Mrs Leavis emphasises the place of Eton – Eton standing for the English Public School system generally. In reviewing a number of books in 1939[44] by Sir Edward Marsh, Logan Pearsall Smith, Cyril Connolly and Louis MacNeice, she points to the significance in this context of knowing the right people. Sir Edward Marsh, for example, 'became an innocent blotting-paper to all literary aspirants he met in the right company, particularly good-looking young men with fetching manners.'[45] 'His representative quality . . . enabled him to produce in the Georgian Poetry-Books something that went like hot-cakes . . . and his classical education gave him an unshakable conception of what poetry ought to be . . .'[46] The complacent inability 'to apply purely literary criticism because of an unconscious acceptance of social values'[47] is as prominent in the much more intelligent Connolly as in the naive Stephen Spender. Connolly himself points out the truth: 'Critics in England do not accept bribes, but they discover one day that in a sense their whole life is an accepted bribe, a fabric of compromises based on personal relationships.'[48] There is a continuity of feeling and value between the public school and the university world into which these young men then moved, and between this and the literary society which they graduate into:

> Mr Connolly and his set expected to succeed Rupert Brooke's, and are now seeing to it that the literary preserves are kept exclusively for their friends. We who are in the habit of asking how such evidently unqualified reviewers as fill the literary weeklies ever got into the profession need ask no longer. They turn out to have been 'the most fashionable boy in the school', or to have had a feline charm or a sensual mouth and long eye-lashes.[49]

In Mrs Leavis's view it is hardly possible to exaggerate the advantages that the Americans enjoy in having 'no public-school system, no ancient universities and no tradition of a closed literary society run on Civil Service lines . . .'[50]

Leavis insisted again in 1940 on the state of affairs, amply recorded and documented in *Scrutiny*, in which the young man from the ancient university could immediately and without any particular sense of change find himself in a fraternity that ran contemporary letters, 'ran them so effectively that he could make a name and a career without even coming in sight of adult standards.'[51] How admirable, he points out, in this world is the example of Henry James, and his

> bewildered and badgered antiquity . . . I can't go into it all much – but the rough sense of it is that I believe only in absolutely independent, individual and lonely virtue, and in the serenely unsociable (or if need be at a pinch sulky and sullen) practice of the same; the observation of a lifetime having convinced me that no fruit ripens but under that temporarily graceless rigour, and that the associational process for bringing it on is but a bright and hollow artifice, all vain and delusive.[52]

It is the sulky and sullen practice of graceless rigour that shows in Leavis's scornful assaults on the British Council, a bureaucratic organisation for administering and propagating associational values. Such a system works not only against the critic but against the creator. The creative mind depends, as Arnold says, on the atmosphere of living ideas. One who is from his school-days persuaded to believe that the Sunday papers can direct him to the source of life and light will be deprived of essential nutriment and be bound to wither. If there was one figure above all whom Leavis chose as the exemplar and determiner of this world, it was John Maynard Keynes – just as one figure who innocently demonstrated all the disadvantages of a young writer brought up in this atmosphere was Stephen Spender. Keynes was the most formidable promoter of this coterie spirit that modern England has known. His genius as economist, logician and financial speculator made him a sought-after patron and gave him immense power which he used to propagate 'the taste, idiom and assumptions of the very inferior coterie *milieu* to which he belonged.'[53] Keynes embodied the taste and had the sources of power and patronage; G. E. Moore provided the intellectual justification for believing that 'the supreme values of life were the states of consciousness involved in human relations and in the appreciation of beauty.'[54] The importance of Keynes above all in English social history in Leavis's view was not just that he promoted in the cultural realm the Bloomsbury idea of the good life but that he used his powerful influence in enforcing the habit of substituting social-personal values for the appropriate ones. It was Keynes's capacities and his use of them which brought about the state of things revealed in Stephen Spender's autobiography:

> To-day the triumph of the social-personal (or 'club', we may now call it) principle is complete. The club is not narrowly exclusive, but you must belong (and keep the rules) if you are to be recognized to exist. And if the club is not narrowly exclusive the system of relations by which it controls the organs and institutions through which the currency-values are established and circulated is comprehensive and complete.[55]

The tone in which *Scrutiny* conducted its guerrilla war against the Establishment was far from accommodating or even civil. Indeed it was felt to be alarming and dangerous. Its vices, again collected by Leavis and given in his *Retrospect*, were said to be narrowness, proneness to negative criticism, offensiveness, the qualities which made it repellent 'to intellectuals, distinctions, and authorities whose recognized status as such depended on an institutionally secured value-convention, feared sanctions and a safe currency.'[56]

The other deficiency frequently charged against the whole *Scrutiny* undertaking was its lack of a central philosophy or coherent extractable doctrine. J. B. Bamborough, for example, writing in *The Spectator* on the assumptions of *Scrutiny*, spoke of 'Leavis's conspicuous failure to state an aesthetic in support of his draconian judgments.' Or as George Watson in *The Literary Critics* said, 'We may despair of a lucid account of a central doctrine from a critic who has always shown himself indifferent to the study of linguistics.' This was, if not identical, related to an accusation which appeared in the body of *Scrutiny* itself. It was made in the March 1937 *Scrutiny* by Dr René Wellek:

> I could wish [says Wellek to Leavis] that you had stated your assumptions more explicitly and defended them systematically. I do not doubt the value of these assumptions and as a matter of fact I share them with you for the most part, but I would have misgivings in pronouncing them without elaborating a specific defence or a theory in their defence. Allow me to sketch your ideal of poetry, your 'norm' with which you measure every poet: your poetry must be in serious relation to actuality, it must have a firm grasp of the actual, of the object, it must be in relation to life, it must not be cut off from direct vulgar living, it should be normally human, testify to spiritual health and sanity, it should not be personal in the sense of indulging in personal dreams and fantasies, there should be no emotion for its own sake in it, no afflatus, no mere generous emotionality, no luxury in pain or joy, but also no sensuous poverty, but a sharp, concrete realization, a sensuous particularity. The language of your poetry must not be cut off from speech, should not flatter the singing voice, should not be merely mellifluous, should not give *e.g.* a mere general sense of motion, etc. You will recognize, of course, in this description tags from your book chosen from all chapters, and the only question I would ask you is to defend this position more abstractly and to become conscious that large ethical, philosophical and, of course, ultimately, also aesthetic *choices* are involved.[57]

Wellek's other criticism of Leavis on this head was that he was disposed by nature towards a realist philosophy and therefore unappreciative of a whole phase of human thought, idealism as it came down from Plato, which makes him underrate the coherence of the romantic view of the world.

I refer elsewhere to Leavis's reply to this charge,[58] but the simple answer to it was given long ago by Eric Bentley when he published in 1948 a selection of *Scrutiny* contributions called *The Importance of Scrutiny*. It may be, he says, that

... those who do know of Leavis sometimes think of him as one who hands out opinions to the young. They miss the point. It may be a fact that some young people have 'stolen' their opinions from Leavis. How could he stop them? The important thing is to remember that such stealing is clean contrary to Leavis's principles. He is not another Irving Babbitt. If there is a bed-rock of doctrine, an absolute, at the bottom of his work, it is not a philosophical system, but a doctrine as to procedure, a methodological absolute. Even the method is far from peculiar or idiosyncratic. The assumption is that literature means something, that the meaning or content is bound up with the style or form, and may therefore be discovered by the trained sensibility. Literature means letters, humane letters, men's words. The best literature, as we have already been taught, is the best words in the best order. Literary study, Leavis concludes, means a study of the words and their order. To use Ezra Pound's phrase, literature is 'language charged with meaning to the utmost possible degree.' Reading literature, Leavis concludes, means being sensitive to the charge, the energy, which the poet gives to his words.

Far from offering a new philosophy of art, or even insisting on a particular old one, Leavis might be described as the anti-philosophical critic. 'No theoretical discussion should be allowed to go on for long at any distance from critical practice,' he writes in 'How to Teach Reading'. People say one should examine one's assumptions, but the literary critic who says this more than three times ends up as a philosopher, and seldom a good philosopher. Here philosophy plays the perennial part of 'the larger and more difficult subject' that lures critics to give up criticism. If we are trying to demonstrate that criticism is itself a discipline we should not give it up for philosophy, even for the philosophy of criticism. In the *Scrutiny* group of writers are men of radically different philosophies.[59]

These men produced a journal striking in its comprehensiveness. Not that it was comprehensive in treating everything. Its own standards and interests focused the material. But without question a serious student or reader could gain from the seventy-six quarterly numbers of *Scrutiny* reprinted in twenty volumes by the Cambridge University Press in 1968, a complete literary education. Some, for example the South African writer Dan Jacobson, in fact used *Scrutiny* as 'a kind of home university.'[60] Its comprehensiveness, in the sense defined, was expressed in a tone of confident authority which had not been heard in English periodical publication since the great reviews (whose nature and influence, incidentally, were treated with scholarly precision and critical understanding by R. G. Cox in the June and September numbers of *Scrutiny* in 1937). The panel of reviewers in *Scrutiny* was, one repeats, not all of a level. It had one genius in F. R. Leavis and probably another in Q. D. Leavis; and it had a number of extraordinarily disinterested, incisive, and committed minds: I am thinking in particular of James Smith, D. W. Harding, John Speirs, D. A. Traversi, W. H. Mellers, D. J. Enright, and Marius Bewley. But there were hangers-on, there were barnacles, and there were parasites. But there were very few of these latter and certainly not enough to lower the general excellence, the consistent independence, and the salutary quality of *Scrutiny* criticism.

5

The Principal Collaborator

Queenie Dorothy Leavis, née Roth, was born in London in 1907, brought up in a cultivated household ('I remember Nelson's cheap reprint with gratitude, for it lay around the house when I was a child and was my own introduction to Henry James')[1], and educated at Latymer School, Edmonton, where her contributions to the school magazine, sketches, reports, poems, show a precocious sensibility. She read English at Girton, took a First in the Tripos in 1928 and was awarded an Ottilie Hancock Research Fellowship, during the tenure of which she engaged in the research which was to be published in 1932 as *Fiction and the Reading Public*, one of the most significant and independent pieces of literary work ever to have come directly from a young research student in the Humanities. When Queenie Roth and Frank Leavis were married in 1929, Leavis was thirty-four and had published nothing of real substance. His own thesis on 'The Relationship of Journalism to Literature: studied in the rise and early development of the Press in England' was decidedly narrower, more academic and less adventurous than his wife's. There is little doubt that his first writings, *Mass Civilization and Minority Culture*, and *Culture and Environment*, were directly derivative from his wife's work. Indeed, her influence on him in these years, as in later critical periods, was substantial and creative. Leavis was a great man but there is as much evidence in the published writings of his wife's influence on him as of his on her.

Fiction and the Reading Public is anthropological in manner, or perhaps one should now say sociological. 'I soon found myself committed,' Mrs Leavis says, 'to a method of investigation which I prefer to describe as "anthropological". It consisted in examining all the material that seemed to bear on this question in an unbiased but inquisitive frame of mind and concentrating on registering shifts of taste and changes in the cultural background, allowing such conclusions as I arrived at to emerge simply by comparison and contrast and analysis.'[2] Mrs Leavis's writing from the beginning was more fluent and nimbler than her husband's, her interests were more current and clearly defined, and even this first work shows the qualities she was to become notable for, originality, independence, and a fine sense, quicker and lighter than Leavis's, of many aspects of the contemporary world. She also shows herself freer than any other prominent *Scrutiny* writer from any set or static idiom.

Her study, which uses fiction as the index of popular taste, derives from a conviction of the enormous importance this category of writing had upon the minds and lives of the English people – the supreme influence in art before the advent of television. It derives too from a strong sense that the history of taste has significance in the light of our current situation. Two elements are prominent in the work. It is informed by a vivid sense of the contemporary position and it is firmly embedded in history. Reading is certainly a contemporary appetite but people now read, not for any particular artistic, spiritual or informative purpose, but chiefly to pass the time. Mrs Leavis quotes a comment from *New Age*: '. . . the novel gives the longest surcease from ennui at the least expenditure of time and money.'[3] Reading to pass the time is the essential condition for producing fantasy fiction, 'the typical reading of a people whose normal impulses are starved of the means for expression.'[4] The processes which Mrs Leavis saw firmly in train in the 1930s, which have now established themselves irresistibly and which have in television, popular fiction and the press descended to depths unplumbed then, she sets in their historical context. The primitive literary market of the Elizabethans and a public too narrow for specialisation meant that the possibilities of the printed word had not been discovered or exploited. The period of the next two hundred years in the history of popular taste was represented at its purest by Bunyan, at its most splendid by Milton, and at its most popular by Defoe. It was an influence which lasted throughout the eighteenth and nineteenth centuries:

> It was the greatest good luck for the English that three of their early literary masterpieces (the Authorised Version, *Pilgrim's Progress*, and *Paradise Lost*) should have been explicitly religious works, so that even the grimmest and poorest Puritan household possessed at least the first two of these; and that a journalist of genius should have been impelled by force of circumstances to make the most fascinating of all games (playing at house) a suitable Sunday book. These four works remained the inevitable if not the only books in the home of the decent working man for a couple of centuries, an invaluable educational influence with whatever purpose they may have been read, for to read Bunyan and Milton for religious instruction, as to attend Elizabethan drama for the 'action', is to receive an education unconsciously.[5]

The autobiographies of the self-educated, of James Lackington, of William Hone, of Thomas Cooper, of Samuel Drew, show how it was possible to acquire a feeling for literature which seems impossible in the twentieth century. Mrs Leavis remarks how struck she is by two things, '... the ability that these barely literate working-men display to tackle serious works, and the absence of any but material difficulties in their way.'[6] When eighteenth-century enthusiasm was replaced by revolutionary idealism some puritan vigour persisted as a shaping force. The Mechanics Institutes, the 'Mutual Improvement' Societies, the Philosophical Institutions, channels in which this Puritan sensibility still ran, turned more and more to purely scientific, spiritual and philosophical themes. The appearance of the modern popular press at the end of the nineteenth century was what finally broke up the Puritan tradition. The decline of this tradition was accompanied by a growing fissure between cultivated and popular taste. The leisure classes read simply for amusement, ordinary working people began to be left without leisure for reading, and with Lytton we see the first of modern bestsellers. Lytton was taken seriously by the general public but his work represented the debasement of the novelist's currency. 'To make a useful generalisation, bestsellers before Lytton are at worst dull but ever since they have almost always been vulgar. A similar distinction is to be made between periodicals before and after Northcliffe entered Fleet Street.'[7] That is, the degeneration represented by the bestseller was reinforced by the brutalisation of the popular press. The competition for circulation, the use of advertising psychology, brought about the disintegration of the reading public and the destruction of a tradition within one generation.

The reading of serious fiction requires sustained and intense effort. Such capacities are formed or destroyed by environment. The degree to which a reader can cooperate with a serious novelist is conditioned by the degree of familiarity with literary technique at which the general public has arrived: 'Where the general reader is concerned the capacity for cumulative reading is formed or destroyed by environment; ability to follow the sense of an author depends on mental habits less personal than social; susceptibility to tone is finally a test of manners.'[8] There are two key passages in *Fiction and the Reading Public* which I should like to quote. The first Mrs Leavis takes from Coleridge:

It is noticeable, how limited an acquaintance with the masterpieces of art will suffice to form a correct and even a sensitive taste, where none but masterpieces have been seen and admired: while on the other hand, the most correct notions, and the widest acquaintance with the works of excellence of all ages and countries, will not perfectly secure us against the contagious familiarity with the far more numerous offspring of tastelessness or of a perverted taste. If this be the case, as it notoriously is, with the arts of music and painting, how much more difficult will it be, to avoid the infection of multiplied and daily examples in the practice of an art, which uses words, and words only, as its instruments.[9]

The second is her own conclusion:

His environment is even more subtly against the twentieth-century reader than this account may suggest. It was affirmed . . . that in the post-war civilisation 'the rate at which cultural news penetrates is surprisingly slow' – surprisingly, that is, considering the elaborate machinery for disseminating such news which that civilisation possesses. But when this machinery is examined, the newspaper, the cinema, and so on are seen actually to form and accentuate the stratification which was noted as a striking peculiarity of the twentieth-century public; whatever their function may be in theory they do in fact harden their public, not render it adaptable, conserve popular prejudice, not correct it, above all, induce attitudes which they may profitably exploit.[10]

Already we see in *Fiction and the Reading Public* qualities to be developed and refined in Mrs Leavis's later work: a buoyant intellectual independence, a very firm and very clear sense of moral value, literary critical insight, and a gift for social analysis. We may note that the political stance, while it is by no means left-wing, is distinctly astringent in attitude towards the grosser aspects of commercial capitalism. Perhaps we may call it what we used to think of as liberal. Dickens, at this stage of Mrs Leavis's development we must also interpolate, hardly comes out much better than business. ('The peculiarity of Dickens, as any one who runs a critical eye over a novel or two of his can see, is that his originality is confined to recapturing a child's outlook on the grown-up world; emotionally he is not only uneducated but also immature.')[11] This comment so out of touch with her later view of Dickens is not on a level with the critical acumen shown in the commentary on the eighteenth-century novel or of the perceptions about, for example George Eliot and James Joyce. The two leading interests of original criticism and social analysis were to be taken up in turn while Mrs Leavis was engaged in pressing duties in the home and as her husband's secretary, research assistant and collaborator.

Let me consider for a moment the sociological theme of her work. 'The sociology of the academic world is a sadly neglected subject,'[12] she observed and Mrs Leavis herself may be considered as one of the chief inaugurators of this study in the modern world. The substance of her contribution appears in five articles in *Scrutiny* written between 1943 and 1947. In a series of case studies she deals with the theme both negatively and positively. Walter Raleigh, the first Professor of English Literature at Oxford and his successor, the much less-gifted G. S. Gordon, Professor of English at Leeds and then Merton Professor in Oxford, President of Magdalen and subsequently Vice-Chancellor, provided clinical examples for the pathology of academic life. Raleigh, says Mrs Leavis, 'never took literature seriously, apart from its succubus, scholarship. He is an example of the most dangerous kind of academic, the man who hasn't enough ability to set up on his own as a creative artist and bears literature a grudge in consequence.'[13] He habitually denigrated literary criticism and he treated the academic life and his own students with a repellently mannered cynicism. Gordon, his successor, 'the able Scots student who collects Firsts and prizes by cannily directed industry,'[14] was backed by Raleigh. An altogether smaller figure than Raleigh, Gordon believed in linguistic-philological studies as an end in themselves, and perfect editing of any text, however insignificant, as the ideal activity of scholarship. Gordon's case, writes Mrs Leavis, 'shows what happens to ability when it is exposed to the atmosphere of Classical studies pursued without any standards other than those of scholarship and of social snobbishness.'[15] For Gordon, Lamb, Stevenson and Johnson – the club Johnson – were the great figures of literature and style, and Bridges, not Eliot, the modern creative artist. In this world social standards and conventional literary and cultural values are only different aspects of the same mentality. 'The Discipline of Letters is seen to be simply the rules of the academic English club.'[16] Mrs Leavis contrasts the Raleighs and Gordons, who were honoured and endowed, with other academic figures who were snubbed and disregarded. In studies of A. C. Haddon, who established the study of anthropology at Cambridge, of the philosopher Henry Sidgwick, and of H. M. Chadwick, she proposes different figures for honour and offers a totally different ideal. Haddon, who died in his eighty-fifth year in 1940, was a brilliant anthropological investigator, a genius as a teacher, and a man of utter disinterestedness. He was indifferent to worldly success. He was able to establish his subject because in his life-time it was still possible for the freelance to make his way in Cambridge. The introduction of the Faculty system made such a career more and more difficult. Chadwick was another Haddon, a shrewd Yorkshireman, a splendid teacher, a great scholar, a linguistic genius. Mrs Leavis was herself taught by Chadwick and she pays tribute to his patience, his consideration, and his singlemindedness. He showed above all 'how literary and linguistic studies could be made most profitable, by successfully correlating them with their social background.'[17] He offended the Raleigh-Gordon connection by insisting that compulsory philology was the natural enemy of humanistic studies and that Anglo-Saxon had no literature sufficient to make it worth the while for students of modern literature.

To these pieces on academics, Mrs Leavis joins studies of Henry Sidgwick and Leslie Stephen. Leslie Stephen she thinks of as one in the direct line of the best literary criticism. He exhibited 'a tone, a discipline and an attitude that were desirable models to form oneself on.'[18] The Leslie Stephen she studied was not the Mr Ramsay of Virginia Woolf. Stephen wanted to confine literary criticism to discussing the nature, the quality, and the world of the work of art. He did not see it as a form of substitute creation. He insisted that moral value was an essential element in literary response and literary judgement. He was connected with a fundamentally Puritan tradition and he brought from this elements which were found sympathetic in Cambridge – as they would certainly not have been in Oxford. His post-Cambridge life as a journalist 'seems to have been a congenial extension of the Cambridge ethos.'[19] His dry, cool manner both fitted with and derived from the Cambridge spirit. The other influence that Mrs Leavis holds up for admiration is that of Henry Sidgwick. She gives a vivid picture of his work for the higher education of women, of his moral independence, indeed of his moral heroism, of his advanced views on education and of the Cambridge in which a Sidgwick was not an isolated and repressed figure but rather 'the most visible point of growth.' 'Behind him was an intellectual ancestry in which John Stuart Mill and Clerk Maxwell counted for much; he was the friend of George Eliot and her novels owe much to this world.'[20] In Sidgwick's educational work in Cambridge, in the disinterestedness and selflessness of Haddon and Chadwick, in the disciplined, level-headedness and commonsense of Leslie Stephen, Mrs Leavis found 'an ancestry or tradition for the enterprise represented by Scrutiny.'[21]

The other side of Mrs Leavis's talent, the literary critical gift, is seen to advantage in her papers on Jane Austen, contributed to Scrutiny between 1941 and 1944, and reprinted in F. R. Leavis's *A Selection from Scrutiny*, Volume 2, as *A Critical Theory of Jane Austen's Writings*. She begins by dismissing the common account of Jane Austen as a miracle, a female Chatterton or Keats, uniquely inspired, whose work, perfect from the beginning, shows no development and whose sunny temper made it impossible for her to write of guilt or misery. Through R. W. Chapman's scholarly labours we now have a text of most of her surviving work and letters. From this it is possible to deduce that Jane Austen wrote without intermission – the only time we have no positive evidence for is 1798 to 1803, and we can't assume she wasn't writing then if she kept to her usual habit. Habits of composition included constant application in turn to pieces of work going on at the same time. She produced consciously and laboriously many separate drafts. She was not 'an inspired amateur who had scribbled in childhood and then lightly tossed off masterpieces between callers.'[22] She was artistically a late developer. Not till *Emma*, written when she was nearly forty, did she compose a work of the highest order. Her invention consisted less in conjuring up the new as in working over the old. Jottings made about characters and situations in her youth worked themselves out in maturity. Her genius lay in 'translating the general into the particular; she proceeds from the crude comprehensive outline and the dashing sketch to something subtle and specialised by splitting up and separating out.'[23] Her power was to seize on everything she came across, whether in life or literature, which, says Mrs Leavis, had something like equal authority for her. An immensely important part in her development was her own letters written from home and to home when away. Those to her sister Cassandra were meant to be read aloud to an audience. In fact, says Mrs Leavis, 'In these letters we can not only find much that later went into the novels, but we can see that material in a preliminary stage, half-way between life and art.'[24] Her letter writing, like her drafting of stories into novels at different stages of composition, were two parts of her unique process of composition. By the most intense and particularised pointing, analysis, and commentary, Mrs Leavis embodies these general observations and deductions into a closely argued, admirably proportioned critique which has quite transformed our – certainly my – understanding of Jane Austen.

Some of the most supple and most educative of Mrs Leavis's criticism comes in the course of her treatment of the novel, and particularly of the American novel. She was among the first, and certainly the best, of the *Scrutiny* writers to devote attention to American literature. And, indeed, a good claim could be made for her as the academic inaugurator of American Studies. Moreover, her work in this sphere, unlike that of a number of other English critics, shows a quite positive American sympathy. All the intelligent criticism of Henry James and all the hard work on him, she observes, except what appeared in *Scrutiny*, was done in the land of his origin.

I spoke of the educative quality of her literary criticism because Mrs Leavis is clearly a remarkable teacher, even if she has never been an officially appointed and paid one, and an educational intention is clearly manifest in her writing. She is concerned to enlighten as well as to display. The educational impulse informing her work brings the reader into intimate and personal connection with her thought. The novel is a peculiarly difficult form for criticism. In its largeness, inclusiveness, multiplicity of kinds, and variety of approaches, it is of all the *genres* the hardest on which to bring to bear an adequate and ordered attention. Let me give two examples of the help which Mrs Leavis gives the reader. The first is a general one, which in the briefest way puts before the reader the essence of what he needs to know about James:

> The briefest account of him should include mention of his descent from Hawthorne, that he is a novelist in the same tradition as Melville; should allude to his deliberate stylization of life; notice the techniques he devised for conveying his special interests, his recurrent symbols, his preoccupation with the ideal of social life and the function of the artist in it.[25]

And secondly, a specific point. She is discussing the brilliant story 'The Lesson of the Master', and she shows how the personal ambivalence inside James conditions the structure of the story.

> Moreover, it exhibits one of James's favourite techniques, the structure built on alternative selves. It is a device for conducting psychological exploration in dramatic form. Even *The Diary of a Man of Fifty*, Mr Garnett's first choice, which he says has a charming flavour of Turgenev, is stamped as unmistakably James's, slight as it is, in the mathematical elegance with which its case is presented. The elderly soldier who is the diarist and had blighted his life by leaving the Italian countess, sees acted out by their younger selves, presented in the same relation – in the forms of the dead woman's daughter and a young Englishman – the opposite solution to the diarist's. I dwell on this technical device because it is a key one – it is a different thing from his use of the portrait as the idealized or dead or

false self, which occurs in a great many novels and stories, starting with the very early *nouvelle, Watch and Ward*. It is not merely a device or literary formula, or, like the portrait, the symbol of an intellectual idea, but a method of artistic procedure. It enables an exploration of certain possibilities of life to be presented dramatically, with the tensions, the contrasts and the psychological surprises that make a work of art instead of a narrative.[26]

Any student, any reader, who brought together Mrs Leavis's writings on Henry James and her treatment of some lesser novelist, for example Edith Wharton, whom she calls Henry James's heiress, would end finely equipped as a critic of the novel – that is if he took the philosopher's advice: 'The point is not to listen to a series of propositions, but rather to follow the movement of showing.'[27] Mrs Leavis's essay on Edith Wharton, robust and sensitive, is an admirable example of her manner and achievement. As with Henry James, she determines first what kind of novelist she is dealing with. It is wrong, she points out, to treat Henry James's novels as Victorian prose fictions descended from Addison and Defoe. They belong to quite another kind of novel, deriving from Emily Brontë and Conrad. As for Edith Wharton, she combined 'sustained anthropological interest with literary ability,' in a way unprecedented before *The Bostonians*. Her best work was not historical – in Mrs Leavis's eye the historical novel bears the same relation to art as the waxwork. Edith Wharton's talents flourished on the contemporary and the changing. Her 'unmannered style and impressive presentation solved the problem of tone by ignoring the reader altogether.' She had a more convincing understanding of the uneducated than George Eliot and a more plausible one than Hardy: 'both these last having a suspicious tendency to humorous effects and George Eliot besides being never quite free from a shade of superiority in her attitude to intellectual inferiors.'[28] Her masterpiece was *The Custom of the Country*, an incisive and vital dramatisation of social disintegration in which New York society, at one time enjoying both a moral and social code, has become infected by philistinism and the worship of wealth. 'The dining-room at the Nouveau Luxe represented on such a spring evening, what unbounded material power had devised for the delusion of its leisure: a phantom "society," with all the rules, smirks, gestures of its model, but evoked out of promiscuity and incoherence while the other had been the product of continuity and choice.'[29] It is the last stages of this social disintegration which Mrs Wharton 'analysed and chronicled and turned into art,' the disappearance of 'the formative value of nearly three hundred years of social observance: the concerted living up to long-established standards of honour and conduct, of education and manners.'[30] The final question about Mrs Wharton, says Mrs Leavis, is this: 'what order of novelist is she? – i.e., not how permanent but how good?' She is certainly a very fine one. She was highly educated, she was bred on the works of Henry James, she had an intimate but detached view of her society, she was subtler in many ways than George Eliot and more socially and morally experienced, 'and therefore better able to enter into uncongenial states of feeling and to depict as an artist instead of a preacher distasteful kinds of behaviour.'[31] She wrote with more grace and economy than George Eliot, she had a more critical eye for the values of her world than Jane Austen. But whereas they are great novelists she is no more than a very remarkable one – not that that isn't saying a great deal. Mrs Leavis's answer to the question she poses is this: 'I think it eventually becomes a question of what the novelist has to offer us, either directly or by implication, in the way of positives.'[32] Mrs Wharton's values emerge only as something opposed to what she exposes as worthless. She has neither the rich and flourishing culture which sustained Jane Austen nor that 'natural piety, that richness of feeling and sense of moral order' which gave validity to George Eliot's diagnosis of her world.

> Mrs Wharton, if unfortunate in her environment, had a strength of character that made her superior to it. She was a remarkable novelist, if not a large-sized one, and while there are few great novelists there are not even so many remarkable ones that we can afford to let her be overlooked.[33]

Mrs Leavis has made a point of not overlooking the not so many remarkable novelists. Her study of Edith Wharton is a case in point. She has been particularly successful in calling back from oblivion, or near-oblivion, certain novels of quite peculiar merit, both historical and intrinsic. Of George Gissing's twenty-two novels she vividly endorses the view of *New Grub Street* as the one impressive piece of art among his *oeuvre*. The analysis in which she defines the tone of the novel – 'irony weighted with disgust' – and its leading idea, the expression of the misery of the artist among the sharp contrasts of modern life, is balanced, perceptive, and revealing. The creative friction in Gissing's work is between a proud and over-sensitive mind and the brutal facts of life. It achieved a proper poise and effect only in *New Grub Street*.

Outside *New Grub Street*, however, you too often feel that the provocation is inadequate to the suffering. Gissing's susceptibilities are not all equally respectable and in some cases he seems only a querulous old maid, too easily provoked on such subjects as bad cooking, slovenly lodgings, ungenteel personal habits and lack of secondary school education. But in *New Grub Street*, just as what is elsewhere merely bookishness becomes transfused into a passionate concern for the state of literature, so his other minor feelings have turned into positive values, and he produced the one important novel in his long list.[34]

She goes on in her Gissing essay to make a very important point about the history of the English novel. She wants to determine what are those novels which an adult can read with the same kind of attention as he brings to the best poetry. She sees *New Grub Street* as an important member of this group. It is one of the ancestors of the contemporary novel:

> In the nineteenth century, to take the high lights, Jane Austen, *Wuthering Heights*, *Middlemarch*, *The Egoist*, *New Grub Street* connect the best eighteenth-century tradition with the serious twentieth-century tradition that Henry James, Conrad, Lawrence, Forster, Joyce and Mrs Woolf have built up. There are inferior novels (e.g. *The Way of All Flesh*) in this tradition as well as good ones, and very minor successes (like Howard Sturgis's *Belchamber*) as well as major contributions, but they are all immediately recognizable as novels, distinct from what we may more usefully call fiction. It is time the history of the English novel was rewritten from the point of view of the twentieth century (it is always seen from the point of view of the mid-nineteenth), just as has been done for the history of English poetry.[35]

Mrs Leavis has made her contribution towards re-writing the history of the English novel from this point of view, and in the course of it towards rescuing the neglected and the significant. Two notable exercises in this mode were her essay on Richard Jefferies published in 1938 and the Introduction she wrote some thirty years later to the Zodiac Press edition of Mrs Oliphant's *Miss Marjoribanks*. Jefferies's genius – a peculiarly English one according to Mrs Leavis – has been masked by his various reputations as a writer for boys (*Bevis*), as a mystic (*The Story of My Heart*), and as a clumsier predecessor of W. H. Hudson. Mrs Leavis, however, takes a totally different view of him and puts him in quite another tradition: 'he recalls or embodies now Cobbett, now

D. H. Lawrence, now Dickens, now Edward Thomas himself, and he has a sensuous nature akin to but more robust than Keats'; he has, too, a strikingly contemporary aspect as social satirist, and he is in the central and most important tradition of English prose style.'[36] In some ways, as a social satirist, he recalls George Orwell. He began as a conservative farmer who came to detest class, social conformism, and the inertness of conservative prejudice. He was passionately patriotic though he detested the Chestertonian kind of Merry England. He collected folklore, dialect, and observed and described dying crafts and old rhythms of life. He was deeply interested in politics, particularly those which had to do with social justice. But he was neither a simple protester nor a romanticist about nature, 'his instinctive humanity and indignant expression of it are controlled by a characteristic irony.'[37] His prose is plain and supple and makes its effect cumulatively. He was only thirty-eight when he died but already there were intimations in his work of the true and subtler parts of Lawrence.

> Nothing came to him through literature, he is as unliterary as Cobbett though of greater personal cultivation and finer native sensibility; a contemporary suggested, says Thomas, that he avoided literary society deliberately in order to preserve his native endowments. And he is an artist in another sense, that compared with his works his life has little interest – all of him that holds value for us exists complete in his writings. He left no revealing letters, he did not mix in any kind of society, his domestic life was happy and normal.[38]

Mrs Leavis considers Jefferies to be an essayist of more weight than Lamb and Pater, and a novelist superior to Hardy. He wrote four novels of considerable distinction, *After London*, *Greene Ferne Farm*, *The Dewy Morn* (his most Lawrentian novel), and his masterpiece *Amaryllis at the Fair*. His villagers are neither conventionalised nor used for comic relief, as in Hardy.

> The portrayer of rustic life who notes the village woman telling the welfare-worker who scolds her for her fecundity: 'That's all the pleasure me an' my old man got' and describes (in *Greene Ferne Farm*) old Andrew Fisher with his *Wuthering Heights* past receiving the clerical suitor for his grand-daughter's hand thus:
> 'Jim! Bill! Jock!' shouted the old man, starting out of his chair, purple in the face. 'Drow this veller out! Douse un in th'hog vault! Thee nimity-pimity odd-me-dod! I warn thee'd like my money! Drot thee and thee wench!'[39]

Strength, vitality and unconventionalism are the notes of the novel that appeal most strongly to Mrs Leavis as a critic. Moreover, she is constantly searching for novels which belong to what she sees as the adult tradition of works of art. One original choice she makes as bridging the gap between Jane Austen and George Eliot – and she sees George Eliot in some aspects as developing directly out of Jane Austen – is the almost unknown *Miss Marjoribanks*, an ironic comedy of a wholly un-Victorian kind, un-Victorian, at least, according to our common prejudice. It brings to bear on the life of a provincial town and on County society the unsentimental sharpness of the Regency period. In technique and style it is witty and fresh. Such a sensibility, Mrs Leavis maintains, could only be produced in the Victorian age in Scotland. Mrs Oliphant's personal life was difficult. She was part of a clan in which the women were tough and the males weak and dependent, 'alcoholics, wastrels, or physically ailing characters who ruin them.' She showed a general disillusionment with the male sex, applying towards men in general her experience with those of her own family:

> First-hand experience of the realities of human nature is always useful to a novelist, but no wonder that in her novels it is women who are generally the admirable or at worst the efficient characters, while the men, unsatisfactory in all sorts of ways, have to be managed for their own good and to avert domestic and social disaster. In her novels loyal men-servants always seem to be Scotch, worthy landowners tend to be.[40]

Mrs Oliphant was an acute observer of the social scene, sharply observing 'the impact of Scottish capacity on English provincial life'. Her heroine Lucilla, 'with her large Scotch bones and her moral solidity, her literal-mindedness, and that characteristic Scotch complacency, based on the consciousness of undeniable superiority, which, makes her able to ignore other people's so-called sense of humour,'[41] is the instrument through which the nature of contemporary society is observed with a cool ironic eye. The psychological acumen, the mobility of the invention, the strong and delicate insight, show a novelist of quite exceptional capacities. The novel has an extensive range, from broadly comic to delicately moving, from ironic deflation to embodied social history, of 'the kind that, in default of the novelist, no historian could supply.'

As in other of Mrs Leavis's critiques of the novel, particular analysis is accompanied by a fine gift for pertinent historical and literary gener-alisation. In the case of *Miss Marjoribanks* the latter part of her essay is concerned with showing that *Miss Marjoribanks* contributed quite considerably to *Middlemarch*. In particular, she believes that George Eliot's treatment of both Dorothea and Gwendolyn, with its new ironic tone and unsentimental attitude, is influenced by Mrs Oliphant. The packed and strongly supported demonstration of this influence is sensitive, imaginative, and carries its own conviction. It is as much a judgement of sensibility as a demonstration of detection.

> It seems to me, to sum up, that creative writers generally and George Eliot in particular (as I have noted before) tend to borrow what, more or less unconsciously, they have been impressed by, not as a matter of miscellaneous items, but as a complex whose value or pregnancy inheres in a unique whole; so that whereas one character in common might be a coincidence and even a couple of no signifi-cance, such a manifold likeness between *Miss Marjoribanks* and *Middlemarch* as I have demonstrated is good evidence of the use of the former by the author of the latter.[42]

But there are novelists whom it is a mistake to recover and about whom one should simply trust time. Charlotte Yonge, whom a group of Christian sympathisers attempted to revive in the forties, was one such. In the course of her trenchant dismissal of the absurdity of this undertaking, Mrs Leavis enunciates with characteristic point and clarity one or two critical principles well worth rehearsing. The sickly Charlotte Yonge as a moralist was 'on a par with pulpit denouncers of short hair and slacks for women'; she had no feeling for the natural sources of healthy life; her picture of human action is both impractical and morbid. Mrs Leavis makes an illuminating contrast with Bunyan or Jane Austen in showing both the cultural conditions and the religious outlook that can and cannot produce art: 'The lack of roots in first-hand experience for her imagination, of substance for her moral passion, prevent her most cherished effects from conveying what she evidently thought they would.'[43] The effort to resurrect Charlotte Yonge, a simple-minded fanatic, leads Mrs Leavis to insist, as *Scrutiny* did with the Marxists also,

> ... that the essential thing in undertaking literary criticism is that you should be a literary critic concerned, with complete disinterested-ness, to demonstrate by the methods of literary criticism exactly what it is that a piece of literary art is doing. This is often quite

different from what it alleges it is doing or undertakes to do, and we have to repeat to the dogmatic Christian discriminator the warning we gave to the Marxist critic, that before certifying a work on the grounds of content or apparent orthodoxy it is as well to be sure that its actual "message", what it inevitably and essentially communicates, is what you thought it was.[44]

She adds to this salutary warning a comment on the critical method which is still very much to the point:

> The method of literary criticism, as repeatedly defined in these pages, is to secure the maximum general agreement for evaluation by starting with something demonstrable – the surface of the work – and through practical criticism to proceed inwards to a deeper and wider kind of criticism commanding assent (or giving an opening for disagreement and discussion) at every step.[45]

In two pieces written as Introductions for the Penguin English Library, the one on *Jane Eyre* published in 1966, and the other on *Silas Marner* published in 1967, Mrs Leavis demonstrates her skill in moving from the surface of the work to some deeper and wider criticism and simultaneously linking learning and the critical act so that each is energised and refined by the other. Let me look first at the later piece on *Silas Marner*.

Silas Marner represents the George Eliot buried in the legend of the masculine blue-stocking, the admirer of *Pilgrim's Progress* and the passionate believer in poetry. In *Silas Marner* George Eliot is the matured artist, fearful of too much schematism, appreciating that a novel is more than psychological portraiture. She is now preoccupied with a theme and the problem of embodying it. In this novel for the first time 'experience and finished faculty' go together. It is a legendary tale suggested by childhood recollection and with the fairytale element suppressed or subdued. '*Silas Marner* sprang from her childish recollection of a man with a stoop and expression of face that led her to think that he was an alien from his fellows'[46] – a clear hint of Bunyan. The protagonist is a poor nineteenth-century Christian who has lost his faith in the community, a faith born in the city and a community unrecognised in the country. George Eliot balances in her study of the solitary soul the problem of a cultural inheritance threatened by the dehumanising machine-work, and of the natural piety of religion threatened by the dominant evangelical outlook coloured by Calvinism:

There is thus a multiple typicality about the case of Silas Marner. In him the dire effects of the Industrial Revolution are examined; the current form of religion, a Christian fundamentalism, has finished the effects of denaturing him by disinheriting him. How can such losses to the race be made good? – it is George Eliot who describes Marner's kind as 'a disinherited race'.[47]

Silas Marner prepares us for *Middlemarch* and *Felix Holt*. 'It is superior to these in an art of concentration that uses always the minimum – the loaded word and the uniquely representative act – an art which puts *Marner* with Shakespeare and Bunyan rather than with other Victorian novels.'[48]

George Eliot presents only in the barest minimum the peasant code of life but it is sufficient for her purpose, although Mrs Leavis insists that the modern reader, with a blank in consciousness and memory about this kind of life, must read himself into it. It is the moral feeling rather than the fullness of village life that *Marner* represents with such superlative exactness and sympathy, and in particular the vitality and generosity of village neighbourliness. The individual struggle in the book which has to do with Marner's achieving reintegration into the community is kept before us with a firm but unobtrusive tact, and by symbolism which is delicate, complex and effective. There are laws of life, George Eliot echoing Turgenev insists, although they cannot be stated, laws which are enacted in the community of the village and in the history of Silas's soul. Silas's connection with these laws, his rehearsal of their operation, is conveyed with humour, pathos (in particular the difficulty of achieving any real communication between people who don't belong to the same culture) and the rarest insight. Nor does Mrs Leavis accept the scepticism of many, for example Leslie Stephen, about the old bachelor's reception of the baby and his return to the bosom of society in consequence. Silas like many children of the poor had been used to looking after his baby sister, and cherished the memory. He is domesticated by habit and handy by virtue of his trade. Mrs Leavis conveys with considerable feeling the recovery and reintegration of Silas:

> We perceive that Silas is vividly imaged as being himself an old winter fly crawling out under the reviving spring sunshine which Eppie is to him. And this passage builds up with what follows to convey Silas's gradual return to a life of feeling, ending by bringing into play again the herbs that not merely recall his mother but represent something like the traditions of the race.[49]

The influence of Bunyan, like that of Wordsworth, is powerful in this novel, but it is an absorbed influence. There is no simple Wordsworthian message in this novel. There are no illusions about the peasantry or the possibilities of its life. Concentration on the peasantry in the first half makes a vivid term of comparison with the gentry when Squire Cass is brought before us. He is typical of a class whose extravagant habits and bad husbandry are preparing the village for ruin when the war is ended. He is a bad landlord, his sons are dissipated, the interior of the Red House is squalid. Mrs Leavis remarks that Mary Ann Evans is peculiarly qualified by her upbringing to appreciate the fine distinctions of the English class system of her day, thoroughly equipped to feel in person all the strains and anomalies of the contemporary social and religious system. The village, when we return to it, shows us charity and fellowship in the Lammeters' 'liberal orderliness'. This gives her further opportunity for the constant play of ironical social criticism enriched by general reflections about human nature so that the devices of the novel, its elaborate parallels and providential arrangements, never intrude: 'Yet without dwelling on these things we do get as we read a sense that these complexities of reference are further illustrations of those laws of life that, as the novel is concerned to demonstrate, so mysteriously exist.'[50]

Mrs Leavis's writings on the Brontë sisters are among her most spirited but also most mellow. Both in *Jane Eyre* and *Wuthering Heights* there is that which appeals deeply to her nature, and the play of this personal feeling upon great art, as we cannot but be convinced after reading Mrs Leavis, produces criticism of a high order, of a very individual character, and of the most enlightening kind.

Perhaps the most important general point made in these critiques has to do with the kind of novels which the Brontë sisters wished to compose. Mrs Leavis makes the point by quoting Charlotte's comment when she had been advised by G. H. Lewes to study Jane Austen and to correct her shortcomings according. For Charlotte, Jane Austen's eighteenth-century control, prudence and skill, work to exclude what her feelings for the Romantics and Shakespeare had convinced her of, the new novel that was necessary.

> She does her business of delineating the surface of the lives of genteel English people curiously well. . . . What sees keenly, speaks aptly, moves flexibly, it suits her to study; but what throbs fast and full, though hidden, what the blood rushes through, what is the unseen seat of life and the sentient target of death – this Miss Austen ignores.

She no more, with her mind's eye, beholds the heart of her race than each man, with bodily vision, sees the heart in his heaving breast. Jane Austen was a complete and most sensible lady, but a very incomplete and rather insensible (*not senseless*) woman. If this is heresy, I cannot help it.[51]

On this Mrs Leavis comments:

As always, criticism has preceded and fostered creation. Here the idea of a novel, the novelist's ambition and the expression of it, are all curiously suggestive of D. H. Lawrence. Charlotte and Emily Brontë were evidently united in their determination not to write novels which give merely a surface imitation of life ('more real than true'), not to be satisfied with studying people in their social and intellectual character. They aimed at achieving through prose fiction something as serious, vital, and significant as the work of their favourite poets, which should voice the tragic experience of life, be true to the experience of the whole woman, and convey a sense of life's springs and undercurrents. To envisage such a possibility for the novel was at that date a critical achievement of the first order; to succeed, however unequally, in carrying it out was surely proof of great creative genius. In order to be great art their novels, these girls realized, must include 'poetry', necessarily employing a poetic method and evolving new prose techniques. This effort in due course led to the novel's becoming the major art form of the nineteenth century.[52]

The importance of *Jane Eyre* is not that of the sport or psychological curiosity. In Mrs Leavis's judgement *Jane Eyre* is coherent, in general totally controlled, and even schematic. The theme, an urgently personal one, generates the form. The organisation of the novel is not based on narrative nor is its theme given to us by logical exposition. Charlotte wanted to show how an embittered charity child comes to maturity in an age which made certain inhuman assumptions about women and the relations between the sexes, about the relations between the young and the old, and about religious and social life. All these themes are subjected to a radical scrutiny during the enactment of Jane's development, which is divided into four sharply distinct phases. Each of these experiences, undergone by a child with 'a fine instinct for what makes for her own psychic health and happiness' initiates the new and adds a further degree of maturity. In the course of it *Jane Eyre* uses means which are symbolic as well as dramatic, calls on a fund of first-hand experience, but also employs imagery and significance derived from literature. These are means supporting a fine faculty both for individual psychological analysis and for social understanding. The writing shows an extreme care in composition: 'Her prose is apt to be a mosaic, noticeably Regency in its combination of eighteenth-century exactness and the new journalistic idiom which is frequently rhetorical and quite likely to contain vulgarisms (like "optics" for "eyes").'[53] And yet Charlotte Brontë, more than Jane Austen and more than George Eliot, uses a cogent poetic language (with all that that implies in the calling on the resources of folklore, fairy-tale and the uncanny), and exhibits what Mrs Leavis calls a 'magical quality' in her writing. Here is part of one of the illustrative passages quoted by Mrs Leavis:

> I thought I had taken a wrong direction and lost my way. The darkness of natural as well as of sylvan dusk gathered over me. I looked round in search of another road. There was none: all was interwoven stem, columnar trunk, dense summer foliage ... no opening anywhere. I proceeded: at last my way opened, the trees thinned a little; presently I beheld a railing, then the house – scarce, by this dim light, distinguished from the trees; so dark and green were its decaying walls. . . . It was as still as a church on a week-day: the pattering rain on the forest leaves was the only sound audible in its vicinage. 'Can there be life here?' I asked.[54]

But the crown of Mrs Leavis's critical achievement, if we leave aside her substantial contribution to the collaborative work on Dickens (1970), was her 'A Fresh Approach to *Wuthering Heights*', published in 1969, from material which she took with her to Harvard and Cornell for seminars and lectures. It is an extensive essay, almost a book in itself. In it we see, as we do indeed in her essays on *Silas Marner* and *Jane Eyre*, a blend of Mrs Leavis's matured capacities: originality and independence, critical insight, swiftly moving intelligence, wit and tartness, a powerful moral base to the thought, psychological acuity, contemporaneity in attitude and reference, and a plain flowing prose style, a more appealing and accessible medium than her husband's.

That *Wuthering Heights* is a great classic Mrs Leavis has no doubt. It is hard, however, to say precisely what kind of classic it is. She is clear as to the flaws of construction and composition which are the result of inexperience, false starts, re-writing, and the youthful effort to include too much and every sort of experience in the single work. There are several minor themes, not all perfectly integrated. There is, for example, the regional version of the sub-plot of *Lear*, there is the romantic theme of incest as part of the impulse of the earliest conception of the novel. When this was rejected, Emily Brontë was left with inconsistencies. Catherine's feelings for Heathcliff are those of sister for brother, Heathcliff's for her always those of a lover. There is also the reminiscence in the prominence given to Heathcliff's goblin character, the premonitions of and obsession with death, of Hoffmann and James Hogg. A further theme is the romantic image of childhood in which we see Catherine and the other Heathcliff, the non-Lear one, innocently roaming the country. There is, as well, the social novel, or the socially developed theme in the novel, which is concerned with the conflict between a wholesome and natural unit of healthy society and its over-refined opposite – the tension between Wuthering Heights and Thrushcross Grange, two different cultures in which the latter is bound to oust the former. So that the romantic and the economic theme are present in different intensities and proportions at different places in the novel, documenting and deepening what Mrs Leavis sees as the psychological or central novel. The sociological novel is not the real novel, and the Heathcliff-Catherine-Edgar relations on the one side and the Cathie-Linton-Hareton one on the other are the most significant parts of Emily Brontë's intention (Mrs Leavis is much against giving the moor any mystical or metaphysical significance. 'The moor is a way of pointing a distinction.'[55]) The focus of the first half of the novel is certainly Catherine, and her case, examined with subtlety and dramatised with impersonal power, is the real moral centre of the book. Mrs Leavis makes an enlightening analogy with Henri-Pierre Roché's *Jules et Jim*. She does this to emphasise her point that this is essentially a novel of relationships and that far too much attention has been given to its wild and metaphysical element. Like Henri-Pierre Roché, Emily Brontë is intensely occupied with the problem of 'what people call love'. Catherine Earnshaw is another Kate. She is totally dominant, she ferments trouble, she is egocentric, she is indifferent to her husband's intellectual tastes, she humiliates him constantly. The difference between the novels is that Roché sees Kate as the absolute and archetypal woman. But Emily Brontë surrounds Catherine with other kinds of feminine natures, for example with the truly normal Nelly Dean. Nelly's sympathies and her gifts are limited but she is the wholesome, classless mother-figure and the correction to the notion of Catherine as representing the essential woman. However, unlike Roché, Emily Brontë shows us in a delicate annotation of human behaviour the strains and deficiencies in Catherine's upbringing which contribute to her particular psychology. We are not meant, therefore, to conceive of her as deserving of nothing but moral blame. Nelly's adult and selfless conduct prepares us for the younger Cathie's evolution away from the possibilities of repeating her mother's disaster. She has similar impulses, almost as bad an upbringing, but she achieves self-knowledge and wisdom – whereas Roché shows Kate's daughter committed to an extensive repetition of her mother's attitude. The novel is firmly placed in the eighteenth century and the remote place and the northern setting help to reinforce the moral and psychological truths which are embodied in it.

In *Wuthering Heights* Emily Brontë is concerned to replace moralistic judgement by compassionate understanding. The aim is subserved by a method of parallelism and contrast, first between the two halves of the book and then by a variety of particular echoes within it. Certainly there is much that is confused and ambiguous. In the interests of a new conception of what the novel could and would be, for the sake of originality of subject and expression, the author was prepared, says Mrs Leavis, to make sacrifices which seemed negligible to her, 'sacrifices of plausibility, of consecutiveness, of proportion, even of consistency'.[56] Mrs Leavis's intention has been to turn attention towards the 'human core of the novel', away from the metaphysical and mystical and below the sociological surface. Emily Brontë's success in dealing with that persuades Mrs Leavis to speak of finding finally in this novel 'the complexity of accomplished art'.

> And when we compare the genius devoted to creating Nelly Dean, Joseph, Zillah, Frances, Lockwood, the two Catherines, and to setting them in significant action, with the very perfunctory attention given to Heathcliff and Hareton as wholes (attention directed only when these two are wheeled out to perform necessary parts at certain points in the exposition of the theme to which – like Isabella and Edgar Linton – they are subsidiary) then we can surely not misinterpret the intention and the nature of the achievement of *Wuthering Heights*.[57]

The complexity of accomplished criticism is also the final impression left on us by Mrs Leavis's criticism, a criticism characterised by originality, lucidity, conviction and point, and a criticism which, perhaps under the huge wing of her husband's reputation, has not had its proper recognition. It belongs with the best of the period.

6

General Characteristics

If the last forty years has been a period remarkable for its criticism, this could hardly have been foreseen at its beginning. Effective criticism depends on good critics and an adequate audience. But in the twenties few good critics had any access to the audience; while those who had mostly possessed neither a rational conception of the critical function nor the capacity to perform it if they had known what it was. 'From Dryden to Jeffrey, and from Jeffrey to Mr. Squire, are two big jumps,' said J. F. Holmes,[1] though the second is less of a leap than a precipitation. Arnold had complained of the audience of his time that it lacked a large and centrally placed intelligence, that it was remote from a centre of correct taste, that it possessed neither fitness nor measure nor centrality. A Victorian critic, he thought, was not related to a coherent audience. He simply addressed himself to 'a promiscuous multitude, with the few good judges so scattered through it as to be powerless . . .' But it is clear that Arnold was describing a process in train rather than one consummated, just as it is clear that the audience had not wholly disintegrated in Arnold's time. He was among the last to speak to an audience which had both unity and range. The completion of the process of decay, which Arnold noted the beginning of, was arrived at in the twenties, when criticism was replaced by journalistic gossip and academic sermonising. J. C. Squire guided the reading public on the assumption that criticism had nothing to do with intelligence, Arnold Bennett on the assumption that it had nothing to do with integrity, and Robert Lynd on the assumption that it had nothing to do with literature.

It may be that as journalists these writers were bound to accept the ethic and the idiom of the press which supported them. But they are not distinguished either in tone or assumption from contemporary academics. There is little to choose between them and, say, the Cambridge critic, for whom criticism was 'a charming parasite' or the Oxford one, for whom a serious attitude to literature was 'an affront to life.'

Criticism without standards means criticism wholly at the mercy of 'personality' and the occasion, and it becomes either an ecstatic recital of the adventures of one's soul among masterpieces, or the effort to reconstruct the special impression made on the critic by a given work, as though it existed absolutely in itself without reference to any order of values or any context in life or literature. Criticism without standards, that is criticism without a public reference, or without a ground in the deepest concerns of men, is not only personal in this restricted aesthetic sense. It is also personal in another, a worse way. The characteristic marks of such criticism were specified at the time by Bertram Higgins as 'a confusion of social with literary qualities; a hatred of unqualified statements; a hunger for 'personal touches'; an ambition to extend a welcome to all sorts of writing, ostensibly out of a desire for comprehensiveness, really with the motive to justify a mixed standard; finally, an over-insistence on the empirical nature of our present aesthetic judgements.'[2]

But the critical product of the time was not limited to the kind of criticism Bertram Higgins is hammering at here. There was also the Bloomsbury Group. And because the attitude of the Bloomsbury Group to literature was the final phase of a certain critical habit, and because modern criticism developed its own identity as much in relation to this as to the state of affairs represented by George Gordon and J. C. Squire, I should like to glance for a moment at a subject many will think – I have some sympathy with the view – already too much written about. I do not find myself jarred by the 'metropolitan' note in Bloomsbury criticism that many *Scrutiny* writers found so distasteful. For me in the 1970s it even has a not unpleasing period charm. As it exists in Lytton Strachey, for example, particularly in his historical writing, it affects me, oddly enough, as a kind of parochialism. I have a curious sense of sophistication carried to the point of naïveté; and, after all, savouring the exquisite all the time can be a dull diet, and detecting hypocrisy in every corner as tedious as the most ingenuous innocence. In any case I accept the Aristotelian doctrine that one should judge a school by its best examples, and there were certainly finer and more complex elements in Bloomsbury than this. Virginia Woolf, everyone will agree, was as a critic quite another kettle of fish. She had her own individual inheritance, a relic possibly of the eighteenth century, something of that clarity about literature, at once independent and socially sanctioned, which we admire in Leslie Stephen. One must not make too much of this, since she also represented in the purest form the mind of Bloomsbury. And this was a mind which associated the critical practice of Walter Pater with the ethical theory of G. E. Moore. It had, therefore, a nimbler capacity for manipulating general ideas than any Pater commanded. But the intellectual instruments were put to much the same purpose as Pater's, which was to test, to taste, freely to experiment with, what the young aesthete in *The Tragic Muse* called 'shades of expression, of appreciation.' Nor is it necessary to be a Marxist to think that there must be some connection between this bias and an unearned income. Nothing, one ruefully reflects, makes so much for the famed 'intensity of living' as not being compelled grubbily to labour at making one.

This habit of mind produced a kind of literary criticism which was picturesque, cultivated, sensitive and untechnical. It was easy and mocking, and its social reference was directly to the initiate. But the strongest impression it makes on the reader is of being admitted to overhear the murmuring of a cultivated amateur as he strolls appreciatively round his extensive library. One gets this impression even from Virginia Woolf's remarkable *The Common Reader*, which also testifies to her ability to be direct, on-the-spot, and distinctly modern in tone and sympathy. Take, for example, her essay on George Eliot. One notices the elegant smoothness of the writing, the careful sense of rhythm, the occasional quiver of a sensitive response, the tact with which she places a restrained classical reference and the incantatory hush of the close. But the strongest feeling it leaves one with is that the literary object is being assimilated into the personality of the critic. One senses the absorption of the strong, stubbly character of George Eliot into the sensitive, fastidious personality of Virginia Woolf.

It is interesting to see what general explicit judgements about literature a critic in this setting, even one as acute as Virginia Woolf, finally delivers. In another Essay, *How it Strikes a Contemporary*, Virginia Woolf contrasts the achievement of the nineteenth and twentieth centuries: '*Waverley, The Excursion, Kubla Khan, Don Juan, Hazlitt's Essays, Pride and Prejudice, Hyperion* and *Prometheus Unbound* were all published between 1800 and 1821. Our century has not lacked industry; . . . But if we ask for masterpieces, where are we to look? A little poetry, we may feel sure, will survive; a few poems by Mr Yeats, by Mr Davies, by Mr De La Mare. Mr Lawrence, of course, has moments of greatness, but hours of something very different. Mr Beerbohm, in his way, is perfect, but it is not a big way. Passages in *Far Away and Long Ago* will undoubtedly go to posterity entire. *Ulysses* was a memorable catastrophe – immense in daring, terrific in disaster . . .'[3]

The view of literature presented by these selections, omissions and qualifications, is in the romantic tradition, though the romanticism is modified by the classical notion of a work of literature as a form, wrought out and finished and faultless at every point. The romanticism, however, lacks all the fire and certainty of romanticism as a living creed, and the classicism has no sanction outside the study. Ideal literary figures on this view are Landor and Flaubert. It was a conception of literature as primarily a function of the gifted and dedicated personality which was to be rejected by influential modern critics. But even more thoroughly and immediately unacceptable to these critics was the kind of critical practice such a view of literature led to. In this criticism the inveterate habit of the critic is to dissolve the work of art into his own sensibility, to subject it to his own tone and idiom. But one of the chief aims – perhaps the chief aim – of modern criticism is to restore the status of the literary object.

To restore the status of the literary object – to rescue it from complete absorption into the sensibility of the critic – required a different conception of criticism and a new method of conducting it. It is in the work of Leavis that these differences of idea and practice are most developed, and in his work that they are so organised as to establish a criticism which is integral, coherent and decisively in a modern idiom. Leavis's career began against the background I have indicated – against in both sense of the word. But it also began within a context of more positive and productive influences which freshened the stuffy atmosphere of current critical thought and practice. Some of these were less immediate, like Coleridge and Arnold, and in a minor way, Henry James and Santayana; some were more immediate, like Pound, Eliot, Lawrence, Richards and the *Calendar of Modern Letters*. But it was in the long run in virtue of a conception of criticism resulting from this variety of influences that Leavis, who has always insisted on the collaborative character of criticism, was able to remodel its practice.

It wasn't simply chance that Leavis's career began when it did. The late twenties was a period of prising and prying at accepted foundations. If in one way it was a lamentable time for criticism, in another it was a time for the loosening of set assumptions and the questioning of habitual attitudes, a time, that is, itself prompting a major reconstruction. If Leavis was the one who undertook that operation and put his personal stamp on it, he could do so because many others had cooperated in making it possible. We can see now, for example, how close in moral tone and bearing Leavis is to Coleridge and Arnold. The family lineaments are there in the acute consciousness of literature as the embodiment of more than literary value, and in the strenuous concern to make criticism an active influence on the side of spiritual health. It is not surprising that the contained, unspeculative Arnold is more sympathetic to Leavis than Coleridge, the critic with the philosopher on his back. It was another philosopher altogether that Leavis associates with Arnold among the first influences to affect him. 'In those early years after the great hiatus,' he writes of himself after the 1914–18 war, 'as in a dazed and retarded way I struggled to achieve the beginning of the power of articulate thought about literature, it was Santayana . . . and Matthew Arnold who really counted.'[4] It is true that he did not find Santayana fundamentally congenial, although he has continued to admire Santayana's brilliance and urbanity, and that rare wit, 'which is the focused sharpness of illuminating intelligence.'[5] But, as he says, 'indebtedness to an influence needn't mean radical sympathy or approval . . .'[6]

This is an observation which has a bearing on Leavis's attitude to Eliot. 'Fundamentally congenial' is decidedly not what Leavis has felt the later Eliot to be. And yet the indebtedness exists. But it exists, tenaciously, in relation to Eliot's poetry and to the criticism in *The Sacred Wood* and *Homage to John Dryden*, which issued from the problems posed in the composition of that poetry:

> Eliot was the man of genius [Leavis writes], who, after the long post-Swinburnian arrest, altered expression . . . it was the poetry that won attention for the criticism rather than the other way round. What the criticism did was to ensure that recognition of the poetry should be accompanied by a general decisive change, not only of taste, but of critical idea and idiom of critical approach to questions of poetry, and the sense of the past of English poetry, and of the relation of the past to the present.[7]

So altering expression, Eliot altered the mind expressed, and prepared a new universe for literature in which a quite different and contemporary criticism could appear. But it was the poetry which was the effective agent of the change. Eliot was the Wordsworth rather than the Coleridge of the new age.

The altered mind and the altered expression meant that the function of criticism must be larger and more serious than it had been in the last fifty years, just as it meant that a new voice, a new idiom, and a new manner must be found for criticism as well as for literature. It had to be moral as well as aesthetic; or rather it had to serve the moral purpose implicit in its nature. As the great midwife of literature Ezra Pound saw it, in *How to Read*, the character of criticism had to be defined as having to do 'with maintaining the very cleanliness of the tools, the health of the very matter of thought itself ... the solidity, and validity of ... words. Without the care of the damned and despised *literati* ... the application of word to thing goes rotten, i.e. becomes slushy and inexact, or excessive or bloated ...'

An astringent and social function in a lax and atomised age – his acceptance of this aim undoubtedly sharpened the edge of Leavis's criticism. But an abstract incisiveness, however tellingly applied, could not have brought about the deep and more than literary effect that Leavis's criticism has had. Mere sharpness, keenness alone, has only a surface effect, as we see, for example, in Aldous Huxley. In Leavis's case the cutting edge has behind it the weight of a nature with a distinct and developed gift for moral experience. Such an endowment is indispensable if a critic is to be equipped with the primary attribute of his office, adequacy of response. An adequate response to great literature calls for power and finesse in thinking, force and delicacy in feeling, and these are powers which cannot be separated from a mature moral faculty. This was a point made by Lawrence when he said, 'A critic must be able to *feel* the impact of a work of art in all its complexity and force. So he must be a man of force and complexity himself. ... More than this, even an articulately and emotionally educated man must be a man of good faith. ... A critic must be emotionally alive in every fibre, intellectually capable and skilful in essential logic, and then morally very honest.'[8] And 'morally very honest' is what the most hostile will certainly allow Leavis to be. In fact the suggestion is sometimes made that his work suffers from an excess of this virtue, or what is the same thing, a deficiency in that melting co-operativeness so necessary in English life. It is clear, however, that the combination of good faith with trenchant and supple awareness makes for a rare capacity of conviction. Serious conviction is always impressive. But in the modern world where conviction is taken to be explicable by reference to 'culture' or to temperament, and where flickering opinion substitutes with most of us for solid conviction, profound conviction, conviction displayed, argued, and articulated, is peculiarly disturbing. And 'profound conviction' very well describes the impression a reader takes away from Leavis's work. As he grows familiar with it he becomes aware of conviction in depth and of certainties implied at every point of the exposition.

But these certainties are *implied*. Or they were at this period of Leavis's critical career. Leavis recognises that a philosophic training, for example, which would enable a critic to state his assumptions explicitly and to defend them systematically might be a valuable addition to the critic's equipment. His fear, however, is that this would be an advantage gained at too great a price. It would lead to 'blunting of edge, blurring of focus, and muddled misdirection of attention: consequences of queering one discipline with the habits of another. The business of the literary critic is to attain a peculiar completeness of response and to observe a peculiarly strict relevance in developing his response into commentary.'⁹ Too hasty a movement towards generalisation upsets the necessary delicate balance. If he avoids generalisations, he claims, this is not through timidity but because he feels they are too clumsy. 'My whole effort,' he reports, 'was to work in terms of concrete judgements and particular analyses: this – doesn't it? – bears such a relation to that; this kind of thing – don't you find it so? – wears better than that.' The critic's first endeavour must be to cultivate a scrupulously exact relationship to the object of his attention. He has to develop a fine, finger-tip sensitiveness, and capacity for particularised, responsive touch.

It is this tact at the point of application which marks Leavis's best critical work, whether he is talking of Swift or Lawrence, Henry James or *Measure for Measure*, George Eliot or Keats. It lets him stand before the object in the posture best fitted to make it available to him. It is a method of adaptive address which promotes superb technical criticism without ever declining into an inflexible technique. When the critical method hardens into an habitual technique the object ceases to exist in its own right and becomes simply an occasion for critical bossiness, something to be bullied into the approved pattern. But Leavis even at his most severely disapproving keeps himself open; he does not operate according to a clutch of preconceived categories or any abstract system. His method cannot be reduced to a formula. Certainly he has his vocabulary (and one cannot overlook the influence on that of terms put into circulation by Henry James, and of I. A. Richards's cleansing analysis of the received vocabulary of criticism), but its terms are malleable and the idiom modulated to the nature of the thing considered.

Leavis's method combines intuition, analysis and judgement. The intuition is made explicit in the analysis and the analysis is resolved in the judgement. These are not stages in a dialectical process, but emphases in the effort to read completely. Nor is there in what Leavis means by and offers in *analysis* anything of a laboratory method. The work of literature, he insists,

> is there for analysis only in so far as we are responding appropriately to the words on the page. In pointing to them (and there is nothing else to point to) what we are doing is to bring into sharp focus, in turn, this, that and the other detail, juncture or relation in our total response. ... Analysis is not a dissection of something that is already and passively there. What we call analysis is, of course, a constructive or creative process. It is a more deliberate following-through of that process of creation in response to the poet's words which reading is. It is a recreation in which, by a considering attentiveness, we ensure a more than ordinary faithfulness and completeness.[10]

The clearest and crispest description of Leavis's critical practice and manner appears in a passage where he defended himself against the charge that many young people had been prematurely encouraged by him to undervalue Milton and compare him unfavourably with Donne:

> You cannot be intelligent about literature without judging. A judgement is a personal judgement or it is nothing – you cannot have your judging done for you. The essential form of a judgement is 'This is so, isn't it?' and the question (it is a real request for confirmation) expects, at best, a reply of the form 'Yes, but . . .' Here, diagrammatically (so to speak) we have given us that collaborative process by which valuations are established as something 'out there' about which we can profitably discuss our agreements and disagreements. Pupils of mine will testify that immeasurably more of our time together in any year is taken up with my offers to enforce, one way or another, directly and indirectly, these truths than is given by me or them to Milton (or Donne), And it is a further truism (they are very familiar with it as such) that only by the collaborative-creative process I have alluded to can a living literary culture – and all that goes with it – be created and maintained.[11]

Implicit in Leavis's studies of the structure of literature, and controlling the method by which they are established, is a number of fundamental convictions. The most important of these are a conception of the poetic use of language, a conception of literature, and a conception of the values appropriate in criticism. I can best convey the quick of Leavis's idea of the poetic use of language by quoting some cogent and illuminating comments on Johnson and Hopkins which have to do with this basic notion. Of Johnson he writes: 'The exploratory-creative use of words upon experience, involving the creation of concepts in a free play for which the lives and configurations of the conventionally charted have no finality, is something he has no use for...'[12] Or of Hopkins he says: '... his use of words is not a matter of saying things with them, he is preoccupied with what seems to him the poetic use of them, and this is a matter of making them do and be ...'[13] And Leavis quotes approvingly a passage from D. W. Harding on Isaac Rosenberg: 'He – like many poets in some degree, one supposes – brought language to bear on the incipient thought at an earlier stage of its development. Instead of the emerging idea being racked slightly so as to fit a more familiar approximation of itself, and words found for *that*, Rosenberg let it manipulate words almost from the beginning.'[14] An essentially poetic use of language, that is, cannot rightly be thought of as a 'medium'. In it there is a coincidence in activity of words and ideas in constructing the poet's meaning. Language, in fact, one could say, takes the initiative: it is active, forming and informing. Words in poetry are not passive objects waiting to be arranged. They themselves quicken the unformed into significance. They do not simply translate the poetic experience. They compose it.

Such an idea is one of the chief criteria by which Leavis discriminates between poet and poet, and between poem and poem. It is an inward, sympathetic understanding of the intimate operations of language at its most intense. In Leavis's system of standards it is the one which corresponds to the element in his response which I called a feeling for textures. It is supported by, or it fits in with, a more inclusive conception, a conception of literature, which in its turn corresponds in his response to his sense of structure in literature. A literature, Leavis contends, is more than an array of distinct and independent works. It is an order expressive of and helping to form a common mind, imagination and sensibility. I must quote here a passage in which Leavis gives the most considered statement of his view. He is making the point that Ezra Pound's definition of literature, as 'simply language charged with meaning to the utmost possible degree,' while it is positively right, is incomplete. He refers in the passage to Eliot, but it is clear that it isn't just Eliot's conception that he is advancing:

> ... literature ... cannot be understood merely in terms of odd individual works illustrating 'processes' and 'modes'; it involves a literary tradition. And a given literary tradition is not merely, as it were by geographical accidents of birth, associated with a given

language; the relation may be suggested by saying that the two are *of* each other. Not only is language an apt analogy for literary tradition; one might say that such a tradition is largely a development of the language it belongs to if one did not want to say at the same time that the language is largely a product of the tradition. Perhaps the best analogy is that used by Mr. Eliot in *Tradition and the Individual Talent* when he speaks of the 'mind of Europe'. 'Mind' implies both consciousness and memory, and a literary tradition is both: it is the consciousness and memory of the people or the cultural tradition in which it has developed.[15]

The poets live in this consciousness and reproduce this memory; and the consciousness and memory live in them and fashion them. Less important poets illustrate the tradition; the more important ones significantly develop it. Literature so conceived takes in much more than writers and writing. And criticism is relevant to our most pressing concerns because to the critic

> ... literature matters, in the first place at any rate, as the consciousness of the age. If a literary tradition does not keep itself alive here, in the present, not merely in new creation, but as a pervasive influence upon feeling, thought and standards of living (it's time we challenged the economist's use of this phrase), then it must be pronounced to be dying or dead. Indeed, it seems hardly likely that, when this kind of influence becomes negligible, creation will long persist. In any case, a consciousness maintained by an insulated minority and without effect upon the powers that rule the world has lost its function.[16]

Given this view of the intimacy of literature with life, it is only to be expected that Leavis would strongly reject any realm of the exclusively aesthetic or any uniquely literary values. Literature engages 'a wide range of profoundly representative experience' and criticism, which is the adequate reading and the profitable discussion of it, has to proceed from 'moral centrality, profound commonsense.' On the one hand, 'traditions, or prevailing conventions or habits, that tend to cut poetry in general off from direct vulgar living and the actual, or that make it difficult for the poet to bring into poetry his most serious interests as an adult living in his own time, have a devitalising effect'[17]; on the other hand, 'to insist that literary criticism is, or should be, a specific discipline of intelligence is not to suggest that a serious interest in literature can confine itself to the kind of intensive local analysis associated with "practical criticism" – to the scrutiny of the words on the page in their minute relations, their effect on imagery, and so on: a real literary interest is an interest in man, society and civilization, and its boundaries cannot be drawn . . .'[18]

Leavis, we know, has so insisted on the necessity for criticism to have a moral centre that he is called a moralist. But if he is a moralist, he is one only in the sense in which Johnson, Coleridge and Arnold are moralists. He believes, namely, that literature being what it is, the critic must bring to bear upon it the full scale of his powers and experience. He has to summon *all* the resources of his humanity. The critic's preoccupation with 'form' must be on a level with the writer's, of whom Leavis asks 'Is there any great novelist whose preoccupation with "form" is not a matter of his responsibility towards a rich human interest, or complexity of interests, profoundly realised? – a responsibility involving, of its nature, imaginative sympathy, moral discrimination and judgement of relative human value?'[19] When a critic turns upon a work of literature the whole of his most developed self, there is bound to be in his relationship to it a moral element.

The question, of course, is not whether there should *be* a morality in critical practice. The real – and double – question is surely this: Is the morality advanced sufficiently complex for its purpose? To the second I should answer that I found nothing offensive to relevance, nothing pushing or intrusive in the morality of Leavis's criticism. The tests he applies seem to me always strictly literary tests. 'He is concerned with the work in front of him,' as he himself says when writing of the critical function, 'as something that should contain within itself the reasons why it is so and not otherwise.'[20] If there are moral references in Leavis's judgements they are there because they are part of the integral response, the due, unforced and natural response. As to the sufficient complexity of Leavis's morality, that is not a question that can be answered directly. I can indicate the character of his morality by declaring that it is an expression of the liberal spirit, and I can define this more accurately by saying that it is the liberalism of Arnold, Sidgwick, and Leslie Stephen. It is of this spirit that Leavis wrote in his essay on E. M. Forster, and I should like to quote from it words which apply very closely to himself. It represents

> . . . the humane tradition as it emerges from a period of 'bourgeois' security, divorced from dogma and left by social change, by the breakdown of traditional forms and the loss of sanctions embarrassingly 'in the air', no longer serenely confident or self-sufficient, but conscious of being not less than before the custodian of something

essential . . . far from the complacency of 'freedom of thought', [but standing] nevertheless, for the free play of critical intelligence as a *sine qua non* of any hope for a human future. And it seems to me plain that this tradition really is, for all its weakness, the indispensable transmitter of something that humanity cannot afford to lose.[21]

7

The Arnoldian Middle

I want in this chapter to concentrate on a group of books written by Leavis between 1952 and 1970, in what I think of as his middle, and mellow, Arnoldian period. The group consists of two collections of general essays, the first drawn substantially from *Scrutiny*, the second less so, each of which is followed by a specialised study, the first on Lawrence, the other, written together with Q. D. Leavis, on Dickens. These works are notable for range, stretching from Shakespeare and the seventeenth century to G. M. Hopkins and E. M. Forster, and from *Pilgrim's Progress* and the eighteenth century to Mark Twain and Tolstoy. There are also general discussions in each of the collections prefiguring the themes to be taken up with an even more impassioned concern in the last phase. Leavis's work at this time is marked by its wit, freedom, and flexibility. There are certainly many occasions both in the earliest and the latest work in which comments of John Stuart Mill, oddly enough on the writing of Bentham, surprisingly apply to Leavis's style. (Leavis himself introduced an edition of Mill's essays on Bentham and Coleridge as the classical documents for understanding the nineteenth century and the Victorian mind.) The comment I am thinking of is this:

> He could not bear, for the sake of clearness and the reader's ease, to say, as ordinary men are content to do, a little more than the truth in one sentence, and correct it in the next. The whole of the qualifying remarks which he intended to make, he insisted upon imbedding as parentheses in the very middle of the sentence itself. And thus the sense being so long suspended, and attention being required to the accessory idea before the principal idea had been properly seized, it became difficult, without some practice, to make out the train of thought.[1]

In Leavis's case one also has to bear in mind the close relation between his written style and his customary speech. The rhythms of the English voice, and particularly of his own version of it – a cultivated and shaded East Anglian version of it – shaped the run, pause and turn of the sentences. And although he did not have anything like a strong or sonorous vocal instrument, he was a most accomplished lecturer and an exquisitely sensitive reader aloud.

As one reads, and rereads, the spare, packed essays of *The Common Pursuit*, one is struck again and again by the way in which Leavis's whole, charged sensibility is alert for what he sees as the essential thing, namely the pulse of life, the impulse of growth. It is his responsiveness to this in the most varied places, whether in the Mulciber passage in Book I of *Paradise Lost*, in *The Vanity of Human Wishes*, or the ode *To Autumn* or the Fourth Book of the *Dunciad* or in Gerard Manley Hopkins, which informs his criticism with a living, nervous and authentic energy. It is this which is the essential constituent of his judgements and values. One of the influences which can most smother 'the disturbing new life, the stir of spirit that manifests itself in unfamiliar forms,'[2] is the presence of the academic mind. The usual faults of academic writing are correctness and decorativeness and the feeling of being under an obligation to import significance, usually by means of reference to the achievements of others, academics necessarily having to use the labour of other men. The academic infection spreads as society shows itself less and less capable of supporting a class of professional writers. The academic artist is apt to be gratuitously explicit, solemnly sincere like a public orator presenting for an honorary degree. But the academic critic has more obdurate and mortal faults. In two essays on Gerard Manley Hopkins Leavis takes up this theme in respect of a supremely academic poet's, Robert Bridges's, treatment of Hopkins. Hopkins was concerned to use 'the current language heightened, to any degree heightened and unlike it, but not (I mean normally: passing freaks and graces are another thing) an obsolete one,'[3] whereas all Bridges's friendliness towards him could not disguise his distaste for what was lacking, namely a prim, literary decorum. Hopkins, in whom vigour of mind was connected with the vitality of concreteness, was considered by Bridges, in confident academic certitude, to be a freak and a sport, and outside the correct and regular tradition. It is a further irony, Leavis points out, that Hopkins's scholarly editor, Claude Colleer Abbott, was himself intensely and characteristically academic – classically so, according to Leavis. 'Hopkins has an editor who betrays radical hostility to what Hopkins stood and stands for.'[4] If Professor Abbott is one kind of academic critic, Dr E. M. W. Tillyard is another, at a point lower down the scale of academism. He manifests the academic habit of providing a problem to which he has discovered a solution – namely, in the case given by Leavis, that the themes of

L'Allegro and *Il Penseroso* were derived from one of Milton's Latin *Prolusions*. Moreover, he exhibits the academic anxiety to be constantly up-to-date and comprehensive. It is reprehensible on this view to criticise adversely accepted authors. When such critics accuse Leavis of putting certain authors on the Index he retorts that they pursue 'the steady aim of putting on the list of works that students must drudge through, and learn to admire, everything that they see a chance of disinterring from literary history.'[5] In addition to disinterring the dead scholars of this kind, industrious specialists in creative genius, authorities blandly unaware of critical limitations, are with 'lumpishly possessive impertinence' capable of 'anti-critical identifications of *personae* and fictive episodes with actual persons and collected facts, gratuitous annotations, useless and betraying vulgarities of insensitiveness and unintelligence . . .'[6] It was for Irving Babbitt, whom he saw as the Platonic academic, that Leavis reserved his severest strictures on the academic response to literature and art. His indignation is provoked by T. S. Eliot's designation of Babbitt as an educated man, such that Lawrence could never have become, however much information he had accumulated. Irving Babbitt, Leavis cries,

> Irving Babbitt, all one's divinations about whom have been confirmed by the reminiscences and memoirs of him that have appeared since his death! Babbitt, who was complacently deaf and blind to literature and art, and completely without understanding of his incapacity; who, being thus in sensibility undeveloped or dead, can hardly, without misplacing a stress, be called intelligent! Even as Mr. Eliot quotes him and comments on him he appears as the born academic (is that what 'by nature an educated man' means?), obtuse – Mr. Eliot seems almost to bring out the word – obtuse in his dogged and argumentative erudition.[7]

But the academic mind is not limited to universities and academics strictly so-called. It has a wider and more menacing existence. It is at the heart of that group of influential contemporaries whom Leavis described as the orthodoxy of enlightenment, and as 'the publicizers, public relations men, heads of houses, academic ward-bosses, hobnobbers with Cabinet ministers.'[8] This set of plumply padded members of the social, literary and educational establishments, adopting a lean and radical look, can accuse Leavis of an uncompassionate harshness and indifference as to whether or not the working class enjoyed a high standard of living, and, assuming a Benthamite approval of advancing science, class him as a Luddite. But if he is a Luddite it is only in the

sense that Dickens was one and his attitude towards the workers he
met in the course of an 'unaffluent and very much "engaged" academic
life,' was one of 'shame, concern and apprehension at the way our
civilization has let them down – left them to enjoy a "high standard of
living" in a vacuum of disinheritance.'[9] It is the enlightened pluralists,
nourished on a soup of abstraction, blending Bentham with Marx,
Freud with the distractedly permissive Lawrence of *Lady Chatterley's
Lover*, Bloomsbury snobbery with egalitarian politics, who have in a
period of social and cultural degeneration displaced the educated class.
The contemporary sensibility as exemplified in them is wholly deficient
in a living touch and a sense of relative value, a situation which makes
the literary tradition and literary criticism all the more important for
the conservation of collective experience:

> Literary criticism provides the test for life and concreteness; where
> it degenerates, the instruments of thought degenerate too, and
> thinking, released from the testing and energizing contact with the
> full living consciousness, is debilitated, and betrayed to the academic,
> the abstract, and the verbal. It is of little use to discuss values if the
> sense for value in the concrete – the experience and perception of
> value – is absent.[10]

If it was his sense alert to the stir and tremble of life which made
Leavis, in reaction, excoriate the inert and the fake, and therefore apt to
invite the hostility of the establishment, it was his taste, both ranging
and full-bodied, which kept him engaged with the best, and therefore
apt to provoke the anger of the defenders of the second best or the
third rate. It was not that he was incapable of appreciating the genius of
Milton or Shelley or the distinction of Tennyson, but that he felt it, in
his pulse and nerves, and in his judgement, to be either not the supreme
thing or to be the development of lesser or more alien capacities in
language and also in civilisation.

Let me produce as one example of living touch, relative valuation
and energising contact with the concrete, Leavis's two essays on
Bunyan, one, 'Bunyan through Modern Eyes' from *The Common
Pursuit*, and the other, 'The Pilgrim's Progress' from *'Anna Karenina'
and Other Essays*. They provide, too, an opportunity for commenting
on the term 'Puritan' so often applied to Leavis. Each takes off from a
specific disagreement with another, in one case Jack Lindsay the
Marxist author of *John Bunyan: Maker of Myths*, in the other with the
scholarly William York Tindall. Lindsay is concerned to show *Pil-*

grim's Progress as an automatic reaction to class war, Tindall to demonstrate that Bunyan was simply one of a huge crowd of preaching and scribbling fanatics. Of Lindsay Leavis writes: 'he proffers emptiness; like most Marxist writers who undertake to explain art and culture, he produces the effect of having emptied life of content and everything of meaning.'[11] The subtleties, delineated by G. R. Owst in *Literature and Pulpit in Mediaeval England,* which helped to produce Bunyan, become in Lindsay's hands a grossly simple and brutal dialectic. Under this treatment *Pilgrim's Progress* is the product of political and religious resentment and Bunyan's art no more than the expression of Bunyan's pleasure, at 'combat without the complications of reality.' Tindall recognises that Bunyan's economic opinions are derived from the moral ethos of the Middle Ages, an aspect which causes embarrassment to Jack Lindsay, 'who as a Marxist has to recognize that Bunyan (though of course we have to cheer him for standing up for his class) was wrong in opposing the development of the new economic order and trying to hold up the dialectic and hinder the growth of a proletariat . . .'[12] If Lindsay is preoccupied with making Bunyan an element in a social force, Tindall is concerned to reduce him to the status of one of a crowd of preaching mechanicks. In each work it is both the art of Bunyan and the conditions which nourished it which are wholly underestimated. It was possible, Leavis remembers, to read *Pilgrim's Progress* as a child, without worrying about Calvin, Predestination, Imputed Righteousness, or Justification by Faith. It is characteristic of the full-bodied quality and the total employment of self in Leavis's criticism that he should bring in, even if only glidingly, this significant childhood memory. Bunyan was one of a crowd, or a tradition, but not merely one, and the culture to which he belonged wasn't simply his own past, but that of a richly creative community in which a revulsion from Vanity Fair did not imply banning the humane arts and graces from life. Bunyan was in a direct line with the homiletic tradition which went beyond the Reformation deep into the Middle Ages:

> Bunyan the creative writer wrote out of a 'moral sense' that represented what was finest in that traditional culture. He used with a free idiomatic range and vividness in preaching (the tradition he preached in ensured that) the language he spoke with jailers and fellow prisoners, with wife and children and friends at home. A language is more than such phrases as 'means of expression' or 'instrument of communication' suggest; it is a vehicle of collective wisdom and basic

assumptions, a currency of criteria and valuations collaboratively determined; itself it entails on the user a large measure of accepting participation in the culture of which it is the active living presence.[13]

The theology of *Pilgrim's Progress* may be unprofitable and even in places repulsive but it remains 'a vitalizing reminder of human nature, human potentiality, and human need.'[14] Bunyan was certainly a predecessor of Defoe in respect of the novel, but Bunyan's realism 'comes from deeper down; his dialogue, in its homely rightness, is much more subtle and penetrating in its power of characterization and has an immensely wider range of tones.'[15] The term 'Puritan', then, if Bunyan is the model for it, should not suggest 'a stern or morose austerity, or, in the preoccupation with Grace, any indifference to the graces of life.'[16] It was a Puritanism which assumed that art was necessary to life. And the preoccupation with Grace itself was much more than narrowly fanatic or sectarian. It affirmed a validity and sacredness in life without which there could probably, Leavis concludes, be no such thing as cultural health.

The Puritanism which was expressed supremely in Bunyan's art was neither sourly exclusive nor grindingly insistent. Intense spirituality was its centre but it also included the joy of children eating their bread well spread with honey, dancing and music, Christiana with her viol, Mercy with her flute, Prudence with her spinet. '"Wonderful! Music in the house, music in the heart, and music also in Heaven" – the exclamation suggests aptly that actual "unpuritanical" sense of earthly life in relation to the eternal which informs *The Pilgrim's Progress*.'[17] In the course of defining the peculiarly glad and human note of the spirituality of *The Pilgrim's Progress*, Leavis compares Bunyan with Defoe, his successor as the great popular writer and bestseller. Certainly we have a sense of there being in 'the order of reality in which this history is enacted, a dimension over and above those of the commonsense world,'[18] but this does not in any way weaken the vision into a dream or diminish the reality of the life Bunyan is engaged with. The theme gives Leavis occasion to speak in a strikingly personal way of the relation of religious feeling to art, which looks forward, I am sure, to deep interests in the latest part of his career. We are aware as we read Bunyan, Leavis reminds us, in a way that we never are with the invincibly sane and decent Defoe, that the appalling abysses and toppling mountains menacing the pilgrim are the negative accompaniments of something missing from Defoe's world, an intense and profound concern for the meaning of life. We have, Leavis tells us, to talk loosely about important matters when no precision is possible (a contention he was to make again and again in the books of his final, philosophical and religious phase), but there is nothing loose, or nothing that could be usefully tightened, when he is moved to state, and movingly states:

> Such a concern, felt as the question 'What for – what ultimately for?' is implicitly asked in all the greatest art, from which we get, not what we are likely to call an 'answer', but the communication of a felt significance; something that confirms our sense of life as more than a mere linear succession of days, a matter of time as measured by the clock – 'tomorrow and tomorrow and tomorrow . . .'.[19]

It would not be possible to achieve 'so confident and exalting a sense of significance'[20] in our time, or indeed with comparable completeness even in the time of Defoe. But this does not imply any slackening of its value for us.

> One of the things we learn from frequenting the great works of creative art is that where life is strong in any culture, the 'questions' ask themselves insistently, and the 'answers' change from age to age, but in some way that challenges our thought; the profound sincerity of past 'answers' will invest them for our contemplation with a kind of persisting validity.[21]

The fresh and breathing vitality of a Bunyan, the irresistible and unanswerable steadfastness of inner life which makes us know 'we do not belong to ourselves'; the deep and urgent theme governing and directing expression, expression which is not merely elaborated by the individual author but engages the powers and resources of the language; an unclouded coherence of psyche; and intelligence, that special use of intelligence in art which Leavis defined as 'the power of recognizing justly the relation of idea and will to spontaneous life, of using the conscious mind for the attainment of "spontaneous-creative fulness of being"':[22] these are the qualities, 'the animating presences' Leavis sought for in great art, these are the grounds on which he discriminated between artist and artist, and specifically between the two great writers of the age, Lawrence and Eliot. No one has written with more subtlety of perception and respect on Eliot than Leavis. He puts him with Lawrence as the two who will be seen in retrospect to dominate the age. But he judged Lawrence to be immensely the greater genius. This view, argued with passionate conviction, supported by some of Leavis's most powerful criticism, developed over many years and reconsidered and refined on several occasions, followed on a concept of

the history of prose fiction in English as well as on the most detailed
scrutinies of the works of both writers. Leavis gives a clear and succinct
account of it in the early pages of his book, *D. H. Lawrence: Novelist:*

> ... if depth, range and subtlety in the presentment of human
> experience are the criteria, then in the work of Hawthorne, Dickens,
> George Eliot, Henry James, Melville, Mark Twain, Conrad – we
> have a creative achievement that is unsurpassed; unsurpassed by any
> of the famous phases or chapters of literary history. In these great
> novelists (I do not offer my list as exhaustive of the writers who
> might be relevantly adduced, but confine myself to those who
> present themselves as the great compelling instances) we have the
> successors of Shakespeare; for in the nineteenth century and later the
> strength – the poetic and creative strength – of the English language
> goes into prose fiction. In comparison the formal poetry is a marginal
> affair. And the achievement of T. S. Eliot, remarkable as it was, did
> not reverse the relation.[23]

There was, for Leavis, therefore, a bitter irony in the fact that Eliot,
the lesser artist but the greater success – it was without permission, he
reminds us, that Lawrence won his fame – should have used this
immense influence consistently to retard and diminish Lawrence's
reputation. After his first flinching distaste, it is true, Eliot speaks of
Lawrence in milder and more appreciative terms – although no obituary
appeared in *The Criterion* on Lawrence's death and the amiable E. M.
Forster was taken to task for his too artless enthusiasm for 'the
greatest imaginative novelist of the age'.

But while Eliot came to see and recommend Lawrence as a serious
and improving author, his essential account of him remained negative
and limiting. He was, Eliot said in *After Strange Gods*, a man with
'acute sensibility, violent prejudices and passions, and lack of intellectual and social training.'[24] Again, as later he writes in the foreword
to Father William Tiverton's *D. H. Lawrence and Human Existence*,
'He was a man of fitful and profound insights, rather than of ratiocina-
tive powers ... drawing the wrong conclusions in his conscious mind
from the insights which came to him from below consciousness ...'
Eliot, that is, saw Lawrence as having a certain genius but of a hasty,
inartistic and fundamentally mystical and intuitive rather than intelligent kind. To Leavis this was totally to misread the nature, as it was to
undervalue the value, of Lawrence's genius. Without hesitation or
hedging he puts the emphasis on Lawrence's art, on his intelligence, and
on Lawrence's 'unfailingly sure sense of the difference between that

which makes for life and that which makes against it; of the difference between health and that which tends away from health.'[25] That Lawrence, who in 'logical stamina, the power to pursue an organizing process of thought through a wide and difficult tract, with a sustained consistency . . .'[26] was superior to Eliot himself, should be judged incapable of what we ordinarily call thinking, seemed to Leavis a gross inversion of the proper order. There was a comparable travesty in the accusation of sexual morbidity made against Lawrence whose art expressed, and whose criticism drew on, a lucid wholeness, harmony and health of the psyche, and particularly when the charge is laid by one 'whose own attitudes . . . to sex have been, in prose and poetry, almost uniformly negative – attitudes of distaste, disgust and rejection.'[27] Leavis does not wish to attribute the sum of human wisdom to Lawrence, although in reaction to Eliot, Wyndham Lewis and David Cecil, and after a life-time spent in getting recognition for Lawrence, he some-times seems to be doing so. He allows that Lawrence can write badly and he finds a due proportion of failure in his art. He acknowledges that Lawrence's preoccupation with sex is excessive and he showed in his strongly unfavourable line on *Lady Chatterley's Lover* how sick-ness, bad writing and a cerebral attitude to sex came together at certain places. But he insisted that Lawrence's concern with spiritual health, as well as his possession of it and his understanding of it, far transcended what is suggested by talk of sex. 'His may be "not the last word, only the first"; but the first is necessary.'[28]

In the work devoted to Lawrence published in 1955, Leavis repeatedly expresses the view that Lawrence was a remarkably fine literary critic, the best of the day – an opinion that those who know *Studies in Classic American Literature* and *Phoenix* will not want to quarrel with – and a more interesting poet than many have allowed, although he is less ardent on this matter than, say, D. J. Enright[29] – as well as a discursive analyst and critic of civilisation of the most perceptive originality – witness *Fantasia of the Unconscious* and *Psychoanalysis of the Uncon-scious.* Nevertheless he puts the supremacy of Lawrence's achievement finally in the fiction, and among the fiction in *The Rainbow* and *Women in Love*, striking works of creative originality, and among the shorter novellas and stories in *The Captain's Doll* and *St. Mawr*, both treated extensively and in detail, and then in an assortment of the tales, consti-tuting, by themselves, a body of creative work sufficient to put Lawrence among the great writers. Leavis comes back again and again throughout the book to his contention that Lawrence's genius, one of the most extraordinary in English literature, was expressed in fiction, was for fiction, and contributed in the most powerful and original way to the extension of the universe of the novel. Of the very large number of comments which refer and enforce this point, let me choose just one in which Leavis is talking of the opening scene between Hannele and Mitchka in *The Captain's Doll*:

> Once again we are made to reflect, with a fresh wonder, that never was there a greater master of what is widely supposed to be the novelist's distinctive gift: the power to register, to evoke, life and manners with convincing vividness – evoke in the 'created' living presence that compels us to recognize the truth, strength and newness of the perception it records. To say that he exercises it incomparably over the whole social range doesn't suggest the full marvel. The women in the opening of *The Captain's Doll* are aristocrats and Germans, and these foreign ladies of high birth and breeding are, as such, immediate actual presences for us; they are *there*, in their intimate encounter, authentic and real beyond question; done – established and defined in our sense of them – by an economy of art that looks like casualness.[30]

It is clear that Leavis's general view of literary history over the last two hundred years is supported and particularised by a concept of the novel which he finds embodied in Lawrence's art. It is also clear that this concept, the result of the actual responses to specific works, was also developed in harmony with the idea of the novel elaborated by Lawrence himself, not before or in separation from his work, but as a reflection and a critical analysis of his own creativity. I want, then, to indicate the main notes of this idea which is both implicit in the fiction and constantly called on in the criticism, and afterwards to illustrate – one can do no more – Leavis's treatment of Lawrence by referring to a notable example, his essay on *St. Mawr*. Before doing that, however, I must interpolate another comment. By concentrating on Lawrence's greatest art, and few would fault Leavis's choice for that, Leavis leaves little room or opportunity for expatiating on Lawrence's weaknesses. Not that he doesn't make it manifest that he is well aware of Lawrence's particular tendencies to imperfection. He questions the impersonality of some of the early work which registers in too direct and untransformed a way Lawrence's personal experience, his relations with his mother or with Frieda; he sees signs of too great a tentativeness in the development or organisation of the later part of *The Rainbow*; and he points, illustrating it from *Women in Love*, to what must seem the most Lawrentian of Lawrence's faults, the tendency to 'an insistent and over-emphatic explicitness, running at times to something one can only call jargon,' betraying that he is 'uncertain of the value of what he offers; uncertain whether he really holds it – whether a valid communication has really been defined and conveyed in terms of his creative art ("Art speech is the only speech").'[31]

In outlining the Lawrence-Leavis idea of the novel I shall draw on Lawrence's account. For Lawrence it was the explication of his own practice; for Leavis a conclusion from the position of many masters. The novel in the hands of Melville, Conrad, James and Lawrence himself, has become a species of poetry, perhaps the form in which the poetic imagination now expresses itself most naturally, fully and powerfully. The transmutation of its nature means an astonishing extension of the universe of the novel. The object of the novel is to be no less than 'the whole man alive' – that is to be its theme and the audience to which it is addressed.

> The novel [Lawrence says] is the one bright book of life. Books are not life. They are only tremulations on the ether. But the novel as a tremulation can make the whole man alive tremble. Which is more than poetry, philosophy, science, or any other book-tremulation can do. . . . Plato makes the perfect ideal being tremble in me. But that's only a bit of me. Perfection is only a bit, in the strange make-up of man alive. The Sermon on the Mount makes the selfless spirit of me quiver. But that, too, is only a bit of me. The Ten Commandments set the old Adam shivering in me, warning me that I am a thief and a murderer, unless I watch it. But even the old Adam is only a bit of me.
>
> I very much like all these bits of me to be set trembling with life and the wisdom of life. But I do ask that the whole of me shall tremble in its wholeness, some time or other . . .
>
> [Novels] in their wholeness . . . affect the whole man alive, which is the man himself, beyond any part of him. They set the whole tree trembling with a new access of life, they do not just stimulate growth in one direction.[32]

Because he is concerned to add to the life of the complete person, the novelist is also concerned in a fundamental way with moral issues. 'Right and wrong is an instinct: but an instinct of the whole consciousness in a man, bodily, mental, spiritual at once. And only in the novel are *all* things given full play, or at least, they may be given full play, when we realise that life itself, and not inert safety, is the reason for

living.'[33] For what, if we think about it, asks Lawrence, does one's life
consist in ? It consists '*in* this achieving of a pure relationship between
ourselves and the living universe about us ... an infinity of pure
relations, big and little ... And morality is that delicate, for ever
trembling and changing *balance* between me and my circumambient
universe, which precedes and accompanies a true relatedness.'[34] It is
the function of art

> ... to reveal the relation between man and his circumambient uni-
> verse, at the living moment. As mankind is always struggling in the
> toils of old relationships, art is always ahead of the 'times', which
> themselves are always far in the rear of the living moment ...
>   Now here we see the beauty and the great value of the novel.... The
> novel is the highest example of subtle inter-relatedness that man has
> discovered.... The novel is a perfect medium for revealing to us the
> changing rainbow of our living relationships.[35]

Clearly the novel so conceived is very different from, more complex
and more important than, the novel conventionally understood. The
names given by Lawrence – Plato and the Sermon on the Mount – help
to define the difference. A constitutive theme of the Lawrentian novel
is that discrepancy between what man is actually, concretely, in his
tissues, nerves, psyche and beliefs, and what man could be. This is in a
radical way a philosophic theme involving a metaphysical conception
and an ethical intention. For Lawrence, as for Leavis, it was all the
more necessary for the novel to offer itself as a centre for such permanent human concerns, since philosophy itself has turned its interests
away from such matters. To supply in fiction what philosophy dis-
regards, to rescue the novel from sentimentality and philosophy from
the deadest, abstract generality – this was an essential undertaking for
the novelist in Lawrence's eyes:

> It seems to me it was the greatest pity in the world, when philosophy
> and fiction got split. They used to be one, right from the days of
> myth. Then they went and parted, like a nagging married couple,
> with Aristotle and Thomas Aquinas and that beastly Kant. So the
> novel went sloppy, and philosophy went abstract-dry. The two
> should come together again – in the novel.[36]

And of course the novel must pursue this end without damage to its
own integrity. Lawrence is not recommending fictional theses or
illustrated propaganda. The novel was to help us develop an instinct
for life not a 'theory of right and wrong.' 'The novel has a future. It's

got to have the courage to tackle new propositions without using abstractions; it's got to present us with new, really new feelings, a whole line of new emotion, which will get us out of the emotional rut.'[37] What makes a novel 'serious', therefore, is an apprehension of reality as deep as this, its organisation about a moral impulse and its construction in the terms of art. It is the novel so understood which can help us to live as nothing else can; no didactic scripture, anyhow.

It is of the novel so understood that Lawrence is the master. It is out of the understanding of the novels that Leavis says, speaking of *Women in Love* and *The Rainbow*, 'These two books would by themselves have been enough to place Lawrence among the greatest English writers.'[38] The immediate context of Leavis's judgement was a claim for the unsurpassed wealth of dramatised social history in Lawrence, marked in *Women in Love* by an astonishing comprehensiveness in presenting the England of 1914, in *The Rainbow* by historical depth in unfolding the transmission of the spiritual heritage in an actual society. I want in speaking of *St. Mawr* to fasten on certain other notes of this kind chosen by Leavis both to illuminate the text and to particularise the creative capacity of the novelist.

I have to start off by noting the heightened vocabulary of appreciation used by Leavis in speaking of this story of some 180 pages, which has to do with a wayward stallion and the threat to tame him by gelding; his owner, Lou Witt, a young American woman living in Europe; her dilettante husband Rico who is playing at being a painter; her sardonic and dominating mother; and a couple of grooms. On this slim basis Lawrence has raised a work of art which Leavis says is an 'astonishing work of genius'[39] and a full and self-sufficient creation, characterised by a creative and technical originality superior to that of *The Waste Land*. (The two works have a certain thematic unity.) Fully to justify this valuation from a critic not given to lavishness would entail reproducing the whole of Leavis's closely-woven supporting argument. I can only, as I say, refer to a number of key features in it.

To begin with, *St. Mawr* combines, says Leavis, pregnancy and concentrated force – a whole view of the civilised world is worked into its narrow space – with a flowing freedom of expression that looks like careless ease. But that ease encompasses a great range of source, use, and tone in the language, 'the slangy colloquialism, the flippant cliché given an emotional intensity, the "placing" sardonic touch, and when it comes (as it so marvellously can at any moment), the free play of poetic imagery and imaginative evocation, sensuous and focally

suggestive.'[40] Of course, the complex theme requires the intricate
instrument, the theme which is implicitly and dramatically defined by
image, action and symbol. It derives from the great Lawrentian preoccupation with the wounded nature of modern man in contemporary
society, a wound of negation, a terrible vacancy. An essential part of a
healthy human nature has been allowed to sink beneath the level of
accessibility and no longer operates in the blocked, starved modern
consciousness. *St. Mawr* stands, says Leavis, for 'deep impulsions of
life that are thwarted in the modern world' and for 'all that deep
spontaneous life which is not at the beck and call of the conscious and
willing mind, and so in that sense cannot be controlled by it, though it
can be thwarted and defeated.'[41] Nor is Lawrence anywhere in this
delicately exact tale guilty of engaging in a polemic against consciousness or a campaign in favour of sex. When the stallion is with Lou –
and his presence is established with uncommon and emphatic power –
he is not merely a sexual symbol, but something which both includes
sex and transcends it. 'The wild, brilliant, alert head of St. Mawr
seemed to look at her out of another world.' It is the great triumph of
Lawrence's supremely intelligent art in *St. Mawr* to make this other
world irresistibly palpable and real. And he does so while showing
himself a master of the manner, the modes, the figures and the comedy
of this world; '. . . creative genius in Lawrence manifests itself as
supreme intelligence,'[42] is Leavis's conclusion.

> What is it but intelligence that we have in that deep insight into
> human nature; that clairvoyant understanding of so wide a range of
> types and of social milieux; that generalizing power which never
> leaves the concrete – the power we have seen exemplified of exposing
> the movement of civilization in the malady of the individual
> psyche?[43]

I want to end this section with a brief consideration of the book on
Dickens which the Leavises published in 1970, the centenary year. The
double authorship reminds us that Leavis for all his isolation, increasing
as it did with the years and especially after he severed his last official
link with Downing, nevertheless was a member of one of the most extraordinary intellectual partnerships in English life, as sustained as that of
the Webbs or the Hammonds and as creative as that of William and
Dorothy Wordsworth. Let me quote the dedication not simply as
proof of personal devotion but also as testimony to the way the
Leavises saw themselves and their place in literary history:

We dedicate this book to each other as proof, along with *Scrutiny* (of which for twenty-one years we sustained the main burden and the responsibility), of forty years and more of daily collaboration in living, university teaching, discussion of literature and the social and cultural context from which literature is born, and above all, devotion to the fostering of that true respect for creative writing, creative minds and, English literature being in question, the English tradition, without which literary criticism can have no validity and no life.

But if it is a combined work, it is only fair to point out that Mrs Leavis's share in it is certainly not less substantial than her husband's. He is responsible for three major sections, on *Dombey and Son*, *Hard Times*, and *Little Dorrit*, one of which, *Hard Times*, is reproduced from *Scrutiny* (1947), and another, on *Dombey and Son*, is a fuller treatment of an essay published in *The Sewanee Review* in 1962; she, for four major sections, on *David Copperfield*, *Bleak House*, *Great Expectations*, and the Dickens illustrations, together with several significant appendixes and a number of the long, illuminating and often witty footnotes characteristic of Mrs Leavis's writing. My own impression, in fact, is that this is Mrs Leavis's book to which her husband has contributed, rather than the other way round. In any case, *Dickens the Novelist* represents the Leavis's final view of Dickens, a view which had transformed itself over forty years from its unfavourable beginning to the point where Dickens assumed the status of Shakespeare of the novel. They disclaim any intention of providing a general survey of Dickens since 'all such enterprises are merely academic, and unprofitable critically.'[44] Their purpose is to demonstrate the creativity, the artistry and the intelligence of Dickens, to cancel finally the reputation of Dickens merely as popular entertainer of genius, and to register a protest in particular against the trend of American criticism from Edmund Wilson onward.

The collaborators acknowledge that they have been guided by what they call 'the spontaneities of the personal judgement and the personal habit of approach'[45] – a fact which adds a refreshing tang of contrast to the work. One notes, for example, a distinct shade of difference in the two judgements on Smollett's influence on Dickens, particularly in respect of the character of Captain Cuttle in *Dombey and Son*, or again, how Mrs Leavis is very much more clearly in possession of, if not much impressed by, the latest Dickens scholarship. For reasons of space and proportion I shall concentrate on their criticism of *Dombey and Son*,

David Copperfield, Bleak House and *Little Dorrit,* which seems best to
me to reveal their collaborative understanding and their differences of
idiom and individuality.

Leavis remembers having heard *Dombey and Son* read aloud – and
admirably so – by his father in the days when family reading was still
an institution (Leavis, we remind ourselves, was born in 1895), and he
confessed to a long abstention from the novel as something belonging
to greener and less sophisticated days. Now he thinks of it as marking
a decisive step in Dickens's development, as his first major novel,
offering an urgent and powerful theme and massive evidence of creative
force. It is a great but imperfect work of art since the creativity was
trapped in an elaborate Victorian plot which licensed childish sensa-
tionalism, luxuries of pathos and lush moral insistencies. Nevertheless it is the vitality, the strength, 'the genial force of Dickens's
inexhaustible creativity,'[46] which must remain with the reader. This is
the source of the sharp immediacy and 'intensity of sensuous and
imaginative realization,'[47] of 'the peculiar strength of the humour in the
supreme ranges of Dickens's art,'[48] of the rich, flexible and endlessly
original expression.

The world created by *Dombey and Son* with 'ironic trenchancy ...
and natural truth'[49] is that of new money-power, class exclusiveness,
utilitarian orthodoxy, the closed-heart and human pride. It is pre-
industrial England – the new railways offer hope and possibility – but
savagely of the City, and it is located in Dombey as cold pride, a force
utterly hostile to life, generosity and even to what it loves. Against this
are the Toodles, standing for all that is repressed in the Dombey case,
human kindness, human feeling, a prosperously human life. Between
them is Paul, whose growth and tragedy are enacted with the kind of
irresistible particularity which comes from overwhelming conviction,
the direct pressure of the theme and piercing and delicate psychological
acumen. *Dombey and Son,* that is, brings in a Dickensian strength that
had not till then been characteristically Dickensian. And yet creativity
in *Dombey and Son,* for all its full and masterly flow, failed to issue in,
or inevitably compel, the form or design necessary to its nature: evidence, surely, of some central flaw in thematic development. (We remember on the personal side that at one point Dickens laid aside his
great new creation to compose a run-of-the-mill Christmas tale for his
avid public.) When, Leavis points out, the theme of money-pride turns
to the theme of the bought bride, Dickens is carried into a realm where
his knowledge is not the product of deep personal engagement but

simply the result of the external, vulgar and conventional. Melodrama takes over from drama, the prosaic ousts the poetic, fabricated plot displaces organic design.

And yet in her singularly original chapter on *David Copperfield*, Mrs Leavis reminds us that Tolstoy himself thought Dickens a master of construction and was deeply influenced by him, above all by *David Copperfield*. She shows how in *War and Peace* the married life of Prince Andrew and Lisa reproduces in Russian terms the relationship of David and Dora. The difference in treatment is greatly to Dickens's advantage for in Tolstoy this relationship is 'quite barely stated instead of, as in *Copperfield*, comprehended in its whole social and psychological context and implications.'[50] Mrs Leavis's judgement on the novel, abundantly illustrated and supported from the text, places the emphasis most firmly on the brilliance of its organisation.

> The masterly construction of *Copperfield* is the more surprising when one reflects that its only predecessor as an integrally conceived novel was *Dombey*, and that that broke down, changing direction and mode, with the death of little Paul, losing its previous steady focus on the theme. *Copperfield* is only a year later but what an advance it shows in planning, complexity of conception and consistency from the first chapter right through to the schematic ending! (leaving out the last chapter, which provides a pantomime transformation scene – a concession to the reading-public which Dickens never again makes. There are no happy endings after *Copperfield*).[51]

Mrs Leavis altogether discounts the view that some specious or accidental unity accrues to *David Copperfield* from its being a disguised autobiography. She finds no evidence of an involuntary or uncontrollable identification of Charles Dickens with David Copperfield of the kind that 'we resent at times in *Jane Eyre* or find embarrassing in *The Mill on the Floss*, for not being David, Dickens is not concerned to make a hero of him.[52] On the contrary, she judges the neutrality or colourlessness of David, so odd in a work by the author supremely capable of communicating a uniquely vivid individuality, a deliberate device (Pip in *Great Expectations* is another example), by which, emphasising the protagonist's representativeness enables Dickens to conduct a characteristic enquiry into the nature of happiness in marriage. 'David incarnates the kind of youth the age demanded – sensitive, modest, upright, affectionate, but also resourcefully industrious and successful in rising in the world.'[53] The theme itself is beautifully and economically organised in a set of delicate parallels and poetic echoings between the Clare and Dora sections, which are themselves preluded in the history of David's own parentage, given resonance and depth by means of a myth rather than fact, by folk-tale and symbolic action, and point and intimacy by the inwardness of an autobiographical method. We are aware at every point of 'the novelist's full consciousness of the living nature of the material he works in, material that he is shaping with the responsibility of a great artist possessed by a theme he must develop.'[54] *David Copperfield* shows us, Mrs Leavis argues, an effortless impersonality, the most careful thinking out of the ideas and human truths the novelist is engaged with, a tone exactly fitted to its purpose, which is not to indict but to question contemporary assumption, nothing of an obtrusive schematic intention, and a marvellous understanding of speech as the index of individuality. Nor, Mrs Leavis concludes, must we fail to acknowledge the pioneering quality of Dickens's art. *Dombey* and *Copperfield* take the novel in conception and idiom out of melodrama and stage rhetoric, and in point of construction, from the picaresque and moralistic into the realm of psychological truth and depth.

The study of *Dombey and Son* brings out Dickens's poetic creativeness, that of *David Copperfield* his mastery of composition; the studies of *Bleak House* and *Hard Times*, the one by Q. D., the other by F. R., bring out the intellectual distinction of Dickens's analysis of the Victorian world. Each is concerned to obliterate the reputation of Dickens as one who is incapable of thought, or as the clumsily Philistine critic of some single, simple abuse. Of the theme of *Bleak House*, a Dostoievskian novel, which is for Mrs Leavis 'the most impressive and rewarding of all Dickens's novels,'[55] she writes:

> Remembering that 'jarndyce' was the old-fashioned pronunciation of 'jaundice', we see that the Jarndyce Case is the case of man in the state of Victorian society . . . The bearing of Justice and Equity on religion, morals and ethics, and on social sanctions and institutions, is a matter explored by Dickens throughout *Bleak House*.[56]

Dickens may have been indebted to the Carlyle of *Past and Present* for the general direction of his theme, but its tightly controlled, characteristically witty, poetically evocative realisation is wholly Dickens, the Dickens who wrote for 'a deeper level of self than the journalist, actor, social friend or even, on the whole, the letter-writer, drew upon.'[57] The plot, 'touching off a chain of cause and effect that exposes a dead past,'[58] is a classical form not before used by Dickens, although he employed this model again in *Little Dorrit*. But it is the theme which is now the deepest influence shaping the novel. Nor is it simply the Law as such but 'the laws of human nature and the society that man's nature has produced as the expression of our impulses,'[59] and above all of the destructive litigating impulse which constitutes the sinister and chilling universe of the novel. Merely being born makes men antagonists, merely living makes them litigants. Some strive for justice – Miss Flite, Gridley – and go mad or die, and others opt out of the struggle – Mr Jarndyce, Sir Leicester – but no one escapes the destructive influence of institutionalised egotism or fails to be touched by the contradictions and absurdities of an utterly competitive society.

For Mrs Leavis *Bleak House* is a triumph of inclusive art as distinguished from the triumph of exclusive art which is *Hard Times*. This pertinent distinction nicely discriminates between her own treatment of *Bleak House* and Dr Leavis's of *Hard Times*. *Bleak House* is strikingly inclusive, comprehending an abundance of topics, insights, and critical, social and historical judgements. Let me simply mention no more than a dozen of the subjects developed with clarity, force, and constant reference to the text. There is her sympathetic account of Esther, the true recording consciousness of the novel; her analysis of the *persona* and function of the terrifying and abnormal Mr Tulkinghorn, the power-hungry lawyer; or of the sinister Mr Vholes, his figure 'chilling the seed in the ground as it glided along.' There is the strength of Dickens's intellectual understanding and searching observation of his age and its strains. It was a society which could still throw up a Mr Skimpole, the first of the Victorian aesthetes, or could signal the aristocracy's final surrender of its place and influence. There is the hope offered by professional competence and humanity, as with the physician. There is the fascinating exploration of the idea of childhood in a utilitarian society and the damage it can do to the child's growth and psyche. There is the treatment of the complexity of the mode of *Bleak House*, where Dickens's vision is served by a combination of brilliantly intelligent analysis, high spirits, grim humour, refusal to sentimentalise, and by prose which is exquisitely concrete and richly suggestive. *Bleak House* makes clear that both in substance and its medium the eighteenth-century influences of Hogarth, Swift, Gay and Smollett are being displaced by greater ones, by Shakespeare, Jane Austen, Disraeli and the Pope of the *Moral Epistles*.

The sharply focused concentration of *Hard Times* and the manifold in-gathering richness of *Little Dorrit* are examined by Leavis in two essays: one is the comparatively brief, classical piece taken from *Scrutiny* (1947) which inaugurated the approach to the novel as dramatic poem; the other, on *Little Dorrit*, expresses Leavis's thought in a much more developed state and is organised round the affinity Leavis discerns between Blake and Dickens. It also brings to the surface themes that were to be taken up and passionately worked at during the latest phase of the critic's career. The pith of these two essays, the one on the world of Bentham, the other on the wider world of Calvinist, commercial Victorian civilisation, is given in some trenchant and economical paragraphs in the essay on *Little Dorrit*. I do not think the passage is too long to quote, and it has the advantage of conveying the authentic tang and idiom of Leavis's mature style of thought and expression. It comes from the place where he is introducing the subject of the relation of Dickens to Blake:

But I am not intending to commit myself to the belief that Dickens had read Blake. What is plain beyond question is that he was familiar with Wordsworth and with Romantic poetry in general, and that his interest and responsiveness were those of an originating genius who was equipped by nature to be himself a great poet. Further, a man of wonderfully quick intelligence, he mixed with the *élite* that shared the finest culture of the age and, when first frequented by him, was like himself pre-Victorian. One can say that his genius, entailing a completeness of interest in human life (Dickens was not 'a solemn and unsexual man'), cities and civilization that it was Wordsworth's genius not to have, spontaneously took those promptings of the complex romantic heritage which confirmed his response to early Victorian England; confirmed the intuitions and affirmations that, present organically in the structure and significance of *Hard Times* and *Little Dorrit*, make one think of Blake.

I have in mind, of course, the way in which the irrelevance of the Benthamite calculus is exposed; the insistence that life is spontaneous and creative, so that the appeal to self-interest as the essential motive is life-defeating; the vindication, in terms of childhood, of spontaneity, disinterestedness, love and wonder; and the significant place given to Art – a place entailing a conception of Art that is pure Blake.

In *Hard Times*, with its comparative simplicity as a damning critique of the hard ethos and the life-oppressing civilization, the identity of the affirmatives, or evoked and related manifestations of life and health and human normality, by which he condemns, with those of Blake is clear. *Little Dorrit* is immensely more complex, and offers something like a comprehensive report on Victorian England – what is life, what are the possibilities of life, in this society and civilization, and what could life, in a better society, be? To elicit the convinced assent to the proposition that here too the underlying structure of value-affirmations (implicit, spontaneous, inevitable) upon which the form and significance depend is Blakean, is not so easy. But the structure is there; for the book *has* organic form and essential economy: it is all significant.[60]

The *Little Dorrit* essay, of which this is a characteristic page, is so packed, so tightly bound together in its parts and so intimately directed by the leading idea, that I can only touch, almost at random, on two or three of the points made here. Take, for example, the point about Dickens's being pre-Victorian. Mrs Leavis had shown in the Preface to *Dickens the Novelist* how Dickens in manner and sensibility exhibited the uninhibited character of the lower middle-class Regency England he was reared in. Dickens and his friends were wildly unconventional and exuberant by later, primmer Victorian standards. But more is meant than this. Dickens no more than Shakespeare started from nothing. Santayana's view of him as a cultural waif was, says Leavis, 'stultifyingly false.' On the contrary, 'Dickens belonged as a popular writer, along with his public, to a culture in which the arts of speech were intensely alive.'[61] And Dickens's indebtedness to the theatre had as its most important aspect an indebtedness to Shakespeare himself 'He read immensely, with the intelligence of genius, and his inwardness with Shakespeare, the subtlety of the influence manifest, and to be divined, in his own creative originality, can't be explained except by a reader's close and pondering acquaintance.'[62] And the deep connection with Shakespeare and a living English culture was made pertinent and present and critically cogent by new and subtle kinds of awareness drawn from Blake and the Romantics.

Or consider the observation about the significant place given to art. Both the Leavises have been at pains in this volume to stress how deliberate and conscious an artist Dickens, the great public entertainer, was; in him, as in Shakespeare, exuberant vitality and flowing creativeness go hand in hand with an artist's finely judged calculation and a marvellous skill, both intellectual and imaginative, in the management of design, in the choice of means and their relation to ends, and 'a subtlety of purpose and touch' he is not as a rule credited with.

We tell ourselves that in presenting the large cast of diverse characters and the interplay between them Dickens is conducting a sustained, highly conscious and subtly methodical study of the human psyche; that he is concerned to arrive at and convey certain general validities of perception and judgement about life – enforcing implicitly in the process the truth that 'life' is a necessary word; that it is not a mere word, or a word that portends nothing more than an abstraction.[63]

Dickens, the intellectual artist of this calibre, exhibiting a close affinity with Blake, gives a profound importance to art as the locus and standard of full creative human life. In *Little Dorrit* this importance is not concentrated in a given character or situation or relationship but is subtly diffused throughout, affecting both the persons and the connections of Doyce the inventor, the woodcarver Cavalletto, and even Pancks and Flora Finching, each of whom is seen as a major value in a comprehensive design and as 'part of a whole finely nerved organism.' Here again, says Leavis, we have the unmistakable affinity with Blake:

Dickens lays the same kind of emphasis on the creative nature of life as Blake does, and insists in the same way that there is a continuity from the inescapable creativeness of perception to the disciplined imaginative creativeness of the skilled artist, and that where art doesn't thrive or enjoy the intelligent esteem due to it the civilization is sick.[64]

And, lastly, let me choose from the key passage quoted earlier the lines which argue that in *Little Dorrit*, a novel with organic form and essential economy in which everything is significant, 'the underlying structure of value-affirmations (implicit, spontaneous, inevitable) upon which the form and significance depend is Blakean.' '"Identity",' Leavis reminds us, 'is the word with which he insists, in the face of the ethos of "Locke and Newton", that what matters is life, that only in the individual is life "there", and that the individual is unique.'[65] A spontaneous and profound understanding of what was meant by Blake's distinction between identity and selfhood was a constitutive element in the mature Dickensian sensibility, a structural principle in *Little Dorrit*'s design and the deeper source of the novel's significance. Identity as ego-free love and disinterestedness, and responsibility towards something other than self, is figured in different forms in Little Dorrit and Daniel Doyce; selfhood, ego-assertive will, is expressed in a variety of modes in the Calvinist Mrs Clennam, the mad Miss Wade, and the formidably proud Henry Gowan, in whom 'insistent consciousness of superiority is an underlying consciousness of nullity.'[66] With this divining instrument, or rather conception, since nothing so alive could be a mere instrument and no instrument so totally incorporated into the material it engages with, Dickens offers the surest and most delicate analysis of the individual human psyche together with an intense questioning of the whole span of Victorian civilisation, its organisation, institutions, classes, privileges and pretensions, each activity modulating into the other and back again in a manner which is natural and supremely intelligent. This art, the art of a major dramatic poet, shows flexibility of tone and mode, complete obedience to the authority of the real, and an instantaneous rapidity in adducing and defining in creative terms criteria appropriate to determine it, as well as Shakespearean energy in evoking person, place, décor and atmosphere, and a spirit that is religious in the way Blake's is.

On this high note I propose to conclude my commentary on *Dickens the Novelist*, which I see as the most positive, the most sympathetic and generous, and the most complete expression of a collaboration of genius.

8

The Coleridgean Conclusion

I call this final phase of Leavis's career Coleridgean, and I want to begin by glancing at Leavis's own essay on Coleridge, which was written as long ago as 1940,[1] and then at those themes in Coleridge which rise spontaneously and assume their own form in Leavis's work. The first will serve in its qualifying and negative pointing to refine our notion of Leavis's own work. The second will show, I believe, that in spite of Leavis's ambivalent attitude to Coleridge, there was certainly much that they had in common, particularly in this concluding part of Leavis's career. Leavis gave a qualified admiration to the Coleridge who combined a creative gift with a rare critical intelligence at an important moment in poetic history. He appreciated that in the religious and intellectual history of the nineteenth century Coleridge exercised a profound and spreading influence. But this *Scrutiny* essay on Coleridge takes its stand on the integrity and autonomy of literary criticism, which is a discipline of the most delicate relevance, focusing intently on what is actually there in this particular place in the poem, moving out from that to the poem as a whole and from the poem as a whole to the context of ideas and sensibility in which it is set. It follows, therefore, that to approach Coleridge through his philosophy of art or through his metaphysics, or through a discussion of his indebtedness to, or independence of, Kant, Schelling, the Schlegels, or Fichte, was in Leavis's view an unprofitable expenditure for the literary student. On the one hand, one would not go to Coleridge for initiation into the key problems of philosophy, and on the other hand 'the literary student who goes to Coleridge in the expectation of bringing away an improved capacity and equipment for dealing critically with works of literature will, if he spends much time on the "philosophy of art", have been sadly misled.'[2] Coleridge's prestige depends too much on an awed vagueness about his transcendental philosophy.

Leavis acknowledged that the 'subtle-souled psychologist' with a particular interest in language who was so brilliant as a practical critic might well not have been able to exist at all at that time in history had it not been for his metaphysics. But Leavis is left with the feeling that Coleridge's actual achievement is disappointingly incommensurate with the rarely gifted mind. Like Eliot, he is unimpressed by the Fancy-Imagination distinction, although he sees it as one way of calling attention to the organic complexities of verbal life. He feels that Coleridge, while he did not inaugurate the Bradley 'character' approach to Shakespeare, certainly lent his prestige to it. And he would never think of proposing even the work on Shakespeare to the literary student as an exercise in classical criticism calculated to make much difference to his powers of understanding and appreciation.

While the discussions in the group of chapters on Wordsworth in *Biographia Literaria* show that Coleridge perceived certain essential truths about poetic rhythm, which are not even yet commonplace, the treatment of Wordsworth's poetry, however interesting, hardly amounts to a profound and very illuminating critique. Coleridge at his best, Leavis believes, is seen in the chapter on 'The specific symptoms of poetic power elucidated in a critical analysis of Shakespeare's *Venus and Adonis* and *Lucrece*'. In this analysis Coleridge shows evidence of his peculiar distinction as a critic. Principle emerges from practice, and 'we are made to realise that the master of theoretical criticism who matters is the completion of a practical critic.' It is a mastery which comes evidently 'from the English critic who has devoted his finest powers of sensibility and intelligence to the poetry of his own language.' In this chapter Coleridge deals with themes which have only recently established themselves as key ones in current critical activity, with the idea of impersonality, for example, with the organic nature of imagery, with the nature of wit in poetry. But Leavis concludes, it is all impressive evidence of what he might have done; no more. This is the depressing conclusion:

> Coleridge's prestige is very understandable, but his currency as an academic classic is something of a scandal. Where he is prescribed and recommended it should be with far more by the way of reservation and caveat (I have come tardily to realize) than most students can report to have received along with him. He was very much more brilliantly gifted than Arnold, but nothing of his deserves the classical status of Arnold's best work.[3]

And yet Coleridge's criticism in assumption and practice had within it much that Leavis admired, for example in the criticism of Eliot. It was modelled upon what Coleridge himself called 'the physiognomy of the being within,' that is, his own creative activity – which itself affected and was affected by his interpretation of the creative activity of

other writers, and supremely of Shakespeare. When he speaks, therefore, of 'an implicit wisdom deeper than our consciousness,' as one of
the profound sources of Shakespeare's creativity, he is making reference to something within himself as a critic as well as pointing to something there in Shakespeare. He is making not only a statement about
Shakespeare but a revelation about himself. This is not only one of the
sources of literary creation but one of the essential canons of criticism.
'An implicit wisdom' is a phrase carrying with it suggestions of
rhythms 'deeper than our consciousness,' of something like a tribal
disinterestedness or a more than personal sagacity, and of a radical
inclusive commonsense. It brings with it the idea of a fundamental
human morality: not the superior morality which Coleridge speaks of,
complacently, as an achievement of the nineteenth century, but something more permanent and significant, more like a central, instinctive
human tradition, of the kind Leavis continually invoked. Coleridge has
in mind here that moral, more than individual life, or moral being
as he called it, which, even more than man's intellectual powers,
distinguished him from the animals and made him truly human.
It is a feeling, as Coleridge explained when writing about women in
Shakespeare of all 'that *continuates* society, as sense of ancestry
and of sex, with a purity unassailable by sophistry, because it rests
not in the analytic processes, but in that same equipoise of the
faculties, during which the feelings are representative of all past
experience . . .' As it disclosed itself in Shakespeare this was a
positive and tremendous *ordinariness*, a centrality of experience and
judgement which was itself never twisted by aberration whatever aberration it was turned upon.

> Keeping at all times in the high road of life, Shakespeare has no
> innocent adulteries, no interesting incests, no virtuous vice . . .
> Shakespeare's fathers are roused by ingratitude, his husbands stung
> by unfaithfulness; in him, in short, the affections are wounded in
> those points in which all may, nay, must, feel. . . . He neither excites,
> nor flatters, passion, in order to degrade the subject of it; he does not
> use the faulty thing for a faulty purpose, nor carries on warfare
> against virtue, by causing wickedness to appear as no wickedness,
> through the medium of a morbid sympathy with the unfortunate. In
> Shakespeare vice never walks as in twilight: nothing is purposely out
> of its place; . . . he does not make every magistrate a drunkard or
> glutton, nor every poor man meek, humane, and temperate; he has
> no benevolent butchers, nor any sentimental rat-catchers.[4]

There is a sentence in *Biographia Literaria* which offers a neat transition to the last of the conceptions I specified as lying at the back of Coleridge's criticism, namely his idea of language: 'in all societies there exists an instinct of growth, a certain collective unconscious good sense working progressively to de-synonymise those words originally of the same meaning . . .'[5] Coleridge's thought on language is in resonance with his thought on the mind. The mind constructs and refines relationships, language constructs and refines meanings. Each has a collective and unconscious base, an individual and conscious crown. Neither is simply a mirror reflecting an object or a garment clothing a form: '. . . to know is in its very essence a verb active,'[6] he affirms, and '. . . words are not things, they are living powers . . .'[7] It was a particular anxiety of Coleridge to show the connection between language and human experience as something closer and subtler than it was commonly taken to be in Locke or Hobbes or Horne Tooke. Language was neither an 'invalid surrogate' for experience nor a veil floating deceptively across and around our ideas. He questioned whether language is no more than an arbitrary attachment of words to thoughts and things, which Collingwood argued would amount to saying that language was a set of technical terms.[8] Of course language is arbitrary in the sense that it is artificial and various, but it is not arbitrary in the same way as a new technical term is arbitrary, or the words in a non-sense language, or the rules of a new game. As he wrote to William Godwin:

> Is *thinking* impossible without arbitrary signs? And how far is the word 'arbitrary' a misnomer? Are not words etc. parts and germinations of the Plant? And where is the law of their growth? – In something of this order I would endeavour to destroy the old antithesis of *Words and Things*, elevating, as it were, words into Things, and living Things too.[9]

'Growth' is a figure which condenses into itself a whole variety of notions – of naturalness as opposed to arbitrariness, of an intrinsic initiative, of the burgeoning of life according to an implicit pattern, of a completion of it which cannot be totally forecast, and of an elaborate complexity of structure. All of which we may claim are implicit in Leavis's own account. Coleridge realised how many more than merely verbal elements go into language. 'I include in the meaning of a word not only its correspondent object; but likewise all the associations it recalls. For language is framed to convey not the object alone, but like-

wise the character, mood and intentions of the person who is representing it.'[10] Language constructs meaning and this gives our experience
its peculiarly human note; at the same time it makes meaning relatively
permanent, preserving in experience a kind of force and density which
otherwise might simply evaporate. Language to some degree and
literature, the most intense form of language, to a much higher degree,
'preserved,' he points out, 'a purity of meaning to many terms of
natural objects. Without this holdfast, our vitiated imaginations would
refine away language to mere abstractions.'[11] Coleridge wished not
only to insist on the part of language in making experiences permanent,
but on the intimacy, on the unity even, between language and human
experience itself. 'For if words are not things, they are living powers,
by which things of most importance to mankind are activated, combined, and humanized.'[12] He rejected the tradition, still current today,
which took the use of language to be the fixing of passive labels to
completed experiences. He wished, instead, to abolish the distance
between language and thought. Language was not only an instrument
but a source of thought, not only an agency but an initiator. And the
more language was this, the more was it significantly human: '. . . the
best part of human language, properly so called, is derived from
reflection on the acts of the mind itself.'[13] And what is true of language
in a general and loose way is true of literature in the most particular and
intense way, and true above all of the language of poetry. Shakespeare's
language, for example, 'was not drawn from any set fashion, but from
the profoundest depth of his moral being.'[14]

All language constructs and continues meaning, all language organ-
ises and humanises things. The language of poetry adds not only a
special harmony or a particular attractiveness of pattern, although it
does add these. The special function of art, 'the figured language of
thought,' is 'to partake of the reality which it renders intelligible.' The
language of poetry adds performance to memory, it is revealing as well
as commemorative. Coleridge distinguished the translation of abstract
notions into a picture language from poetry in which language itself is
a symbol 'characterised by a translucence of the special in the individual,
or of the general in the special, or of the universal in the general.'[15]
Translucence, an actual shining through: the language of poetry does
not merely refer outside itself to objects and thoughts and feelings. It
performs what it hints at and it undertakes what it promises. If this is
the nature of the language of poetry, its condition, its health, is to stand
in a relationship with life which is direct but also detached. Not the

direct, naively realist relationship that Wordsworth argued for, not the active adoption of the very language of life or of any particular set or class, and certainly not a selection of the language of mountaineers and peasants. (*Peasants*, Coleridge seems to sigh.) No, the language of poetry must be intimately connected with life. It must draw on real rhythms and vital uses. Coleridge wholly rejected any remote or mandarin diction. He wrote to Thomas Wedgwood, 'I should think your judgement on the sentiment, the imagery, the flow of a Poem decisive ... but in point of poetic Diction I am not so well s[atisf]ied that you do not require a certain aloofness from [the la]nguage of real Life, which I think deadly to Poetry.'[16] Neither aloofness, therefore, nor identification, but rather a language involved with life, quickened by imagination and disciplined by reflection. Such a language in Coleridge's generous interpretation could occupy a point on a great range stretching all the way from Milton to Massinger.

> The style of Massinger's plays and the *Samson Agonistes* are the two extremes of the arc within which the diction of dramatic poetry may oscillate. Shakespeare in his great plays is the midpoint. In the *Samson Agonistes*, colloquial language is kept at the greater distance, yet something of it is preserved, to render the dialogue probable: in Massinger the style is differenced, but differenced in the smallest degree possible, from animated conversation by the vein of poetry.[17]

Assumptions of the sort I have sketched – on the character of criticism itself, the organic in art, the relevance of morality, the nature of language – are present and vivifying throughout Coleridge's critical writing. As we shall see, there is indeed a quite astonishing degree of similarity between Coleridge's interests, practice, aims and presupposition, and those of the important works of the last decade of Leavis's life. This was a richly productive period. Between 1969 and 1976 there appeared not only the collaborative *Dickens*, but *English Literature in Our Time* (1969), *Nor Shall My Sword* (1972), *The Living Principle* (1975), and *Thought, Words and Creativity* (1976), evidence surely of a creative energy of thought and application of the most extraordinary kind. In this Coleridgean phase, the Leavis who had been criticised for not exposing his deepest convictions, devoted himself to making them explicit and unmistakable. Themes dealt with glancingly in other places recur again and again, his circular and swooping habit of thought being evident in each book and from book to book. These have to do with society, the collapse of cultural continuity, education, the university, the necessity of literary studies, their essential quality and function in producing an educated class, and the nature of human experience as it is embodied in language.

In our period, growth, change and mutability, the conditions and drives of modern civilisation, are taken for granted as good in themselves, so that 'the profounder human consequences and significances of unceasing rapid and accelerating change escape notice.'[18] England, which Arnold felt was in danger of becoming a greater Holland, Leavis sees as rapidly turning into a little America. Leavis's 'fierce, informed and resolute conviction' was of the overriding necessity for a conscious opposition to the blankness about the human condition introduced by change proceeding at such a rate. We still had a model for a living continuity in our language, and supremely in our literature, together with an institution, the university, by which the processes of change if they could not be arrested could at least be influenced by minds possessed of a sense of humanity. 'The problem is to maintain the full vital continuity of our culture.'[19] Such a strong, informing sense of human reality and life in conditions in which it is not inherited has to be created, nourished and sustained.

Certain terms insistently repeat themselves throughout these works in such a way, indeed, as to make them, appearing as they do in all Leavis's starts and restarts, turning and circling, retracing and recalling, not only parts but actively unifying elements of the same *oeuvre*. Two of the most important are responsibility and creativity, and Leavis, true to his own literary critical habit of thought, which he claims and, in fact, demonstrates, to be as valid and autonomous as the historian's, or philosopher's, or the scientist's, appeals in his argument for point and support to certain great writers – though not, in spite of what I have said, to Coleridge. This is the method of which Leavis says: 'it licenses an elliptical economy on my part; it frees me for a tactical flexibility – I needn't make a show of sustained expository method.'[20] The writers are Blake, Dickens, Eliot and Lawrence. Of Blake and Eliot he writes with strong but definite qualification (far more severe, of course, in the case of Eliot than Blake), of Dickens and Lawrence, with a full and committed enthusiasm. He sees Blake as bringing into creative continuity and culture a new sense of human responsibility of which romanticism was the matrix. This sense was as different from the Byronic defiance as it is from 'the hubris of technologico-positivist enlightenment.'[21] The conscious and intense creativity of the artist that we see existing at its height in Blake is continuous with and inseparable from human perception itself. It is this which makes art, and supremely literature, utterly necessary to mankind. It is, then, both continuous with perception and always concerned with the real. In Blake this genius manifests itself in 'a profound communicated insight into the nature of human life, the human situation, and human potentiality.'[22] Blake offers us compellingly an understanding of human nature as it is. Where he is at a loss is in attempting to speak of what it might become. The Eternal Man and Jerusalem could not be presented in minute particulars but only in generalisations, abstractions and clouded vagueness. 'This is the aspect of Blake to which Lawrence's sharp comment applies: Blake is committed to knowing where knowing is impossible.'[23] And again Leavis writes: 'insistent prophetic vehemence, the thickening of symbolisms, can only give us the antithesis of the "wiry bounding line".'[24] Blake as an artist of the actual is the vindicator of human creativity and human responsibility, and what Blake stands for is vital and essential for us precisely because what Blake's prophetic insight saw is now our constant state and condition, 'cultural disinheritance and the meaninglessness of the technologico-Benthamite world.'[25]

Blake, says Leavis, echoing Coleridge, is 'the protest of life against the world of Newton and Locke,'[26] a world, says Coleridge, in which man is 'a lazy looker-on at an external universe.' Perception itself, Leavis repeats again and again, is creative, and he calls Blake to witness that 'there is a continuity from the creativeness of perception to the creativeness of the artist.'[27] (He could easily have called Coleridge in to witness to the same truth.)

But Blake who saw, as clearly as Coleridge was to see later, what was happening could not affect the transformation taking place, and indeed completed by 1700. The bias of civilisation was altered and the processes initiated by Locke and Newton which were to lead in due course to a Benthamite ethos were set in train. The eighteenth-century poets, as Eliot pointed out, cultivated in poetry the virtues of prose. These prose virtues entailed above all an insistent politeness. A writer was a polite artist addressing a polite audience on polite subjects. Eliot, says Leavis, misdirects when he identifies these prose virtues with the wit which led back to Marvell and Jonson. What was positive in this new culture had no reference to the court and all that is entailed in Marvell, but rather to the salon, the coffee-house and the club. It was certainly a positive culture but it 'had no place for the distinctively poetic use of language, the exploratory-creative, exemplified supremely by Shakespeare . . .'[28]

By 1700 a transformation as momentous as any associated with the development of modern civilization had taken place, never to be reversed. The new Augustan culture represented by Pope and *The Tatler* entailed an unprecedented insulation of the 'polite' from the popular. There *could* be no reversal: the industrial revolution, which by the end of the 18th century was well advanced, worked and went on working inevitable destruction upon the inherited civilization of the people. Dickens was the last great writer to enjoy something of the Shakespearian advantage.[29]

Blake, in this context, leads directly to Dickens. In this context means first, as Leavis points out, the situation in which 'collaborative and creative renewal, the cultural consciousness and the power of response ... fade into nullity, and technological development, together with administrative convenience ... *impose* the effective ends and values of life, at the cost of an extreme human impoverishment';[30] and secondly, the new development of creative expression which indeed in the nineteenth century engages the major geniuses, and prose in the form of the novel 'takes over the supreme function of poetic creation ... The achievement in the English language is one of the great creative chapters in the human record. In England the novelists from Dickens to Lawrence form an organic continuity; the intelligent study of them entails a study of the changing civilization (ours) of which their work is the criticism, the interpretation and the history: nothing rivals it as such.'[31] It is in *Hard Times* that the relation between Blake and Dickens is, in Leavis's eye, unmistakable. It is in that book that the Benthamite calculus and the quantitative interpretation of human life are found and demonstrated to be inadequate, sinister and crippling. In Dickens as in Blake there is an unbroken connection between perception, self, and the major creativeness of the great artists. Leavis insists

> ... once again that for Dickens as for Blake there is a continuity from the creativeness of perception (I represent by that the elementary manifestations of life) to the developed and disciplined creativeness of the artist, in whom spontaneity goes with trained skill, and that the genuine representative of art in *Little Dorrit* is Daniel Doyce, the inventor – as opposed to the bogus artist, Henry Gowan, who *hasn't* disinterestedness, energy or love (he *has* instead plenty of ego).[32]

Of course Dickens was a social critic as well as a dramatic novelist but his social criticism invoked values which transcend the social, values which cannot be stated abstractly and which reflected a concept of

human life wholly beyond the statistical and Benthamite. The essential
thing was not the reformer's preoccupation, powerful as that was, but
the instinctive grasp of, the magnificent understanding of, and the
brilliant rendering of human life and creativity.

> One asks, as one reads and ponders: what are the things, the qualities,
> the human manifestations that Dickens positively values, and in
> relation to which he orders his criticism of Victorian life and society –
> finds himself ordering it as he feels his way into the organization of
> his novel? and how are they related to one another? The deep
> affinity with Blake comes out in the answers. I remember noting
> down, as the text prompted me with them, the words that registered
> the answers that took form. The words, of course, in themselves do
> little: they point to the charged and definite significances that the
> novel, the dramatic poem, creates and conveys. The words I set
> down are 'disinterestedness', 'love', 'spontaneity', 'energy', 'creative-
> ness', 'art'.[33]

Leavis used to admit that he was no philosopher while observing
this betokened no great modesty on his side. In his last book, *Thought,
Words and Creativity*, he writes: 'I think of myself as an anti-philoso-
pher, which is what a literary critic ought to be – and every intelligent
reader of creative literature is a literary critic.'[34] It is the anti-philoso-
phic part of his nature that Michael Tanner blames for Leavis's claim in
The Living Principle – one of the greatest of his books – that his
admired Michael Polanyi had resolved the disabling Cartesian doctrine
of the ghost in the machine by dissolving or denying its existence: 'His
mind is the mind of his body, and his body is the body of his mind. The
dualism that has defeated so many epistemologies is eliminated here.'[35]
Nevertheless, Tanner maintains, Leavis's instincts and his ideas for
dealing with 'the relations between thought, language and objectivity
are those of a first-rate philosophic intelligence':

> The overwhelming truth that emerges from that valuable though
> disfigured part of *The Living Principle* is the priority of language in
> what makes us distinctively human, and therefore the continuity of
> the artist's activities with those of everyone else, in so far as the rest
> of us use language responsibly. When Lawrence said 'Art-speech is
> the only speech,' whether or not he meant it literally doesn't matter;
> what does matter is that he was substantially right. There can't be
> great art in a society whose language is very primitive, or in an
> advanced state of decline. Artists are dependent, no matter how
> great their genius and originality, on non-artists.[36]

Leavis's account of language seems to me strikingly in harmony with Coleridge's. Its aim is to exorcise the Cartesian-Newtonian dualism from the Western mind. "'The child's discovery, and construction, of the world" is possible because the reality he was born into was already the Human World, the world created and renewed in day-by-day human collaboration through the ages.'[37] (How close this is to the sense of the early rhythms of growth communicated by Wordsworth in the first books of *The Prelude*.) The instrument of that day-by-day collaboration through the ages is language, the creative, living tissue of thought and feeling.

> The nature of livingness in human life is manifest in language – manifest to those whose thought about language *is*, inseparably, thought about literary creation. They can't but realize more than notionally that a language is more than a means of expression; it is the heuristic conquest won out of representative experience, the upshot or precipitate of immemorial human living, and embodies values, distinctions, identifications, conclusions, promptings, carto-graphical hints and tested potentialities. It exemplifies the truth that life is growth and growth change, and the condition of these is con-tinuity. It takes the individual being, the particularizing actuality of life, back to the dawn of human consciousness, and beyond . . .[38]

Language, he continues, is 'more than a "means of expression": it embodies values, constatations, distinctions, promptings, recognitions of potentiality.'[39] and if you ask whether it exists, Leavis says you have to reply, since you cannot point to it, or find it, or see it, that 'It is concretely "there" only as I utter the words and phrases chosen by the meaning (*in* me, but outward bound) which they convey and you take them.'[40] Language is the immediate and continuing creator of the third realm in which minds meet, and literature, the most powerful and inclusive form of language, works in the same dimension. 'The poem is a product, and, in any experienced actual existence, a phenomenon, of human creativity, the essentially collaborative nature of which it exemplifies in diverse distinguishable modes. And yet it is real.'[41]

If language is the paradigm of a lost cultural continuity, and one of its few remaining vital forms, then literature is the metaphor, the gathered force, of that continuity which still gives access to what Leavis calls 'the living principle'. The living principle, he defines as 'an apprehended totality of what, as registered in the language, has been won or established in immemorial human living.'[42] All major writers, he maintains, strive to achieve a fuller and more penetrating consciousness of it; and 'where there is an educated public the living principle will be a living presence and have some influence.'[43] The major writer attempts both an intimacy with the living principle through the language which becomes alive in a full sense with hints and apprehensions and intuitions that go back to earlier cultural phases. And yet, 'The writer is alive in his own time, and the character of his response, the selective individual nature of his creative receptivity, will be determined by his sense – intensely individual – of the modern human condition.'[44] True to his intention and his method, Leavis continues his argument throughout by means of constant close engagement with particular major writers. In this last part of his life and work the two who concern him most are Eliot and Lawrence.

Leavis did more than most, and earlier than most, to establish the rank and nature of Eliot's genius. Before *Scrutiny* began, throughout its history, and after its decease, Eliot's work received constant, active and discriminating attention. Eliot's place as one of the two great creative geniuses of the age could not, in Leavis's eyes, be disputed. But there were elements in Eliot's personality, American, Establishment, sexual and religious in a formal sense, the effect of which was to distort and diminish the achievement. Eliot was a major genius disabled by inner contradictions.

His achievement makes plain both the unquestionableness of the genius and the frustrations that life suffered in him. The genius and those conditions together make his involuntary testimony challenging in a highly significant way; that is, consideration of the plight his poetry reveals sharpens our understanding of our civilization.[45]

Leavis's witness to the genius is nowhere more delicate and subtle than in the sustained treatment given to *Four Quartets* in *The Living Principle*. In this restrained but utterly engaged commentary Leavis pays tribute to Eliot's 'creative resource in making language serve him in a basic exploration of experience.'[46] The poem offers us the most profound and rigorous thought but it is 'musical' thought, Leavis insists; that is, it works with meanings in a way that music does not but it is released from a simple logical or discursive organisation. Eliot's purpose requires of him, and of course of the reader, a most intense alertness of consciousness. But we mustn't suppose, Leavis points out, that consciousness in Eliot himself is wholly identified with the creative purpose. There is a certain opaqueness at crucial points as to what the poet himself is doing. Let me give a single short instance, from the essay on *Burnt Norton*, of Leavis's finesse and subtlety in making the movement of the poem present to us.

His gift with language appears in the way the paragraph opens:

> *Other echoes*
> *Inhabit the garden. Shall we follow?*
> *Quick, said the bird, find them, find them,*
> *Round the corner.*

If we saw the first sentence by itself, insulated, we should read it as if it were general statement, and 'distant'. But the eye of the reader sees forward; we take simultaneously the sharp practical question and the urgent 'Quick', and know that we have moved back into a presented immediate as unquestionable as

> *My words echo*
> *Thus.*

The difference is that *this* immediacy imposes decision and instant action – action as a result of which we find ourselves *in* the rose-garden. We are given no account, narrative, dramatic or discursive, of how this changed relation to the rose-garden has been brought about. Nor do we ask for one, for the 'music' imposes itself on us: we recognize its authority. We perceive by now that the musical organization is a means of developing, in the exploratory-creative way, the significance of 'memory'. This is a key-word for Eliot; we note how it goes with 'echo', and we shall soon have noted other associated words. In 'Burnt Norton' he invokes our experience of the creativeness of memory, and gives new life to our knowledge that creativeness isn't necessarily irresponsible.[47]

But if Eliot was a genius, he was also a 'case', a term that it is very rare to have to apply to such a masterful talent. The case has to do with the presence in Eliot of what Leavis, quoting D. W. Harding, calls 'the pressure of urgent misery and self-disgust.' Memory, a great creative impulse in *Four Quartets*, is mixed with regret, regret with guilt, and guilt with a flinching repulsion from life, particularly in its sexual aspects. Here are two instances of this failure in Eliot. How can such a master of the language, asks Leavis, one capable of writing like this:

> Now the light falls
> Across the open field, leaving the deep lane
> Shattered with branches, dark in the afternoon,
> Where you lean against a bank while a van passes,
> And the deep lane insists on the direction
> Into the village, in the electric heat
> Hypnotised—

how can such a master be so innocently ignorant as to reduce the
English civilisation and the language which made Shakespeare possible
(and, of course, Eliot himself) to the lumpish yokels heavily disporting
themselves in the passage which presents the people of pre-industrial
England as 'clumsy, crude, gross, and incapable of the spiritual or
cultural graces.'[48]

> Rustically solemn or in rustic laughter
> Lifting heavy feet in clumsy shoes,
> Earth feet, loam feet . . .
> . . . Feet rising and falling.
> Eating and drinking. Dung and death.

The truth is, according to Leavis, that Eliot though subtler was like
Pound an American and shared an essential blankness about the kind of
human world, the living principle, that has vanished. Moreover, the
phrase 'dung and death', with its unequivocal recoil (which had started,
Leavis notes, with the 'visionary contemplation of the open field'),
links in the poem and in Eliot himself with the quivering, uncontrolled
disgust at the thought of sex evident, in so many places, from beginning
to end in his work.

  This negation is a function of some frustrating self-contradiction in
Eliot which expresses itself also in both self-accusation and in a profound sense of human impotence and nullity. It is sound wisdom,
Leavis points out, for Eliot to tell us that the knowledge derived from
experience has only a limited value, but he slips (and Leavis points out
that 'slips' implies a degree of unconsciousness) into affirming that it
has no value. Eliot's personal plight involves a certain nihilism so that
Eliot was both a diagnostician of genius of the sickness of the time and
also a sufferer from it. So great a poet, of course, was not wholly con-
strained by his own and the world's sickness. There are moments of
liberated illumination. One of the supreme ones comes in *Little
Gidding* where Eliot with the help of Dante, assuming the roles both of
Dante and Brunetto Latini,

> . . . the brown baked features
> The eyes of a familiar compound ghost
> Both intimate and unidentifiable,

achieves full self-recognition and a total and unclouded identification
with the living principle.

  At this point I would like to call in aid Henry James whose writings on literature, before the narcissistic, looping-the-loop prefaces of his later years, are a granary of critical hints and tips. He says about Trollope: 'He must have had a great taste for the moral question; he evidently believed that this is the basis of the interest of fiction.'[49] This is a view which many have taken of Leavis's own interest in fiction: wrongly, I believe. Elsewhere, writing about Flaubert, James says: '... he tasted of the knowledge by which he was subsequently to measure everything, appeal from everything, find everything flat. Never probably was an impression so assimilated, so positively transmuted to a function; he lived on it to the end ...'[50] Not morality, then, in any narrow sense is at the root of Leavis's criticism of fiction but this knowledge, impression and function. He himself called it the living principle, and it was this which he found constricted in Eliot and creatively free in Lawrence. For Lawrence the writer's thought was identical with his creativity. The logic of what is commonly taken to be thought, the abstract, discursive and cerebral, is 'too coarse to take care of the subtle distinctions life demands' and creativity makes. Lawrence's thought, then, was a concrete thought, a spontaneous thought, and a responsible thought. The instrument of that thought, but more than the instrument, the tissue and nerve, was the English language. 'Without the English language waiting quick and ready for him, Lawrence couldn't have communicated his thought: that is obvious enough. But it is also the case that he couldn't have thought it. English as he found it was a product of an immemorial *sui generis* collaboration on the part of its speakers and writers.'[51] Art and explanation, the novels and the expositions, spring from the one root in Lawrence, 'are vitalized by the one sap, and . . . there can be no question of a genetic or dynamic priority to be assigned to either of them.'[52]

For Leavis, Lawrence was essentially English, Eliot both American and also too much an irritating Francophile. Lawrence in his innumerable communications with others showed an ease and spontaneity that came from genuine interest, '... they were humanity and life, and *he* was obviously without pretensions or designs.'[53] It was this, says Leavis, which was the secret of his dramatic power, and ease and dramatic power distinguish him from Eliot who had neither. In fact Lawrence came at a moment in literary tradition when the nature, form, purpose and scope of the novel had been transformed. Life, as we have seen, meant for Lawrence achieving a disinterested purity of relationships of every kind between man and the living universe, relationships which were to be kept in balance and order by the delicate morality which precedes and accompanies a true relatedness. It is the business of art to reveal this living relation and the art which does this supremely in the modern world is the novel. 'The whole is greater than the part. And therefore, I, who am man alive, am greater than my soul, or spirit, or body, or mind, or consciousness, or anything else that is merely a part of me. I am a man, and alive. I am man alive, and as long as I can, I intend to go on being man alive. For this reason I am a novelist.'[54] This is the Lawrence that concerns Leavis so strongly and so intimately, the necessary Lawrence, the novelist who took his art so seriously, whose intentions were so radical, and whose powers were equal to his intentions. The Lawrentian art, like the Lawrentian imagination, were, Leavis concludes, 'concerned intensely for the real, being an indispensable mode of the intelligence that explores and tests experience with a view to establishing what the real, for our best insight and apprehension, is.'[55]

There are two characteristics of Lawrence, marking him off sharply from Eliot, which Leavis deeply admired and which in their own form are characteristic of Leavis's own work. The first I can make clear with the help of George Santayana, who distinguished between 'that antecedent integrity which is at the bottom of every living thing and at its core' and 'that ulterior integrity . . . which might be attained at the summit of experience . . .'[56] The fruit of the former is 'vitality' and of the latter 'the spiritual life.' Lawrence had an unparalleled sense for this antecedent integrity in many kinds of existence and many sorts of human beings and a full and subtle apprehension of the characteristic vitality of each. What his art makes clear is that unless antecedent integrity, the primary core of innocence and naïveté, was sound and free, had scope and room, then ulterior integrity, the life of reason, of the intellect and of the spirit, could only be thwarted, starved:

> It is only from his core of innocence and naïveté that the human being is ultimately a responsible and dependable being. Break this human core of naïveté . . . and you get either a violent reaction or as is usual nowadays a merely rational creature whose core of spontaneous life is dead. . . . It is one of the terrible qualities of the reason that it has no life of its own, and unless continually kept nourished or modified by the naïve life in man or woman, it becomes a purely parasitic and destructive force.[57]

The second characteristic of Lawrence's art was that it issued from and itself sustained a religious connection with the universe. For Eliot, that universe, it is not too harsh to say, tended to narrow itself down to an ecclesiastical dimension. Leavis, who was not religious in any formal or Eliotic way, manifests in his work a profoundly religious note in the Lawrentian way:

> And I do think that man is related to the universe in some 'religious' way even prior to his relations to his fellow men. And I do think that the only way of true relationship between men is to meet in some common 'belief', but physical not mental. . . . There is a principle in the universe towards which man turns religiously – a life of the universe itself. And the hero is he who touches and transmits the life of the universe.[58]

The severance of a religious connection with the life of the universe produces increasingly disorder in man's psyche and disharmony in his surroundings, soiling what Lawrence called 'the clarity of being' and producing and confirming what Leavis sees as the Benthamite mechanical uprooted world of modern man.

Religion, then, in Lawrence was more inclusive, more natural, more wholly the issue of a flow of life than it was in Eliot, so that there is an unbroken connection between his deepest instincts and his highest art. In the same way in Leavis deep human instincts, profound common-sense, natural piety, inform the highest flights of intellect and the subtlest practice of criticism. Each in this regard, in a way that Eliot was not, is all of a piece throughout.

In Leavis this characteristic wholeness showed itself both in the nobler way I have specified and in a lesser way which brought into his criticism not only the boyhood memory of watching a top spinning, which helped to illuminate Eliot's still point of the turning world, or the memory of hearing a Victorian ballad rendered in childhood which contributed to understanding sentimentality, but other things, slights, injustices, ignorings and neglect, and the common faults of less gifted opponents. These things are unimportant in comparison with the genius for intensity, the moral passion, the clairvoyant insight into human capacity realised in literature, and above all in Leavis's incessant engagement with issues that were real and significant. There is a passage in Lawrence's letters which, as I re-read it, seems to me to apply, in a way the modern world needs very much to advert to, to Leavis himself. It occurs in a letter written in 1917 and it is about an old Viennese lady:

> The world doesn't matter; you have died sufficiently to know that; the world doesn't matter, ultimately. Ultimately, only the other

world of pure being matters. One has to be strong enough to have the just sense of values. One sees it in the old sometimes. Old Madame Stepinak was here yesterday. I find in her a beauty infinitely lovelier than the beauty of the young women I know. She has lived and suffered, and taken her place in the realities. Now, neither riches nor rank nor violence matter to her, she *knows* what life consists in, and she never fails in her knowledge.[59]

Notes

I: ON THE PERSONAL SIDE

1 F. R. Leavis, *Letters in Criticism* (ed. John Tasker), London 1974, p. 87.
2 R. Hutchins, at one time President of the University of Chicago.
3 F. R. Leavis, 'The "Great Books" and a Liberal Education', *Commentary* Vol. XVI, July 1953–December 1953, p. 228.
4 Eric Warmington, 'Society and Education in Cambridge 1902–1922', *Universities Quarterly*, Winter 1975, p. 31.
5 'Elites, Oligarchies and an Educated Public', *The Human World* 4, 4 August 1971, p. 18.
6 'The 1917 reforms achieved by Stewart, Chadwick and 'Q', though partial, enabled the first examination in the new English Tripos to take place in the Easter Term of 1919. What was now required for a degree was Section A (English literature, medieval and modern) together with Section B (early literature and History, but no compulsory Philology). However, relatively few undergraduates struggled with Section B, since Section A, together with part of another tripos, sufficed. Thus, F. R. Leavis of Emmanuel, after war service as a stretcher bearer, followed a II.ii in History with a first in English, and Basil Willey of Peterhouse, wounded and taken prisoner as a Lieutenant in the West Yorkshires, had firsts in both History and English. The tripos lists for 1920 and 1921 contained the names of G. B. Harrison, J. B. Priestley, Frank Kendon, Gerald Bullett and Rosamond Lehmann, as well as those of Leavis and Willey.' (T. E. B. Howarth, *Cambridge Between Two Wars*, London 1978, p. 117.)

7 F. R. Leavis, *English Literature in Our Time and the University, The Clark Lectures, 1967*, London 1969, Introductory, pp. 14–15.
8 *Letters in Criticism*, pp. 97–98.
9 F. R. Leavis, to *The Times Literary Supplement*, March 3, 1972, in *Letters in Criticism*, p. 147.
10 D. W. Harding, *The Listener*, 24 July 1975, p. 107.
11 William Walsh, *ibid*.
12 D. J. Enright, *New Statesman*, 21 April 1978, p. 536.
13 The biographical data on this head have been given by Ronald Hayman (*Leavis*, London 1976, pp. 16–17), who acknowledges his indebtedness to Lord Annan on the matter: 'The Probationary Lectureships could be held for a maximum of four years, but in 1928, when three University Lectureships fell vacant, Enid Welsford, T. R. Henn and L. J. Potts were promoted. Together with Joan Bennett and Basil Willey, Leavis stayed on as a probationary lecturer until 1931. Basil Willey was the first of the three to be offered a permanent position, but he had to wait until 1934. When another lectureship fell vacant, in 1935, an outsider, George Rylands, was given precedence over both Leavis and Joan Bennett. He had to wait until 1936 and she until 1937.'
14 Basil Willey, *Cambridge and other Memories*, London 1968, p. 29.
15 *Letters in Criticism*, p. 84.
16 *The Listener*, 24 July 1975, p. 107.
17 *Letters in Criticism*.
18 F. R. Leavis, *Nor Shall My Sword*, London 1972, p. 30.
19 *Letters in Criticism*, p. 106.

20 D. J. Enright, *Conspirators and Poets*, London 1966, pp. 33–4.
21 F. R. Leavis, 'Memories of Wittgenstein', *The Human World*, No. 10, February 1973, pp. 66–67.
22 *ibid.*, p. 72.
23 *ibid.* pp. 71–2.
24 *ibid.* p. 76.
25 F. R. Leavis, *Nor Shall My Sword*, p. 63.
26 I give two contrasting judgements of this work, one by Leavis himself, the other by T. Howarth and F. L. Lucas:
(i) 'The product of a wholly original kind of research, it was a "socioliterary study" that did indeed "break new ground" and introduced new ideas and new methods: among other things it made a pioneering inquiry into the old working-class culture of which the new processes of civilization were eliminating the traces – an inquiry that was greeted with angry contempt by Harold Laski and the left-wing intellectuals of the nineteen-thirties.' (*Letters in Criticism* p. 58)
(ii) 'Q. D. Leavis by way of emphasizing her stern condemnation of contemporary culture (except for that enjoyed by what she unhappily called "the high-level reader" and "the sensitive minority") exaggerated the refinements of Elizabethan civilization and the critical acumen of eighteenth- and nineteenth-century journalists. This enabled Lucas to observe that "it is surely a great deal better to like the trashiest fiction than to enjoy seeing a witch burn, to go to the silliest cinema than to soak in an eighteenth-century gin shop". He also had much fun over her evaluation of H. G. Wells as useful for "keeping the lower levels posted with news of what is stirring higher up".' (*Cambridge Between Two Wars*, p. 195)
27 F. R. Leavis, '"Scrutiny": a Retrospect', *Scrutiny* Vol. XX, Cambridge University Press, 1963, p. 3.
28 *ibid.* p. 4.
29 *ibid.* p. 5.

30 T. E. B. Howarth, *Cambridge Between Two Wars*, pp. 194–5.
31 *ibid.* p. 195.
32 *ibid.* pp. 195–6.
33 cf. *Letters in Criticism*.
34 *Letters in Criticism*, pp. 37–38.
35 'We sold out, and could certainly have sold at least twice as many as we printed. In the 1930's we printed 750, a large proportion of which went to subscribers, the rest selling out in due course. This figure tells nothing about the size of the actual public, for very many copies – including many of those subscribed for – went to key places and had, each of them, a great many readers in sixth forms and universities all over the world. It was with the war that the demand began to grow pressingly, and the irony we had to stomach was that the very strict rationing of paper vetoed any increase in the printing: we had a battle, in fact, to maintain the established printing without an insufferable reduction in the number of pages and a cramped make-up. The paper restriction, of course, outlasted the war, but by 1950 we had been able to raise the printing to 1500.' (F. R. Leavis, 'A Retrospect', *Scrutiny* Vol. XX, *Retrospect and Index*, C.U.P. 1963, p. 21.)
36 'A Kind of Valediction: Leavis on Eliot, 1929–75', *Universities Quarterly*, Winter 1975, p. 79.
37 Richard Poirier, *Robert Frost: The Work of Knowing*, New York, 1977, p. 45.
38 F. R. Leavis in *Eugenio Montale: New Poems* (translated and introduced by G. Singh), London, 1976, p. xxiii.
39 *Letters in Criticism*, p. 28.
40 T. E. B. Howarth, *Cambridge Between Two Wars*, p. 198.
41 cf. Fred Inglis, 'Attention to Education: Leavis and the Leavisites', *Universities Quarterly*, Winter 1975, p. 97:
'. . . Leavis not only wished to attack the deathly uncivilization of ruling class gentility as he found it thriving

in Cambridge, and to speak of history and morality in ways that would ensure that men lived better, he also and deeply wished to resist the advance of Marxism, as the only intellectual creed with the muscle and stamina to fill the absent centres of belief and knowledge. And here again he spoke straight to the hearts of his audience: he provided ways of accounting for life and death in industrial society without necessarily invoking the class war, historic necessity, or a materialist universe. There remains as much to be said for such vocabulary in the seventies of the Vietnamese war and *Gulag Archipelago* as for what it meant in the thirties of Stalin's U.S.S.R. and the thousand year Reich.'

42 *Letters in Criticism*, p. 111.
43 *ibid.* p. 110.
44 *Letters in Criticism*, p. 45.
45 *ibid.* p. 43.
46 *ibid.* p. 35.
47 *Letters in Criticism*, pp. 78–79.
48 *ibid.* p. 149.
49 D. J. Enright, *New Statesman*, 21 April 1978, pp. 536–7.
50 Ian Parsons, 'On being F. R. Leavis's publisher', *Universities Quarterly*, Winter 1975, pp. 26–27.
51 D. J. Enright, *New Statesman*, 21 April 1978, p. 537.
52 F. R. Leavis, 'Prefatory Note', *Two Cultures? The Significance of C. P. Snow*, Pantheon Books, New York, 1963, p. 17.
53 *ibid.* p. 27.
54 'All good critics are natural authoritarians. They shape literature to the mould of their own personalities, and cajole the kind of reader who does not know what he thinks into sub-

mission or rebellion, but at least into making up his own mind. ... F. R. Leavis combined this necessary confidence with his own kind of devastating simplicity: in his own way he really was in the great didactic tradition of Dr. Johnson or Blake. But in no sense was he a "committed" critic in the continental style of Belinsky or Lukacs or Sartre. His ideology could seem bizarre, but there was never anything secondhand or institutionalised about it: it rested on a true idiosyncrasy of common sense. And he had marvellous taste.' (John Bayley, *New Statesman*, 21 April 1978, p. 537.) 'The admirer of Leavis will feel able to apply to him some of the observations he has himself made on Johnson (*Scrutiny*, Summer 1944): not only "... the traditional notion of the arbitrary Great Cham of criticism, narrow, dogmatic and intolerant", but also "Johnson is not invariably just or complete; but the judgement – and he never fails to judge – is always stated with classical force and point, and based beyond question on strong first-hand impressions. He addresses himself deliberately and disinterestedly to what is in front of him; he consults his experience with unequivocal directness and always has the courage of it".' (D. J. Enright, *Conspirators and Poets*, London 1966, fn. p. 30.)
55 *The Function of Criticism*.
56 Coleridge, *Aids to Reflection*: Preface, London 1884.
57 *Conspirators and Poets*, p. 34.
58 *Letters in Criticism*, p. 124.
59 'Obituary', *The Times*, 18 April 1978.

2: EDUCATIONAL PURPOSES

1 'How to Teach Reading' in *Education and the University*, London 1943, p. 105.
2 'Marxism and Cultural Continuity', in *For Continuity*, Cambridge 1933, p.5.
3 *ibid.* p. 7.
4 *ibid.* p. 9.
5 *ibid.* p. 49.
6 *ibid.* p. 108.
7 *ibid.* p. 64.

8 *ibid.* pp. 164–5.
9 'How to Teach Reading' in *Education and the University*, p. 108.
10 *For Continuity*, p. 67.
11 *ibid.* p. 14.
12 *ibid.* p. 64.
13 *ibid.* pp. 72–3.
14 *ibid.* p. 69.
15 *ibid.* pp. 177–8.
16 *ibid.* p. 57.
17 *ibid.* pp. 57–8.
18 *ibid.* p. 188.
19 *Culture and Environment*, by F. R. Leavis and Denys Thompson, London 1933. Mr Thompson, Leavis's collaborator in this book, tells me that his part was to advise on school conditions and possibilities. His view is that in conception and method the book is essentially Leavis's.
20 *Education and the University*, p. 23.
21 *ibid.* p. 18.
22 *ibid.* p. 16.
23 F. R. Leavis, 'The "Great Books" and a Liberal Education', *Commentary*

Vol. XVI, July 1953–December 1953, p. 227.
24 *ibid.* p. 228.
25 *Education and the University*, p. 30.
26 *ibid.* p. 38.
27 *ibid.* pp. 33–4.
28 *ibid.* p. 35.
29 *ibid.* pp. 58–9.
30 *ibid.* p. 35.
31 *ibid.* p. 55.
32 *D. H. Lawrence: Selected Literary Criticism*, ed. Anthony Beal, London 1955, p. 290.
33 *ibid.* p. 291.
34 *Education and the University*, p. 37.
35 *ibid.* p. 56.
36 *ibid.* pp. 48–9.
37 *ibid.* p. 60.
38 *ibid.* p. 70.
39 *ibid.* pp. 82–3.
40 *ibid.* p. 113.
41 *ibid.* p. 78.
42 *ibid.* p. 107.
43 *ibid.* p. 126.
44 *ibid.* p. 131.

3: CRITICAL DIRECTIONS

1 *Scrutiny*, Vol. II, pp. 432–433.
2 F. R. Leavis, *English Literature in Our Time and the University*, p. 95.
3 F. R. Leavis, *Revaluation*, London 1936, p. 55.
4 *ibid.* pp. 56–57.
5 *ibid.* p. 83.
6 *The Living Principle*, London 1975, p. 97.
7 *ibid.* p. 99.
8 *ibid.* p. 100.
9 *The Common Pursuit*, London 1952, p. 110.
10 *Revaluation*, p. 164.
11 'Wordsworth: The Creative Conditions', in *Twentieth-Century Literature in Retrospect*, ed. Reuben A. Brower, Harvard English Studies 2, Harvard University Press, 1971, pp. 323–324. (First appearance of this essay was as the Bicentenary Lecture at the University of Bristol.)
12 *ibid.* pp. 325–326.

13 *ibid.* p. 326.
14 *ibid.* pp. 326–327.
15 *Letters* (ed. M. B. Forman), 3rd edition, London 1947, p. 108.
16 *Revaluation*, p. 244.
17 *ibid.* p. 246.
18 *ibid.* p. 263.
19 *The Times Literary Supplement*, 17 October 1936. (Unsigned.)
20 *Heinrich Heine*.
21 *The Common Pursuit*, p. 213.
22 *ibid.* p. 214.
23 *New Bearings in English Poetry*, London 1932, p. 16.
24 *ibid.* p. 44.
25 *ibid.* p. 56.
26 *ibid.* p. 59.
27 *ibid.* p. 68.
28 *ibid.*
29 *ibid.* p. 76.
30 *ibid.* p. 84.
31 *ibid.* p. 119.
32 *ibid.*
33 *ibid.* pp. 124–125.

34 *ibid.* pp. 127–128.
35 *ibid.* pp. 138–139.
36 *Revaluation*, pp. 43–44.
37 *ibid.* p. 112.
38 *ibid.* p. 161.
39 *ibid.* p. 164.
40 *ibid.* p. 245.
41 *ibid.* p. 251.
42 Keats's letter to his brother George, 21 September 1819. (Quoted in *Revaluation*, pp. 266–267.)
43 *Revaluation*, pp. 48–49.
44 *ibid.* p. 272.
45 *ibid.* pp. 164, 165.
46 *ibid.* p. 166.

47 *The Great Tradition*, London 1948, p. 1.
48 *ibid.* p. 2.
49 *ibid.*
50 *ibid.*
51 *ibid.* p. 5.
52 *ibid.* p. 7.
53 *ibid.* p. 9.
54 *ibid.* p. 10.
55 *ibid.* p. 11.
56 *ibid.* p. 12.
57 *ibid.* p. 16.
58 *ibid.* p. 157.
59 *ibid.* p. 163.
60 *ibid.* p. 16.
61 *ibid.* p. 19.

4: THE SCRUTINY YEARS

1 Q. D. Leavis, *Scrutiny*, Vol. VII, p. 210.
2 F. R. Leavis, Prefatory, *A Selection from Scrutiny*, compiled by F. R. Leavis, C.U.P. 1968, Vol. I, p. xi.
3 *Scrutiny*, Vol. XX, p. 2.
4 *ibid.* p. 4.
5 'Retrospect of a Decade', *A Selection from Scrutiny*, vol. I, p. 175.
6 *ibid.* p. 175.
7 *ibid.* p. 176.
8 *ibid.*
9 *Scrutiny* Vol. XIX, p. 257.
10 *Scrutiny*, Vol. XIX, p. 256.
11 *Letters in Criticism*, p. 125.
12 'A Retrospect', *Scrutiny*, Vol. XX, p. 12.
13 *Scrutiny*, Vol. X, pp. 234–247.
14 *ibid.* Vol. VI, pp. 259–283.
15 'A Retrospect', *Scrutiny*, Vol. XX, p. 12.
16 *Scrutiny*, Vol. XII, pp. 249–260.
17 *Scrutiny*, Vol. IV, pp. 365–76.
18 *ibid.* p. 369.
19 F. R. Leavis, 'Tragedy and the "Medium"', *Scrutiny*, Vol. XII, pp. 251–252.
20 *Scrutiny*, Vol. XVII, pp. 186–202; 298–317.
21 *Scrutiny*, 'A Retrospect', Vol. XX, pp. 11–12.
22 *Scrutiny*, Vol. III, pp. 358–369.
23 *ibid.* Vol. VIII, pp. 346–362.

24 *ibid.* Vol. IX, pp. 334–342.
25 *Scrutiny*, Vol. II, pp. 222–239.
26 *ibid.* Vol. VII, pp. 33–55.
27 'A letter on the Music Criticism of W. H. Mellers', by Boris Ford and Stephen Reiss, *Scrutiny*, Vol. XI, pp. 109–116.
28 *ibid.* p. 110.
29 W. H. Mellers, 'A Reply', *Scrutiny*, Vol. XI (pp. 116–124), p. 124.
30 'Dickens, Drama and Tradition', *Scrutiny*, Vol. X, pp. 358–375.
31 'The Novel as Dramatic Poem(II): *Wuthering Heights*', *Scrutiny*, Vol. XIV, pp. 269–286.
32 *Lectures in America*, F. R. Leavis and Q. D. Leavis (London, 1969), pp. 87–88.
33 *A Selection from Scrutiny*, Vol. I p. 132.
34 *ibid.* p. 139.
35 *ibid.* p. 147.
36 *ibid.* p. 151.
37 *ibid.* p. 142.
38 *ibid.* p. 145–6.
39 *ibid.* p. 138.
40 *ibid.* p. 136.
41 *ibid.* pp. 137–8.
42 *ibid.* p. 160.
43 *ibid.* p. 161.
44 *ibid.* p. 162. *A Number of People*, by Sir Edward Marsh (Heinemann); *Unforgotten Years*, by Logan Pearsall

Smith (Constable); *Enemies of Promise*, by Cyril Connolly (Routledge); *Modern Poetry*, by Louis MacNeice, (O.U.P.).
45 *ibid.* p. 163.
46 *ibid.* p. 163.
47 *ibid.* p. 163.
48 *ibid.* p. 164.
49 *ibid.* p. 165.
50 *ibid.* p. 166.
51 *ibid.* p. 176.
52 *ibid.* p. 178.

53 *ibid.* p. 191.
54 *ibid.* p. 193.
55 *ibid.* p. 196.
56 A Retrospect, *Scrutiny*, Vol. XX, p. 18.
57 *Scrutiny*, Vol. V, p. 376.
58 p. [125].
59 Eric Bentley, 'Introduction', *The Importance of Scrutiny* (ed. Eric Bentley), New York 1948, p. xxii.
60 cf. D. J. Enright, *Conspirators and Poets*, p. 36.

5: THE PRINCIPAL COLLABORATOR

1 *Scrutiny*, Vol. XIV, p. 228.
2 *Fiction and the Reading Public*, London 1932, Introduction, p. xv.
3 *ibid.* p. 49.
4 *ibid.* p. 209.
5 *ibid.* p. 97–8.
6 *ibid.* p. 114.
7 *ibid.* p. 164.
8 *ibid.* p. 215.
9 S. T. Coleridge, *Biographia Literaria*, Ch. XXII.
10 *Fiction and the Reading Public*, pp. 228–9.
11 *ibid.* p. 157.
12 *Scrutiny*, Vol. XI, p. 308, fn.
13 *ibid.* Vol. XII, p. 15.
14 *ibid.* p. 12.
15 *ibid.* p. 16.
16 *ibid.* p. 19.
17 *Scrutiny*, Vol. XIV, p. 207.
18 *ibid.* Vol. VII, p. 404.
19 *ibid.* Vol. VII, p. 410.
20 *ibid.* Vol. XV, p. 8.
21 *ibid.* p. 11.
22 *Scrutiny*, Vol. X, p. 65.
23 *ibid.* Vol. X, p. 66.
24 *ibid.* p. 69.
25 *Scrutiny*, Vol. XIV, p. 224.
26 *ibid.* p. 226.
27 Martin Heidegger, *On Time and Being*, New York 1977, p. 2.
28 *Scrutiny*, Vol. VII, p. 273.
29 Edith Wharton, *The Custom of the Country*.
30 Edith Wharton, quoted in *Scrutiny*, Vol. VII, p. 270.

31 *Scrutiny*, Vol. VII, p. 274.
32 *ibid.* p. 275.
33 *ibid.* p. 276.
34 *Scrutiny*, Vol. VII, p. 79.
35 *ibid.* p. 80.
36 *ibid.* Vol. VI, p. 437.
37 *ibid.* p. 443.
38 *ibid.* p. 444.
39 *ibid.* p. 445.
40 Introduction to *Miss Marjoribanks*, London 1969, p. 5.
41 *ibid.* p. 6.
42 *ibid.* p. 20.
43 *Scrutiny*, Vol. XII, p. 154.
44 *ibid.* p. 156.
45 *ibid.* pp. 157–8.
46 Letter from Major Blackwood to his wife in 1861, quoted by Mrs Leavis in her Introduction to *Silas Marner*, Penguin English Library, 1967, p. 13.
47 *ibid.* p. 16.
48 *ibid.* p. 14.
49 *ibid.* p. 27.
50 *ibid.* p. 38.
51 Quoted in Introduction to *Jane Eyre*, Penguin English Library, 1966, pp. 10–11.
52 *ibid.* p. 11.
53 *ibid.* pp. 26–7.
54 *ibid.* p. 26.
55 *Lectures in America*, London 1969, p. 102.
56 *Lectures in America*, p. 135.
57 *ibid.* p. 138.

6: GENERAL CHARACTERISTICS

1 *Towards Standards of Criticism*, Selections from *The Calendar of Modern Letters*, London 1933, p. 161.
2 Bertram Higgins, *Towards Standards of Criticism*, p. 62.
3 Virginia Woolf, 'How it Strikes a Contemporary', in *The Common Reader*, London 1925, p. 297.
4 *Commentary*, New York 1959, p. 399.
5 *The Common Pursuit*, p. 121.
6 *Commentary*, p. 399.
7 *ibid.*
8 *D. H. Lawrence: Selected Literary Criticism*, pp. 118–119.

9 F. R. Leavis, *The Common Pursuit* p. 213.
10 *Education and the University*, p. 70.
11 *Letters in Criticism*, p. 89.
12 *The Common Pursuit*, p. 109.
13 *ibid.* p. 51.
14 *Scrutiny*, Vol. III, p. 362.
15 *Education and the University*, pp. 118–119.
16 *ibid.* p. 119.
17 *The Common Pursuit*, p. 215.
18 *ibid.* p. 200.
19 *The Great Tradition*, p. 29.
20 *The Common Pursuit*, p. 224.
21 *ibid.* p. 277.

7: THE ARNOLDIAN MIDDLE

1 *Mill on Bentham and Coleridge*, introd. by F. R. Leavis, London 1950, p. 97.
2 *The Common Pursuit*, p. 60.
3 *ibid.* p. 46.
4 *ibid.* p. 59.
5 *ibid.* p. 39.
6 '*Anna Karenina*' and Other Essays*, London 1976, p. 172.
7 *ibid.* pp. 238–239.
8 *Lectures in America*, p. 25.
9 *Nor Shall My Sword*, p. 79.
10 '*Anna Karenina*' and Other Essays*, p. 224.
11 *The Common Pursuit*, p. 209.
12 *ibid.* p. 208.
13 '*Anna Karenina*' and Other Essays*, p. 41.
14 *ibid.* p. 47.
15 *ibid.* p. 48.
16 *ibid.*
17 *ibid.*
18 *ibid.* p. 44.
19 *ibid.* p. 46.
20 *ibid.* p. 47.
21 *ibid.*
22 *D. H. Lawrence: Novelist*, London 1955, p. 310.
23 *ibid.* pp. 17–18.
24 T. S. Eliot, *After Strange Gods* London 1934, p. 59.
25 *D. H. Lawrence: Novelist*, p. 311.

26 *ibid.* p. 309.
27 *The Common Pursuit*, p. 245.
28 *ibid.*
29 cf. 'A Haste for Wisdom: the Poetry of D. H. Lawrence', in *Conspirators and Poets*, pp. 95–101.
30 *D. H. Lawrence: Novelist*, p. 197.
31 *ibid.* p. 148.
32 *D. H. Lawrence: Selected Literary Criticism*, ed. Anthony Beal, London 1955, p. 105.
33 *ibid.* p. 108.
34 *ibid.* p. 109.
35 *ibid.* pp. 108–113.
36 *ibid.* p. 117.
37 *ibid.* pp. 117–118.
38 *D. H. Lawrence: Novelist*, p. 145.
39 *ibid.* p. 225.
40 *ibid.* p. 226.
41 *ibid.* p. 231.
42 *ibid.* p. 234.
43 *ibid.* pp. 234–235.
44 *Dickens the Novelist*, London 1970, Preface, p. ix.
45 *ibid.* p. xii.
46 F. R. Leavis, 'The first Major Novel: *Dombey and Son*', *ibid.* p. 2.
47 *ibid.* p. 4.
48 *ibid.* p. 5.
49 *ibid.* p. 9.
50 Q. D. Leavis, 'Dickens and Tolstoy:

The case for a serious view of *David Copperfield*', *ibid*. p. 42.
51 *ibid*. p. 43.
52 *ibid*. p. 47.
53 *ibid*. p. 46.
54 *ibid*. p. 96.
55 Q. D. Leavis, '*Bleak House:* A Chancery World', *ibid*. p. 136.
56 *ibid*. pp. 124–125.
57 *ibid*. p. 123.

58 *ibid*. pp. 126–127.
59 *ibid*. p. 131.
60 F. R. Leavis, 'Dickens and Blake: *Little Dorrit*', *ibid*. p. 228.
61 *ibid*. p. 214.
62 *ibid*.
63 *ibid*. p. 219.
64 *ibid*. p. 236.
65 *ibid*. p. 229.
66 *ibid*. p. 232.

8: THE COLERIDGEAN CONCLUSION

1 *Scrutiny*, Vol. IX, pp. 57–69.
2 *ibid*. p. 58.
3 *Scrutiny*, Vol. IX, p. 69.
4 *Literary Remains of S. T. Coleridge*, 4 vols. 1836–39, Vol. II, p. 80.
5 *Biographia Literaria*, IV.
6 *ibid*. II.
7 *Aids to Reflection*, Preface.
8 cf. Collingwood, R., *Philosophical Method*, London 1933, p. 203.
9 Griggs, E. L. *Collected Letters of Samuel Taylor Coleridge*, Oxford 1956–59, 4 vols. Vol. I, pp. 625–6. (Henceforth cited as *Letters*.)
10 *Biographia Literaria*, XXII.
11 *Table Talk*.
12 *Aids to Reflection*, Preface.
13 *Biographia Literaria*, XVII.
14 *Literary Remains of S. T. Coleridge*, op. cit., p. 94, vol. II.
15 *The Statesman's Manual*.
16 *Letters*, Vol. II, pp. 876–7.
17 *Table Talk*.
18 *English Literature in Our Time*, p. 1.
19 *ibid*. p. 7.
20 *Nor Shall My Sword*, p. 105.
21 *ibid*. p. 12.
22 *ibid*. p. 14.
23 *ibid*. p. 19.
24 *ibid*. p. 18.
25 *ibid*. p. 104.
26 *ibid*. p. 124.
27 *ibid*. p. 124.
28 *English Literature in Our Time*, p. 104.
29 *Nor Shall My Sword*, p. 130.
30 *English Literature in Our Time*, p. 172.

31 *ibid*. p. 170.
32 *ibid*. p. 178.
33 *ibid*. p. 178.
34 *Thought, Words and Creativity*, London 1976, p. 34.
35 *The Living Principle*, p. 39.
36 Michael Tanner, 'Literature and Philosophy', *Universities Quarterly*, Winter 1975, p. 63.
37 *The Living Principle*, p. 34.
38 *ibid*. p. 44.
39 *ibid*. p. 49.
40 *ibid*. p. 37.
41 *ibid*. p. 36.
42 *ibid*. p. 68.
43 *ibid*. p. 69.
44 *ibid*. p. 68.
45 *ibid*. p. 197.
46 *ibid*. p. 198.
47 *ibid*. p. 160–161.
48 *ibid*. p. 196.
49 Henry James, *The House of Fiction*, London 1957, p. 94.
50 *ibid*. p. 190.
51 *Thought, Words and Creativity*, pp. 26–27.
52 *ibid*. p. 28.
53 *ibid*. p. 32.
54 *D. H. Lawrence: Selected Literary Criticism*, pp. 104-5.
55 *Thought, Words and Creativity*, p. 60.
56 George Santayana, *The Life of Reason*, Vol. 3, pp. 115–118.
57 *Phoenix*: The Posthumous Papers of D. H. Lawrence, London 1937, p. 245.
58 *Letters of D. H. Lawrence* (ed. A. Huxley), London 1932, p. 688.
59 *ibid*. p. 405.

Index